*Winthrop Rockefeller,
Philanthropist*

Winthrop Rockefeller, Philanthropist

A LIFE OF CHANGE

John L. Ward

THE UNIVERSITY OF ARKANSAS PRESS

FAYETTEVILLE

2004

Copyright © 2004 by The University of Arkansas Press

08   07   06   05   04   5   4   3   2   1

Designed by Ellen Beeler

⊗ The paper used in this publication meets the minimum requirements of the
American National Standard for Permanence of Paper for Printed Library Materials
Z39.48-1984.

Library of Congress Cataloging-in-Publication Data

Ward, John L., 1930–
    Winthrop Rockefeller, philanthropist : a life of change / John L. Ward.
       p. cm.
      Includes bibliographical references (p.   ) and index.
      ISBN 1-55728-768-6 (cloth : alk. paper)
    1. Rockefeller, Winthrop, 1912–1973. 2. Governors—Arkansas—Biography.
    3. Arkansas—Politics and government—1951– 4. Philanthropists—Arkansas—
    Biography. 5. Charities—Arkansas—History—20th century. 6. Endowments—
    Arkansas—History—20th century. I. Title.
    F415.3.R62W378 2004
    976.7'05'092—dc22

                                                                   2004001709

Contents

Foreword

WINTHROP PAUL ROCKEFELLER

In the Parable of the Talents, Jesus described three servants: one given five talents, or units of wealth; one given two talents; and one given one talent. The man given five talents doubled his share to ten talents and was richly rewarded for it. "Well done, good and faithful servant," his lord said. The one given two talents also doubled his share and likewise was rewarded. The one given one talent simply buried it. He was punished not because of where he started but because of what he produced—nothing. The point of the story was simple: The greater your gifts, the more that is expected of you. Aside from my grandfather, perhaps no one understood that better than my father.

Although Dad was a member of one of the world's most famous families, he strove to be the sort of person who could make the farm worker as comfortable in his presence as a king or queen. He entered school burdened with impossibly high expectations and a mild case of dyslexia. At times he struggled in school, finally leaving Yale to roughneck in the Texas oil fields. Somehow, he managed to fit in with the hard men who no doubt wondered what a Rockefeller was doing there. When restaurants would not serve his black coworkers, he would go in to order the meals and ate with them outside. While in the army in the South Pacific, he survived a kamikaze attack on his ship that killed or wounded all the naval officers. Though wounded himself, he took command. Later in the war, he took food and provisions to communities of Philippine civilian war victims.

On June 9, 1953, he set his suitcase down in the old Sam Peck Hotel and began a love affair with Arkansas that would last the rest of his life and into mine. When he arrived, Arkansas was one of the poorest states in the Union, and many of its citizens could not see how to overcome its hillbilly image and inadequate educational system. I think merely by his presence, Dad made changes in the state's self-perception.

He immediately began multiplying his talents wherever he could. He turned a beautiful but depleted corner of Petit Jean Mountain into a showcase farm. As head of the Arkansas Industrial Development Commission, he helped recruit 90,000 industrial jobs to what was then a farm state. Although he lost his first race for governor, he subsequently won two terms as Arkansas's first Republican governor since Reconstruction. Despite being faced with an obstructionist legislature, he nevertheless began reorganizing state government and reforming the prison system, improved wage scales for public employees, and made Arkansans begin to believe that there could truly be an Era of Excellence in their state.

Perhaps I'm most proud of the fact that he alone among southern governors brought together black and white leaders to publicly mourn the death of Dr. Martin Luther King Jr. As a result, Little Rock did not suffer the violent reactions that many metropolitan areas did.

Though his political successors would be the ones to receive the credit for his work, the vision was my father's.

It was in philanthropy where Dad most effectively multiplied his talents. Of course, he gave away millions of dollars, but many wealthy people do that. My father was different because he felt personally compelled to make sure his gifts mattered and that those who received them would be able to help others multiply their own talents. The Arkansas Arts Center is a good example. Envisioned as a modest Little Rock museum by the Junior League members who proposed it, he insisted on something the entire state could enjoy with a mobile collection and world-class art. He also insisted on statewide support so that Arkansans—not Winthrop Rockefeller—would own it.

There was an optimistic spirit to his giving. He didn't write checks to cleanse a guilty conscience like slapping away a mosquito. He immersed himself in the needy as much as the need, he talked with them, he held their hands, and he gave thoughtfully. He solved problems with Yankee ingenuity and southern grit.

Dad died way too young in 1973 at the age of sixty. At the time, I was only twenty-five years old, still trying to find my way, and having what seemed to me to be a singularly difficult time of it. For my twenty-first birthday, he gave me a small book, *A Letter to My Son,* that he wrote so that I might better understand how he became the person I knew as "Dad," in which he described his life from his birth through the war. He was very candid, but remarked that history would be the best judge of his life after his arrival in Arkansas.

Through the different stories and insights in the book, he gently reminded me of his life's message: The greater your gifts, the more you are obliged to do.

At the point of Petit Jean, near our home sits a plaque bearing his mother's favorite biblical quotation from Micah, "And what doth the Lord require of thee but to do justly, love mercy, and walk humbly with thy God." Despite his human frailties, my dad's life was spent doing exactly that, and very well, I might add.

I know that I was lucky to be born a Rockefeller, but I am luckier to have been born Winthrop Rockefeller's son. Dad's greatest gift to me was not my last name but my first, because with that name, he left me a great heritage, and at the same time, an equally great challenge . . . to follow his vision and shape my own, but always to serve, and do so with love.

—APRIL 2003

Acknowledgments

I am deeply grateful for the support of the Winthrop Rockefeller Foundation and to Sybil Hampton, president, and to a number of other persons, in particular these:

Linda Pine, chief archivist at the University of Arkansas at Little Rock, and her fine staff; the late Jane Bartlett, Winthrop Rockefeller's assistant for many years, whose notes and lists and other materials were of great value; the late Mary McLeod, whose significant influence on the philanthropy of Winthrop Rockefeller helped to shape his ideas, particularly in education, and whose guidance led to the creation of the Winthrop Rockefeller Foundation; and my wife, Betty, who was always both patient and encouraging.

—JOHN L. WARD

1

Introduction

Winthrop Rockefeller's moving to Arkansas on June 9, 1953, was neither the ending nor the beginning of his philanthropic life; but for him personally it was a new start, an opportunity for a more intense focus, a transition from being a Rockefeller in New York to an Arkansas Rockefeller.[1] It was quite a change, and he spent the remainder of his life—some twenty years—making the most of it.

As the only Rockefeller brother to transplant himself and his ideas to a permanent spot far removed from New York, there was no blueprint and very little guidance and support from the family as he trudged through the complexities endowed by his wealth and name in an environment that might have seemed almost like a third-world country to him and his friends and family. His move was a bold one, unlike any made by his brothers or sister or his parents. And it was questioned by those he left behind in New York and elsewhere, who wondered why a rich man named Rockefeller would choose to live in what they perceived as a God-forsaken place like Arkansas. Indeed, many Arkansans wondered the same thing: why would a Rockefeller want to live here? He could live anywhere in the world, so why had he chosen to share their life in Arkansas. They tried, some throughout his lifetime, to find acceptable reasons for his adopting Arkansas as his home. He was "running away," maybe, but that didn't make much sense because he could go and live anywhere in the world. He felt that Arkansas was such an obscure dot on the world map, they reasoned, that he would simply disappear from view and wouldn't surface again to attract the attention of his family or the media or anyone else. And then there were those who believed he was trying to make a new start with his life, to locate somewhere that would allow him to build a new life. The bottom line is, they never arrived at a useful answer to the question, for the most part. They saw that he was so different from them. He had interests and habits they didn't or couldn't understand. Thus, they held him apart, in a kind of awe, because of his name and his money. Even as he set out to use his wealth for their benefit, most of them treated that charity and him somewhat cautiously. Some years would pass before all but the money-grubbers would recognize that here was a man unlike any they had known before. He wasn't trying to make a buck, they finally came to see, but rather was determined to give away that buck and many more like it to bring about positive change in Arkansas. And not just his money, they saw. He was willing to invest himself as well, and clumsy and awkward though he could be—especially when it came to public speaking—his sincerity most often came through and his listeners began to trust him and accept him for the leader he became. Granted, a few grabbed onto him immediately and directed him and his deep pockets to those enterprises that would provide him a philanthropic "opportunity" and at the same time benefit their organizations. It was, of course, a way for him to work his way into the fabric of Arkansas at a high level, and he took advantage of it. Rockefeller proved himself to be in many ways the very kind of leader many had hoped for but never counted on. He gave away some $20 million right out of his own pocket during his lifetime, a good bit of it after he got to Arkansas. He spent much more on things that could not be included for income tax purposes but which nevertheless worked to benefit his fellow Arkansans. Much more of his wealth was and is being distributed through the entities created for that purpose. During his life, he took many actions that could have been considered self-serving were it anyone else; but even his critics—and there were plenty of them—saw that with Rockefeller so much of it had a more unselfish purpose. With all his mistakes, his errors of judgment, his inability to read the political winds, and his stubbornness in clinging to ideas that required the compromise he seemed unable to make as those ideas and proposals sank from sight, Rockefeller accomplished a great deal anyway. He used his wealth, his leadership, his significant connections for the benefit of Arkansas, and it paid off for Arkansas big time.

Yes, Rockefeller was different. He didn't seem to care if he was, evidenced by the fact that he didn't change much at all during his life in Arkansas. He enjoyed a certain freedom that seemed to emanate from the expectation that he was different. From flying over the state in his jet airplanes to his home atop a tall mountain with no close neighbors, he stayed apart unless it was his wish, his initiative to mix and mingle with others. He was never really accepted as a "regular guy." Perhaps he didn't try very hard, because there were just too many obstacles—his name, his wealth, his shyness, his heavy agenda, the people around him. One thing for sure, he had had enough of urban life and crowds of people anyway. New York had worn on him, frazzled his nerves in some kind of permanent way that inhibited him from wanting to go back, and he did so infrequently and mostly just when it was necessary. A lot of the problem was his family. Rockefeller didn't exactly leave under a shower of good will; indeed, most likely, many of them were glad to see him go. His name and photographs in pulp magazines from time to time didn't endear him to his parents, in particular. So, Rockefeller just didn't make pleasure trips to New York, and he even resisted participation in Rockefeller Brothers meetings as often as he could. It wasn't his kind of life there anymore, even in the café society circuits he had trekked through from time to time. Of course, his life in Arkansas probably wasn't the "sacrifice" that folks back in New York and other places imagined. First of all, there didn't have to be any inconvenience for him, and there wasn't. He built an airport that would accommodate his jet and his other airplanes, so he could get anyplace he wanted to go with probably more ease than most of his friends back in the big city. He financed the paving of the road to his homestead from the high-way a few miles distant. He pumped water up the mountain from Petit Jean River and hauled in great quantities of topsoil to develop his farm into the showplace it became. Rockefeller constructed a style of living that suited him. He was just following family tradition. Rockefellers could pretty much order their own worlds, and still do. It had been that way since John D. Rockefeller made his fortune, and the pattern for that approach to life was passed on down through the generations. There were some differences. In Arkansas he was surrounded by green grass and awestruck neighbors rather than neon and asphalt; and the sounds he heard for the most part were the bellowing of his big red cows and whatever noises he and his friends and family might create, rather than the clanging and banging of urban life.

He wanted to relieve the tensions with his family, and had he been able to do so, it might have made him less isolated; but he didn't try very hard. With the exception of his younger brother David, he seemed never able to have an honest, open and warm relationship with any of them. As David states in his autobiography, "Winthrop faced an unusually difficult situation within the family. Nelson and Laurance were a club to which he wasn't invited . . . He was teased unmercifully . . . He was, as was I, somewhat overweight and awkward, and received a great deal of ridicule from Nelson and Laurance, who gave him the nickname 'Pudgy.' . . . Later in life, after Win had been governor of Arkansas for two terms, and was suffering from chronic alcoholism, Nelson made some gestures of support, but Win saw them as halfhearted and very belated. Win was deeply embittered about the condescending treatment he felt he had always received from Nelson."[2]

On the occasion of his arrival in Arkansas, Rockefeller said he was here to learn more about the state and its problems. "Perhaps I can make some useful contribution when I learn about it," he suggested in a news conference in the Sam Peck Hotel in Little Rock, where he took up temporary residence. Rockefeller added that he had a lot to learn—a great deal to do. "This is a happy experience," he said. "I want it to continue to be. I am happy here."[3]

"Dad was viewed as a maverick," his son Winthrop Paul says, "not only by the family but by many others. He was the only member of the family to enlist before the war; he was the only member of the family who went to work as a roughneck in the oil fields and the only member to engage in outdoor or in physical activity. While all his brothers were off in banking and other similar fields, Dad took a different tack."[4] (David enlisted in 1942, and served as an intelligence officer in North Africa and France.)

His brother Nelson told *Time* in 1966, "Win found himself in Arkansas." And brother David added, "It was just what he wanted and needed." Later in the same article, David stated, "Win was basically the nonconformist. He was rebellious against the stereotype of what we are."[5] In New York, Winthrop suffered by comparison with his brothers. His education never amounted to much, for himself or his family, and he "disappointed" them in many other ways as well. "Dad was probably hitting the Copacabana, El Morocco . . . the circuit, with engaging, lovely, wonderful women," his son speculated.[6] *Family Weekly* magazine in 1958 described him this way: "Winthrop is a handsome, hearty, 45-year-old giant, gregarious and convivial, who used to frequent café society and once teamed up with actress Mary Martin to win a dance contest."[7] It is worth noting that this reference was in the past tense. He "used" to frequent café society, the article states.

Years earlier, Rockefeller headed for the Texas oil fields when things just didn't appear to be working out for him in New York. It was to "learn the business," it was said, but the fact is, in getting away from New York and out on his own, Rockefeller began to discover something about himself and to take some pride in himself as a man who could hold his own with others and who could earn their respect by dint of his own efforts and not merely his name and money. He found friends among his fellow workers and a common

Winthrop Paul Rockefeller shares much of his father's philosophy, serves as the state's lieutenant governor, is vice chairman of the Winthrop Rockefeller Foundation and a trustee of the Winthrop Rockefeller Charitable Trust, and continues to own and operate Winrock Farms. He and his wife, Lisenne, and their children also have a home in Little Rock. (Photo courtesy of Winthrop Rockefeller Foundation)

thread that would equip him well for his infantry days and, for that matter, the rest of his life. He said about the oil fields, "That was an experience I loved. That was what I had been looking for. From the lowest roustabout to the highest executive, men were working with their hands and their minds, producing something real, something of value."[8]

After the oilfields Rockefeller returned to New York for a time and through his brother Nelson became involved in the Greater New York Fund. This was his first real experience at raising money and organizing others to do so. In material he dictated in the early 1950s, which now reposes among his papers in the archives at the University of Arkansas at Little Rock, he elaborated on the experience this way:

> I had an opportunity to work with the Greater New York Fund and where, for a variety of reasons, I did have some valuable experiences. There were some 450-odd charitable organizations independently soliciting

In the oil fields Rockefeller (at right) seemed to discover things about himself that would sustain him through the rest of his life. He never forgot those days. He worked himself up to "roustabout" before he went into the infantry. (Photo courtesy of University of Arkansas, Little Rock, Archives, WR VII 1.666.c.1)

---

funds in New York, a city whose population was almost evenly divided between Catholics, Jews and Protestants. New York's bill for charitable purposes at that time had reached something like $85 million, and the deficit was about $10 million a year. Many of the organizations had exhausted their possibilities for additional appeals. Also, it was all but impossible for so many different organizations to make efficient, separate appeals to industry. So, the organizations were brought together in the Greater New York Fund to make a united appeal to this largely untapped source of funds—corporate and employee groups.[9] In organizing the committee for the drive, an outstanding Catholic layman and a leading Jew were selected, and the name "Rockefeller" was picked as an appropriate one to represent the Protestants. Nelson was asked to take part, but he said that other commitments would make it impossible. However, he very generously suggested that he thought he had a natural for them in the person of his little brother, who had just returned from Texas.[10]

The opportunity appealed to me. I had been away from New York so long that my acquaintances were limited, and this offered an excellent chance to get to know a wide number of people whom it might have taken years for me to meet through normal contacts. I agreed to go on the committee; and before I knew it, the responsibility for the whole show was on my shoulders. For one reason or another, the other members of the committee found their time otherwise occupied and little Winthrop was left to do the job. In fact—if not in title—(I was executive vice chairman) I conducted the campaign on my own for several months. I was only 25, and I'd never been in one of those things before. We worked like dogs at it, and—as I recall—we raised something over $4 million.[11] In the 1958 *Family Weekly* article, he is quoted as saying, "Welfare is everybody's job. It's not enough to contribute money. People must make the gift of themselves, of their own time, their creative talent and spiritual strength."[12]

Philanthropy was in Winthrop Rockefeller's very psyche from almost Day 1, growing up in the environment of what could be called philanthropic creation. The ideas of the Rev. Frederick T. Gates influenced and helped to guide John D. Rockefeller. Later on, more of those ideas were translated into original enterprises through John D. Rockefeller Jr.'s convincing his father of the continuing worth of Gates's ideas. The Rockefeller Institute for Medical Research would make significant discoveries to benefit mankind (it later became Rockefeller University) and then there was the General Education Board, created to improve southern education, particularly among blacks, the theory being that "education was seen as the bootstrap by which the south could pull itself out of the mire of poverty left by the Civil War," to quote Melissa Smith, then an archivist for the Rockefeller Archive Center in New York State in a presentation to the Winrock International Institute for Agricultural Development in 1991.[13]

Later, the Rockefeller Sanitary Commission was created, and its work in effect eradicated hookworm in the south. That "south" included Arkansas, and here as in other states—in the beginning—Arkansas doctors weren't all that thrilled about northerners coming down to the Bible belt and telling the rustics about health problems and how to treat them. Later, of course these doctors and other health officials saw the value of it and participated throughout Arkansas and the other states.

The family lessons of philanthropy, though sometimes subtle, nevertheless effectively and permanently imprinted Rockefeller. He would say this in 1964, when he announced his candidacy for governor of Arkansas:

A huge rally of New Yorkers and others marked a high point in the Greater New York fund-raising. Rockefeller ran the successful effort, and appeared here at the General Post Office with New York politicos Albert Goldman and Jim Farley and movie stars Jimmy Durante, Jane Froman, and Ray Bolger. (Photo courtesy of University of Arkansas, Little Rock, Archives, WR VII 1.664)

True, we were born to wealth, but from my earliest recollection we were taught to respect the value of the dollar and to recognize that inherited wealth was in a sense given to us in trust—that we were stewards—that while we would live comfortably with that which we inherited and earned, we had the responsibility to see that these resources were also used wisely in the service of our fellow man. I am proud that as a family we learned the lesson of service and in humility have attempted to follow the example of our parents.[14]

Long before entering into the political fray in Arkansas, and indeed some two years before moving to the state, Rockefeller provided this insight from dictation in 1951:

Thinking back over my own life, I can't remember any given point where I became conscious of interest in people or a desire to give of myself to others; but I do think that a very definite example was my mother and my father and, to a lesser degree, my grandfather. At no time in my entire life can I remember an occasion where my mother did not have the time to stop and be interested in what other people were doing, and expressing to them her respect for the job they were doing well. This suggests that a mutual regard resulted in a very real satisfaction—really so obviously thinking of me as an individual . . . I have the personal qualities which are sensitive to these influences and as a result of it have all of my life—either consciously or unconsciously—attempted to echo these very fundamental qualities.[15]

Rockefeller made it a point to show interest in what was going on around him, in the people of high or low station with whom he came in contact. This was especially evident during the political campaigns when it was expected, but it was a pattern to his life that preceded those political years. He got that from observing and appreciating that quality in his mother, in particular. His father, and of course his grandfather, seemed too detached from the rank-and-file folks around them to get close. So his sensitivity to others, his efforts however to interact with them on some kind of personal level (often ineffective because the people just couldn't feel close to one such as he) was not something he learned in Arkansas. He brought it with him, from his mother's knee, so to speak.

And the speculation about why he was here persisted right to the end. An editorial in the *Arkansas Democrat* (one of the two statewide newspapers at that time) in 1971, after he had been defeated in his bid for a third term as governor, observed, "One wonders why an inheritor of millions has ambition, but Winthrop Rockefeller had a strong one—to erase the playboy image and to gain the same stature as his brothers, who already were busily involved in carrying out the family tradition of public service. So philanthropy led to active involvement in the affairs of government, and this naturally led to politics."[16]

Winthrop Paul says his father "didn't necessarily practice philanthropy in a conventional manner of writing out a check. Dad took a somewhat unconventional approach to how he could serve his fellow man."[17] "Remember his mother's favorite quotation from Micah: *And what does the Lord require of thee but to do justly, and to love mercy and to walk humbly with thy God.* I think that colored his perspective quite a bit. To him, philanthropy was not simply the concept of writing a check and waiting for the next person to come through the door. It was a real tangible sort of activity in which one engaged on a momentary, hourly, daily basis . . . something that was visceral more than merely cerebral."[18] Anne Bartley, Rockefeller's stepdaughter, did not view him as a strategic thinker in terms of philanthropy or other things. "He was a visionary," she explained, "somebody who had passion." Bartley said he never started with A and went to B, then C, then D. "He was painting a picture, a big picture," she said, "and he could ramble around in it but you knew it was connected to something deeper."[19] She said Rockefeller needed people around him who could help translate, first of all, exactly what he was trying to accomplish; and second, to take the big picture and then implement it into reality. Those working with him would come back to him and say how much money it would take and describe everything else that would have to go into it, including how much of his own time and leadership would be required. Bartley said Rockefeller never liked to make phone calls to raise money but he could and would do it. "Somehow or the other, either with a dinner event at the farm or something," she added, "he would create the circumstances where other people could follow up with other prospective donors."[20]

Marion Burton—who worked with Winthrop Rockefeller through most of his years in Arkansas and continues on as a trustee of the estate—says he was always surprised and impressed that Rockefeller had such a great sense of dedication to Arkansas and the development of the state. "He was very responsive to various needs that he detected or became aware of in terms of programs or things that he saw as great voids that needed to be filled," citing such things as medical care, education, industrial development, culture—"just a broad spectrum of interests."[21] He added that "we have some other people in this state who had resources too, but they weren't willing to take the risk or make the commitment to do many of the things that he did."[22]

The landscape of Arkansas on which Rockefeller would practice his philanthropic activities was fairly grim. Delivery of social services in the mid-1950s was generally presided over by paternalistic, political appointees with little or no professional background or real concern for the people served, according to a study by the Rockwin Fund, an educational philanthropy created in 1956 by Rockefeller. Many local leaders feared the loss of underpaid domestics and part-time workers and worked with local welfare officials to keep people dependent rather than enable them to get assistance from the government. Education was poorly financed, and capable teachers and education administrators made a beeline for the state's borders and beyond to better pay and conditions as soon as they could. There were no publicly financed kindergartens, and some schools didn't even have enough money to provide textbooks to all students. Rockefeller was distressed and frustrated by all of this. His new friends in Arkansas, one way or the other, had "gone along." He knew that. They had benefited from the low-wages pattern in particular, and they generally shared the opinion of many others that Arkansas didn't have the capacity, the smarts, or the motivation to do much better. Rockefeller started with those he had come to know, but soon broadened his attack and intensified it through the years to reach all with whom he came in contact. It was his personal war against what he often described as his adopted state's "vast inferiority complex." He was impatient and sometimes angry with even his closest aides about it. Most of them were native Arkansans, and they at first reflected what Rockefeller could not tolerate—a defeatist attitude about the state and a comparatively low opinion of the great majority of those who could do something about it. He would pound his fist on the desk on occasion and turn red in the face to get the attention of those around him so he could push his view on them that this was wrong, that Arkansas and Arkansas people were better than this, and to subjugate them and keep them in almost a slave status to enrich a few was to condemn the state to a rotten future, just as it had been a rotten past and present. While he might have been exaggerating the situation somewhat, he believed it with passion, and that passion began to win them over to the idea that Arkansas and Arkansas people had promise, had potential, and that leadership and someone with fresh eyes and a fresh outlook and vision could begin to change things. That he set out to do. Rockefeller found many ways to serve, to promote his agenda of progress and change, and while that agenda was not limited to generous giving to worthy causes, certainly that was at the core of his efforts. It served to validate him to the people. He put his money where his mouth was. He was quite different from other wealthy Arkansans with which Arkansans were familiar. Rockefeller would not attempt to use or take advantage of them. And he was different in this way from the other moneyed citizens with whom they had any contact or knowledge. The "big boys" had co-opted the Democratic Party in Arkansas many years earlier, and used their prestige and money to ensure that officials were elected to office who would not harm their businesses and would perhaps even help them as they continued with the process of making as much money as they could. Rockefeller's election—coming after several years of tough work to at least start a real two-party political system—ended that. He had already spent lots of money on legal costs to accomplish certain objectives for the state, which included cleaning up the election process (a huge project in itself), and brought in topflight professionals to occupy important positions in government. As top professionals, they could not accept the pitifully small salaries paid by state government, so Rockefeller supplemented their salaries while he was governor. Indeed, before he became governor he supplemented the salaries of highly qualified others (at the University of Arkansas Medical Center, for example) in order to attract and hold them in Arkansas. This was highly controversial, if only because he replaced the "good old boys" with those who understood how to manage government without consulting or considering applicants for those positions who were, in many cases, no more than political hacks. He financed many "study" trips that utilized his airplanes and resources to ascertain how folks were doing things in other parts of the country that might be helpful if applied to Arkansas problems. His corporate leadership cost many millions of dollars. He led in the development of low-cost housing through Winrock Enterprises, played a major role in another low-cost housing program in Central and South America called International Basic Economy Corporation, Winrock Farms, and Winrock International Livestock Research and Training Center, which morphed into Winrock International Agricultural Development Institute. Winrock International has served to leverage money from the charitable trust through contracts and grants for development programs everywhere. In particular, its mission has been to teach subsistence farming to local people throughout the world.

The trust—created from Rockefeller's remaining assets after his death—has distributed $165 million so far, for purposes described broadly in Rockefeller's will, and the Winthrop Rockefeller Foundation has distributed more than $65 million, with the same connections to the expressed intent of Winthrop Rockefeller. Clearly, his vision has continued to dominate their policies in many respects. Both entities are ongoing and will continue distributions of the Rockefeller wealth and earnings in perpetuity. In addition, there is the Arkansas Community Foundation (ACF), created by gifts from the foundation but now growing significantly on its own as a mechanism by which others with smaller philanthropic gifts to provide can do so through ACF so that their funds are managed centrally and are directed to the charitable purposes they designate without the need to create separate foundations to accomplish the same objective.

Lessons from his family in philanthropy, by example mostly, might have sometimes been subtle to Rockefeller, but there was no subtlety in those childhood years about morality and church-going, about Bible reading and of course about the keeping of accounts. This had all been ingrained in Junior by his father, and he in turn sought to hammer it into his children. Winthrop didn't take to it all that well, and was among those least likely to have his accounts in order when it was time to meet with "father" and go over them, even though his older sister Abby was more openly rebellious than any of the

Rockefeller, a student at Loomis, found a sense of belonging and security there. Throughout his life, he spoke fondly of his years at Loomis and provided substantial and consistent support. (Photo courtesy of University of Arkansas, Little Rock, Archives, WR VII Album: WR-A-1–17)

boys. Winthrop wrote in his letter to his son: "At Loomis (preparatory school) I was having money trouble, too. Father was always very strict about our personal accounts. Our allowances were inflexible, and we had to keep a record of everything—our expenditures, our charitable contributions and our savings."[23] The father tried with relentless patience to teach his children to look after themselves, to learn to mend clothes, prepare meals, and so on. And with mixed results, they adhered to the discipline this imposed upon them, but it was apparently quite difficult to carry on such mundane activities in an environment of opulence and a bevy of servants. The children were instructed and reminded constantly that as Rockefellers they had a special obligation to others, and this lesson was very much in the mind and heart of Winthrop, even before his life in Arkansas, and most assuredly in the remaining years after he moved to his new and final home.

In Cary Reich's biography of Nelson Rockefeller, *The Life of Nelson A. Rockefeller,* discussing John D. Rockefeller Jr., he states:

"Junior's rectitude and good works indeed set a rather daunting example for the children . . . The range of Junior's activities was mind-boggling. He funded the restoration of the palace of Versailles. He financed a museum in Jerusalem to house priceless artifacts of biblical times. He rebuilt the library of Tokyo's Imperial University, destroyed in the earthquake of 1923." Junior also contributed to the construction of New York's magnificent Riverside Church and financed the building of the Memorial Bell Tower. Reich also writes that Junior anonymously backed Margaret Sanger's Birth Control Clinical Research Bureau, and he purchased and donated much of the land (some 11,000 acres) needed to establish Acadia National Park on Mount Desert Island, the site of his Seal Harbor retreat.[24]

While Rockefeller in some respects remained out on the fringe of Rockefeller Brothers activities and the lives of his family in general (although quite generous to family causes with his share of the wealth), he projected a pretty good attitude about it all. It is fair to say, however, that he was crushed that his father was never able to work into his travel plans a visit to Winrock Farms to see what his son had built in Arkansas. More hurt than frustrated, Rockefeller had a documentary film produced about Winrock for his father, who reportedly asked to see it a second time. This was a matter of great pride to Rockefeller and to his dying breath he seemed always to be gripped in a process of doing the things he did so his late father and mother would be proud of him, he said more than once in impromptu remarks. Rockefeller had changed his life; he wanted them to know and appreciate it and to see how significant results were coming from his efforts to improve the lot of his fellow citizens. He wanted his father in particular to see that first hand, but it was not to be. David Rockefeller writes in his "Memoirs" that his brother "desperately craved Father's approval, but his academic failures and undisciplined comportment with friends of whom my parents did not approve meant that Father rarely granted him the acceptance and approval he sought."

Rockefeller's first impression of Arkansas was a good one. Responding to the importuning of a wartime buddy—Frank Newell of Little Rock—who knew he was chafing at New York life and wanted to get away, he came to the state and put up in the Sam Peck Hotel (now the Legacy) in Little Rock while he looked around. Here was a bucolic landscape, unshaped in many ways, and a man with ideas and a philosophy that might be lost in the caverns of the skyscrapers built by somebody else could very well find a place for his ideas to grow and flourish and take root and have effect here—and he could grow right along with them. "He saw this as a place where he could make a differ-ence," Marion Burton said. "I think he was frustrated with where he had been living. I think he simply got tired of the routines."[25] It was a long, long step, no matter how driven he was to get away from New York. He would leave the cocoon of the family. That Rockefeller name really cut ice in the big city. He could have just about anything he wanted at the snap of a finger. He was tall and handsome and of course very rich and never found himself wanting for attention. Yet, here he was in Arkansas. Was he prepared? Could he accept the moist heat of Arkansas summers, the mosquitoes and other bug life that had plagued citizens for so long they wrote songs about them. "The boll weevil am a little black bug . . ." one of them went. Rockefeller was a man who sweat a great deal. He could be out for just a short time and be wringing wet with sweat. He would mop his head with his handkerchief until it was soaking wet as well, and then wave it in the air as best he could to dry it out and keep going. All this was particularly obvious as he trekked up and down the streets and roads in his political campaigns, but he wanted the outside life at other times as well, and being in the cattle business compelled him to be out in the heat. Much of this was in his future, and he couldn't really see it coming as he settled into that Sam Peck penthouse, which by the way had a view of the state Capitol down Capitol Avenue to the west. That he would wind up there in the big office on the second floor, as governor, of course never crossed his mind as he and Newell began poking around the state looking for a good place to put down permanent roots. When he headed up Petit Jean Mountain, to check out a place for sale on one of the prominent brows with an eye-popping view of the Arkansas River Valley, he was hooked.

G. Thomas Eisele, legal advisor to Rockefeller, his campaign manager in 1964 and senior advisor to Rockefeller during his public life, said there was no question but that Rockefeller wanted to "live up in his own way to the tradi-tions of his family." Eisele noted that Rockefeller brought a lot of resources other than his playboy reputation that preceded him. He was very sharp on economics and business, according to Eisele, and "in his approach to charitable contributions, you will find that economic education was a big thing that he tried to support and felt was much neglected in America."[26] It was reported when Rockefeller made the move to Arkansas that it had to do with Arkansas's "quickie" divorce laws and his intention and that of Mrs. Rockefeller—"Bobo" as most people knew her—to get a divorce. In fact, the divorce took place later in Reno, Nevada. His first wife, and his second, Jeannette, were both divorcees.

Rockefeller married Jeannette Edris of Seattle, Washington, in 1956. The daughter of a well-to-do West Coast theater magnate, she brought two children

Rockefeller's coming to Arkansas was a mystery to those he left behind in New York. The state featured a weak economy, hot and mosquito-infested summers, and an attitude that was defeatist at best. (Photo courtesy of University of Arkansas, Little Rock, Archives)

to the marriage—Bruce and Anne—and the family seemed to meld together quite well, although Rockefeller's only child—Winthrop Paul—was in and out because he divided his time between his divorced parents. Winthrop and Jeannette divorced amicably after the 1970 campaign.

In his announcement as a candidate for governor of Arkansas in 1964, Rockefeller referred to the various areas in which he had attempted to contribute of himself to a better Arkansas. As he put it, "I have participated in the industrial development program," adding that he had been keenly aware of the aspirations of people in the field of education and that he had "attempted to be of assistance in areas ranging from the efforts to make the Morrilton School District a model program and his participation in the Arkansas Foundation of Associated Colleges and the development of the Arkansas Opportunity Fund and other scholarship programs."[27] Rockefeller saw Arkansas as full of promise but not much hope; of a people he described as being afflicted with a mass inferiority complex, and a people out of touch with, and perhaps not particularly interested in, the world outside. Segregation of the races was hardly even discussed: it was just a given. He would try to change that and many other things as well. Philanthropy was one way, he reasoned. "He was not just giving his money to something," Burton explained. "He was getting other people to give their money to it as well. I mean that's how he developed a kind of philanthropic culture in Arkansas that did not exist when he arrived here."[28]

There were many things in Arkansas he did not understand at first, and a fair number he never did understand, including the "good ole boy" system of government and the attitude of the people generally to just accept their circumstances with no thought of challenging the status quo or attempting to upgrade their situation and make things really better for themselves and others. All this flew in the face of his family background and his own interests and determination. It is fair to say that he had difficulty understanding people for another profound reason. He had been reared in such circumstances that his need to compete with others—all kinds of others—was denied him. Consequently, his ability to "read" people, his judgment about them, was flawed. That he succeeded as he did despite this is testimony to his unwavering determination to make good things happen and to convince his fellow Arkansans that there were better ways. The result was that, through his efforts, he opened their eyes to the exciting potential of a new Arkansas in a new South. "Dad took the approach," Winthrop Paul says, "all right, this needs to be done; this needs to be taken care of and dealt with; how do we market Arkansas? How do we bring Arkansas out of the nineteenth century and into the twentieth? How do we move Arkansas from being a predominantly agrarian society? If we are going to progress, if we are to have the economic resources to move our state forward, we must move out of an agriculture-dependent world of the nineteenth century into the technological world of the twentieth century."[29] Before he came to Arkansas, Rockefeller was only nominally interested in politics at best; but in his adopted state, he quickly got involved and stayed that way through thick and thin, through the rigors of politics that could and did become dirty and replete with name-calling and misrepresentations that sometimes just befuddled him; it was so foreign to all he knew and believed. He was convinced early on that the noncompetitive one-party political system in place in Arkansas could never produce significant progress —economic or otherwise—because it was so cynically controlled by those who were protecting their businesses and gaining ever more favors from government. Through the trauma of trying to lead in the development of a two-party system to change this pattern of subjugation and control, he learned how jealously it was guarded by those holding the powers of public office and by those who controlled them in using the offices of government to protect and enrich the few at the expense of the many. A review by the Rockwin Fund pointed out that during the twelve years Orval Faubus served as governor, "state government was almost completely controlled by boards and commissions composed of men who could profit, through their vested interests, from commission and board activity."[30] In that environment, professionalism in government was virtually nonexistent. He often pointed out that it would have been much easier for him to involve himself in Democratic Party politics in Arkansas. It was the dominant party and he could have cut a wide swath there almost immediately. But he was convinced that the state needed a competitive two-party system and that just playing the game that the old pols played would not benefit the people of Arkansas. Indeed, it had worked to their detriment all along.

The education system was, according to the Rockwin Fund study, one of the most poorly financed in the nation. Arkansas's population was declining, owing in part to the increasing mechanization of agriculture and the fact that the laborers freed from all that labor-intensive effort had to go elsewhere to find work. The economy was stagnant and median family income in 1949 was $1,315, according to the Rockwin Fund study.[31] Rockefeller set about to change things soon after he arrived, and it is somewhat ironic that Governor Faubus gave him an important tool by appointing him to the newly created Arkansas Industrial Development Commission in 1955. He was elected chairman and results were quick in coming.

He brought with him to Arkansas in 1953 a highly developed range of interests and involvements that he did not forsake throughout the remainder of his life, although he added such things as industrial and economic development that addressed a particular need in his adopted state. In the letter he wrote to his son, Rockefeller stated, "I have enjoyed the personal use of money. But I have gotten the greatest satisfaction from using it to advance my beliefs in human relations, human values."[32] He advised Winthrop Paul that the biggest returns from the investment of money come in what we can call "philanthropic achievements" in the "encouragement of people who make our business grow, making jobs and security for others, and in the development of men, their happiness, their usefulness and their freedom."[33] Very high on that list was racial equality. From his earliest years he had a great interest in the welfare of blacks, in particular, and other minorities. As an example, he and his brothers very early in life pledged a portion of their modest allowances to help needy black students at the Hampton Institute. In addition to adding his wealth and leadership to bring about a greater degree of racial equality, Rockefeller concentrated his philanthropy in seven other broad areas of human need as well. Listing them does not reveal near all that he did, in terms of leadership, encouragement, gifts that could not be claimed on his income tax reports, and in particular the catalyst quality of so much of his giving. He was planting seeds with every cent he gave, or so he intended, and the institutions he created or supported in a major way have for the most part continued and grown and provided their own philanthropic support to the worthy causes he espoused in his lifetime. With causes aimed at bringing about racial equality, he also concentrated on education and youth, culture and the arts, physical and mental health, religion, military and veterans' services, support for programs that would positively strengthen America's place in the world, and in general the building of Arkansas.

Providing substantial amounts of money was one mechanism for improving things for his fellow man. But along with the gifts sometimes there was follow-up, an insistence of learning how things were going, how the money was being utilized, and he also did another thing that set him apart—at least in Arkansas—in terms of philanthropy. As has been previously stated, he gave of himself. He took positions of leadership and aggressively sought the support of others in worthy causes—their money, and their leadership as well. Rockefeller and his wife, Jeannette, traveled the state raising money and interest in development of the Arkansas Arts Center, for example. It was a huge success and owing in no small part to his and Mrs. Rockefeller's relentless efforts. "Philanthropy," Winthrop Paul commented, "is more the concept of helping someone to meet a need and accomplish something greater than their original dream. A person would walk in to Dad with one idea of what they thought they wanted to do, and by the time they left, they had a vision, a concept of what they might be able to do. Dad was a great believer in the value of vision, the value of looking beyond one's self-perceived limitations."[34]

When Rockefeller set about to improve the educational situation in his home county, he insisted on leadership that could accommodate the changes and ensure that the resources he poured into the Morrilton School District were well spent and properly utilized. The Reynolds Elementary School was a consequence of his interest in improving educational opportunity in his hometown, and he provided $1.2 million to make it happen and with quality and sustainability.

He observed that health care in his neighboring county was not easily available, so in 1955 he helped to build a health clinic and saw that it was staffed with a physician and that other medical services were provided. It was an example of his leadership that Perry County citizens (one of the poorest counties in Arkansas in terms of per capita income) contributed some $13,000 to the project. He was quite proud of their participation. He had often encountered the attitude that if he were involved—with his deep pockets—then no one else need kick in anything. He worked hard throughout his Arkansas years to overcome that attitude among his fellow Arkansans. Much of the problem had to do with his expectations and with his abysmal lack of understanding of his fellow man. He just never got it, you might say.

Bruce Bartley, his stepson, sums it up this way:

"In many circumstances I think he was a horrible judge of character, and would stay with those judgments to a painful extent."[35] An editorial in the *Arkansas Democrat*, on the last day of Rockefeller's governorship, stated it this way: "He was loyal to too many people who didn't deserve it."[36] It truly appeared to be hit or miss with his choice of people who would work with him. He had some outstanding people who stayed with him throughout, and then there were a whole range of characters that would float in and out and with whom he would keep maddeningly close company, to the dismay and consternation of others around him. He would ask sometimes for one of those around him to check somebody out, find out if they were on the level, so to speak, and if what they were trying to persuade him to do was on the up and up. Some of those folks should have been perceived at a thousand yards as out-and-out con men (or women) with one objective—to get a hand in his pocket; but he would cling to his first impression, his erred judgment, until it was exceedingly difficult to get the hand out of his pocket and send his "friend" on his or her way.

Bruce Bartley, stepson, quickly became close to Rockefeller, traveled a good deal with him, and shared his life on Petit Jean Mountain. Bartley was a close observer of the man and his philanthropy. (Photo courtesy of Bruce Bartley)

Perhaps part of his problem was his generous spirit, Bartley says, adding this:

He was taught from the very beginning that his obligation, his duty, was to give back. I think he felt that almost to a fault. So, on any given day, when I would go by the office, he would as likely be involved in some sort of philanthropic or charitable effort as he would be in business or politics. Mostly likely, he would be doing some sort of good work contributing his time, not just his money. I remember him and Mom working with the Urban League and the extremes to which they went to travel and invest themselves, not just their money. Mom was right there with him in terms of contributing their lives and time here on earth to good works as opposed to spending it on the Riviera or being members of the jet set. They wanted to improve everyone's life. They wanted to do as much good as they could for other people.[37]

Bartley said Rockefeller's philanthropy "wasn't like a spice that he put on certain dishes in his life. It was a part of his life. His attitude was, if there is a problem either with an individual or with a part of society, how can I help resolve it, how can I improve it, how can I make it more equitable and productive? That was a life attitude, one that he practiced 24 hours a day, seven days a week."[38]

In the Rockwin Fund study, this view of Rockefeller's philanthropy was offered: "He introduced a style of philanthropy that helped give birth to a broad scale social and cultural awakening in Arkansas. In so doing, he shattered the image of Arkansas millionaires as self-serving recluses and created among them a thirst for new ideas and a willingness to participate, along with him, in the achievement of a better life for their fellow Arkansans."[39]

2

Racial Equality

Rockefeller's views on racial equality ran deep, reaching all the way back to his earliest memories from childhood. His parents ingrained in him the idea of equality and that all differences—including skin color—were irrelevant in judging others. Throughout his life he saw the person—not the color or the wheelchair or place of origin or anything else. It was obvious to all who knew him and especially those who worked with him. He didn't have one face for the public and another in private; but neither was he the "limousine" or "knee-jerk" liberal that detractors described him as when he moved to Arkansas and began to preach moderation and fairness in an atmosphere not too far removed from sheets and burning crosses. Rockefeller was not unmindful of the effect on Arkansans his comparatively liberal views and actions in terms of race was having. Indeed, he evolved in his thinking and in the practical application of his ideas as he wrestled with the attitudes he encountered. Many a session with his close aides and others who had a better grasp on Arkansas attitudes was held to discuss the issue. He was told that blacks had been disenfranchised in Arkansas from Day 1 and that comparatively speaking they didn't for the most part have a prayer of achieving economic success, that they would never be accepted in a social sense, and that all the smart blacks had long since moved north where their talents could be recognized and their skills could be parlayed into a good living. This was hard to take for Rockefeller, and his stubbornness would kick in when he hadn't a chance at all to prevail with his attitudes. Yet, he was not paternalistic toward blacks. He knew too much for that, and sensed that his help when offered in that spirit would be rejected out of hand. With very limited success he tried to help in 1957, before and after, when desegregation of Little Rock Central High School had the attention of virtually every person in Arkansas and beyond. His efforts to work with Gov. Orval Faubus and others were wasted and to no avail, and may have stiffened already strong opposition to integration even more. This "Yankee race-mixing multi-millionaire" wasn't about to tell Arkansans what to do about racial justice and equality. Any appeals he made to the finer instincts of the players in those days were lost in the quagmire of political expediency.

One of the most dramatic moves he made came when he brought in a black friend from New York—Jimmy Hudson—to serve as manager of Winrock Farms. To say that a black manager directing the activities of whites who worked at Winrock triggered all kinds of reactions and difficulties would be to put it mildly. This was just too much and he was told so by virtually everyone who was bold enough to shell down the corn for him. Rockefeller wasn't about to let popular opinion drive his decisions, of course, but Hudson finally returned to New York on his own after the difficulties related to social acceptance just couldn't be solved so quickly. As long as he was on the farm and associating with his friends and colleagues it worked pretty well, but the minute he drove into town—any town—it wasn't good.

One example Rockefeller's son tells about is when Hudson went to a car dealership in Little Rock to select and buy (for Rockefeller) a vehicle. The salesman had some serious awkwardness in his manner as he tried to confirm that Hudson could really make the deal and so on, and asked if he might call Mr. Rockefeller. "Sure," Hudson said. Rockefeller let the salesman fumble around for an eternity before saying that Hudson could make a deal up to a million dollars, if that's what it took. The gulping salesman finished up the business very quickly indeed, Winthrop Paul recalled.

Rockefeller clung tenaciously to his convictions. It wasn't a kind of desperation mode, however. He was supremely confident even when the noise of the White Citizens Council and other race-baiting organizations reached deafening proportions. Rockefeller held firm and let his views be known far and wide. When the *Arkansas Gazette*—reviled by the segregationists throughout Arkansas for its liberal stance in terms of race relations—won two Pulitzer Prizes for its courageous reporting (in the categories of community service and editorial writing) during the desegregation crisis, Rockefeller was delighted to preside at a dinner honoring Harry Ashmore, who wrote the editorials, and

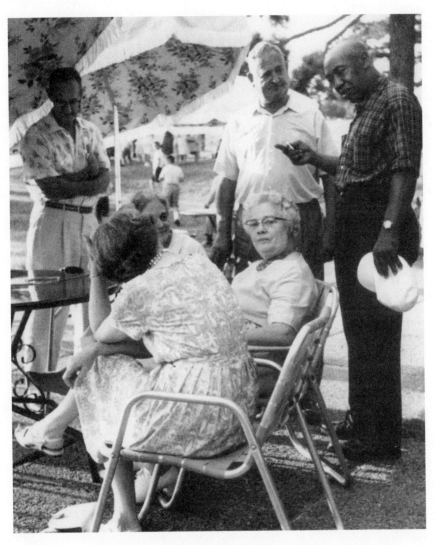

Rockefeller brought Jimmy Hudson (at right) to Arkansas from New York to manage Winrock Farms. At this social gathering atop the mountain, Jim Brand (standing next to Hudson) supervised the moving of large trees onto the homestead premises. Mrs. Brand and Mr. and Mrs. William Worth, friends of the Rockefellers, are also pictured. After a time the Hudsons returned to New York. (Photo courtesy of University of Arkansas, Little Rock, Archives, WR III 412)

the *Gazette*. In a letter to Rockefeller from Mrs. Adolphine Terry, prominent civic leader in Little Rock who stayed the course of desegregation and equality for the races in general, she stated: "As chairman of the committee which arranged the dinner for our Pulitzer Prize winners, I want to thank you for presiding over the occasion. Since these are top awards in the newspaper world, it was eminently fitting that you, our first citizen, should take part in the celebration. There was more involved, however, than simply honoring the *Gazette* and its staff. Some of us are weary of being represented by a crowd which seems to have taken over as spokesmen for Little Rock since last fall. This dinner, we felt, would give another group an opportunity to be recognized; it would also be an encouragement for the fearful. One of the finest things you have done—and there are many—was to give your support and influence to this effort to regain in some degree our good reputation. We are sincerely grateful to you."[1]

Describing Rockefeller's "deep sense of values and right and wrong," Anne Bartley, his stepdaughter, noted that when he believed that something needed to be done that was right, he just turned his considerable resources, not only financial but also personal and the people who worked for him, to get that thing done. And Bartley says there was no hypocrisy about this in either him or her mother, Jeannette, Rockefeller's wife. "What they said and did in private was totally synonymous with what they were doing in public."[2] Anne Bartley was struck immediately by the contrast with the way blacks were treated in Arkansas as compared to where she had spent the earlier years of her life, and said these dramatic differences were evident to her mother and stepfather as well. For the most part, blacks were just simply invisible, nonentities. They had no power and perhaps no hope for a better future. The only times they were noticed was when they got in trouble, and then they would be dealt with rather harshly.

Henry Jones, now a federal magistrate in Little Rock, was a bright and highly educated black man who was tempted as were many others to move on from Arkansas.

"When I was about to leave college [first Yale University, then Michigan Law School]," he explained, "one of my options was not returning to Arkansas. I didn't see returning here; but people were talking about this governor, Win Rockefeller, who had the idea of changing the landscape of Arkansas—that is, making it a place where people who didn't feel very welcome before feel really welcome now. When I told my father (who was a waiter at an exclusive private club in downtown Little Rock) that I was coming home instead of going somewhere else, he mentioned to me someone at a bank who was interested

Anne Bartley, Rockefeller's step- daughter, had keen observations about him and his philan- thropy, and was involved in decisions about his gifts to programs in which she shared an interest. (Photo courtesy of Anne Bartley)

in my coming to work there. When I got back, I went by to talk, but it was clear from the first moment that these people had no place for a young black man in Arkansas to work. That just wasn't within their realm of reality."[3] But Jones wasn't yet discouraged. He was soon talking to folks about working for Governor Rockefeller, and then to Rockefeller himself. "From the very first moment I met him," Jones said, "I felt that he was in fact about dealing with people fairly, about looking at them for what they were and not for what other people thought about them. That's the kind of thing that just made me believe that there was a new day in Arkansas." Jones remembers that Rockefeller was determined to help traditionally black colleges in Arkansas survive, but noted that his philanthropic effort was not limited to the giving of money. "One of the things I saw was that he wanted to deal with Arkansas in a way that people felt they could choose their place, that things were possible for them that had not been possible before."[4]

Rockefeller arrived in his adopted state with ideas developed through the nurturing of his parents and then further worked out on his own. As stated earlier, Arkansas was a state with one-party politics and a segregationist mentality that was in serious conflict with Rockefeller's philosophy. He felt compelled to explain himself in 1964, to find some middle ground, as he offered himself for governor. It was a delicate moment.

"For three generations my family has been interested in the problem of race relations. Over that period of time my family has made contributions of many millions to segregated schools and colleges because of the belief that only through education can the races live in peace and harmony." He further explained that he had opposed the Civil Rights Bill (of 1964) because of the police powers it granted to the executive branch. He promised that when he was governor he would abide by the law "because I must . . . I will have given my sacred oath to do so."[5] The statement in part was a kind of accommodation to the Republican Party, which for the most part was not enamored of desegregation and to vast numbers of Arkansans as well. In retrospect, Rockefeller wasn't especially happy he had said just what he did. His record and his public and private statements and actions after that showed a compassion for racial equality and leadership that he could be proud of throughout the remainder of his life.

He set about in the very beginning to change things and enjoyed both success and failure as he attempted to show his fellow citizens the way toward racial equality, before mandates and legislation and confrontations forced the issue. Before Rockefeller took office as governor in January 1967, blacks were still forbidden from eating in the state capitol cafeteria, for example. The new governor quickly got that practice changed. He shot down many other "customs" with determination and some glee as well. Blacks were not considered for any but the most menial jobs in state government, for the most part. Rockefeller saw to it that they were not only considered—but placed—in more important and more visible jobs.

In 1940, Rockefeller's contributions included a small gift to the Colored Orphan Asylum in New York and a gift of $100 to the National Urban League. But the lifetime of support for black causes began much earlier. Here, in Rockefeller's own words (dictated in the early 1950s), is the early influence and example of his family to this cause:

> The earliest trip I can remember—one that had a great influence on
> my later thinking—was a visit during an Easter vacation to Hampton

Institute—a Negro normal school in Hampton, Virginia. The school program started with grade school and went on through high school, with special emphasis on agriculture and vocational trades. The head of the school was Major Moulton (the name may have been Moton), a wonderful, elderly Negro gentleman; a man of tremendous stature physically, with a spirit as great as his body. We lived on the campus at Hampton and visited many of the classes in agriculture, industrial arts, home economics and similar fields. In the evenings some of the young Negro students were invited to the guest house where we were staying, and told us a little of their lives and their difficulty in getting an education. Many of them had come from extremely poor families, in which mere existence was a struggle. Yet all had a very real optimism and hope for the future. Before we left Hampton, each of us decided that he'd like to help a student. We couldn't have given much out of our allowances.[6]

Rockefeller figured his was about $25 a month. He went on, in the letter to his son, Winthrop Paul: "The honesty, the courage and confidence of the Negroes we met on that trip and subsequent trips I made to Hampton also helped me to develop, early in life, a relaxed feeling in my associations with people of a different race, which has been invaluable to me."[7]

Throughout his lifetime he would donate $734,594.12 to the Urban League, which included $659,458.10 to the national organization, $73,834.91 in Arkansas, and small amounts to Omaha, Nebraska; Seattle, Washington; and White Plains, New York. As a board member, Rockefeller served as a leader as well as a contributor, and was described by Lester Granger, former executive director of the Urban League, in an article in *Time* as "as good a board member as the Urban League ever had."[8]

The Urban League was set up in 1910, to "tear down racial prejudice, eliminate discrimination and create a climate in which doors are opened to new job opportunities, to decent housing, to better education, and to sounder family living." These principles were adopted and followed by Rockefeller to the fullest extent of his power to do so. "The surest barometer of the success of our democracy," Rockefeller wrote in the early 1950s, "is the progress we achieve in making it an equal reality to all people. Today, more than ever, we must demonstrate our willingness to accept the responsibility of democracy by taking an active—rather than a passive—attitude."[9]

Even near the end of his life—in 1972—he provided $1,683 to the Urban League of Greater Little Rock and $20,000 to the national organization. During his lifetime he developed great affection for the late Whitney Young, leader of the National Urban League for many years, and Young was often a guest at Winrock Farms. Young seemed to Rockefeller to be moderate in his approach to race relations—certainly the approach shared by Rockefeller, who had little use for firebrands and sought ways to restrain and re-direct them to accomplish the goal of equality without the heat and danger that went along with fiery polemics. After the assassination of Martin Luther King Jr., and when marches and other demonstrations were getting traction among blacks in Arkansas, Rockefeller and his wife, Jeannette, instead proposed a memorial service on the steps of the state capitol and he as governor and Mrs. Rockefeller and thousands of blacks and others sang "We Shall Overcome" and showed that the deep sorrow and anger at the act of assassination was shared, that it would not be forgotten, and in fact would be a strong catalyst for further changes in the months and years ahead—as indeed it was. During the service he grasped the arm of one of the fiery speakers and firmly moved him back away from the microphone, when it seemed that his oratory was becoming inflammatory rather than uplifting. In this and other ways he insisted on moderation as the way to go in bringing about the racial equality he so longed to see established and to which he consistently made generous contributions of money, time, and leadership.

Rockefeller made many gifts, large and small, to black causes, black churches and colleges, and other entities during his life. It cannot be nailed down whether a number of these gifts proceeded from his being cornered in one place or another by a persistent black who knew of Rockefeller's soft heart when it came to matters of race and efforts to improve opportunities for blacks in Arkansas. Those around him knew of worthy causes that would be appropriate for his charity, and recommended those to him, and he tried to approach that giving with perhaps more organization and planning than he gave to other causes. Beneficiaries covered a wide range, from churches to educational institutions particularly for blacks, to farm organizations and to asylums and of course those organizations in which he had confidence would work for the same causes he was supporting sometimes piecemeal. Many of them were still controversial in a segregationist state like Arkansas. Many churches benefited from his charity, in part because the preachers who headed them were also political activists who knew how to cut through the red tape and the phalanx of aides around him to make the request somewhat forcefully and in person. Most of the black or mostly black institutions of higher education in Arkansas, which he supported, were weak and not particularly promising. One exception was Arkansas A&M College in Pine Bluff, which became the University of Arkansas at Pine Bluff in later years. Another was Philander Smith College, which suffered from leadership with which Rockefeller was singularly unimpressed. On one occasion when he was being solicited for a gift at a meeting of administrators and faculty there, he got up from his seat, took the arm of one of the Philander Smith folks, and led him to a nearby window. Then he dragged the man's hand down the very dusty pane of glass and made a point about getting the house in the best possible order before asking for more money from anyone. Nevertheless, he was a supporter, and the college has continued to develop into a good institution. Major gifts from the Winthrop Rockefeller Foundation, in particular, and the trust, have been aimed at continuing the effort to bring about racial equality. Details are presented in chapters under those headings or in the appendices pertaining to each.

When Rockefeller took office as governor, many who had been denied the promise of an equal chance saw hope in him. In large numbers, they came to him in one way or the other. Many were black, most were impoverished and needed basic things for their houses. They wanted Rockefeller to help them. His philosophy—based on that old saw that if you give a man a fish, you feed him for a day, but if you teach a man to fish, you feed him for a lifetime—was about to be given the acid test. Bob Fisher, who worked closely with Rockefeller on race relations during that period, recalls that

> there were many people in the black community who felt they were entitled to a handout from Rockefeller, just because his name was Rockefeller. They would come to him, wanting $5 or $5,000 or whatever was available, and of course if they got that, then they would disappear for a time and the money would disappear with them and then they would be back. To sort of thwart that, it was his thinking that his money could best be spent and they could best be served by first putting it into education. He supported Shorter College, for example, and supported it and held it up when he was about the only supporter. Shorter College at that time was in direct competition with Philander Smith College, which he also helped. But Shorter College was really striving to survive more than anything else, and he supported that college even though they might be suspect as far as teaching credentials are concerned. He supported the college with the idea that the best way to help the poor, the downtrodden and the impoverished was by giving them an education so that they could get jobs.[10]

Meanwhile, as aides and others told him about the needs of these blacks who were calling on him at the capitol for such basic things as furniture, Rockefeller proposed to help them find or make their own. He employed a man skilled at pulling scrap lumber from construction sites and fashioning furniture from it. The press published various stories about how the governor had launched a program to show those in need how they could find free materials and were given instructions about how to build their own furniture. "Furniture for Families," the program was called. It was precipitated by a delegation from the Welfare Rights Organization who staged a demonstration in the governor's office demanding that furniture be provided for people too poor to buy their own. Rockefeller's idea was to place the manager in a leased building and organize things so that if the welfare folks would provide the labor, materials could be rounded up from scrap piles, donated lumber, and discarded or donated furniture. "New" furniture could be built and old furniture refurbished there. Examples were built to show how it could be done and how good the furniture would look in their homes. It bombed. Aides insisted to Rockefeller that those folks who were demonstrating weren't really that interested in building furniture themselves; they just wanted financial help. At first, Rockefeller didn't believe that, and he persisted with the program until it clearly was a failure.

Jones commented about that philosophy about teaching a man to fish rather than just giving him a fish, saying, "The feeling that I got was that sometimes people get the wrong impression when you talk about teaching a man to fish rather than giving him a fish. I think that's true and that's what he did and what he believed. But that's used sometimes to justify teaching a person to fish when they have no access to a fishing pole or being able to cut down a tree and make a fishing pole."[11] Jones said Rockefeller believed in making those things accessible to a person so that he could in fact fish. "He wanted to be able to make the kind of impact that was possible only if you made opportunity available to people," Jones explained, adding: "I think that many of the things that happened in Arkansas when Win Rockefeller was governor were caused by people having hope because he provided opportunity."[12]

William L. "Sonny" Walker was the first black to be appointed to an important position in state government. He was controversial, to say the least, and Rockefeller really took some heat from his staff and others as he contemplated making Walker the head of the Office of Economic Opportunity (OEO). Walker had compiled a track record of effectiveness in working with both blacks and whites, and Rockefeller surmised that his strengths were of more importance than was the controversy surrounding him. "I was always in the news," Walker said in a 2001 interview, "so I became a very high profile figure. In some instances, I was not thought of very highly by a lot of people . . ."[13]

Rockefeller defended Walker strongly, and Walker remembers Rockefeller saying, "There have been times when Sonny Walker and I have differed on things, but I have found him to be a person who does what he says he will do. I take his word that he has made a commitment to me and will be a seasoned and responsible person in operating the state agency."[14] Walker was so controversial that even before Rockefeller named him to head the state Office of Economic Opportunity, a group of Little Rock businessmen chartered a bus and headed over to Kensett to prevail upon Rep. Wilbur Mills (then described as the most powerful man in Washington, owing to his chairmanship of the House Ways and Means Committee) to help them remove Walker from his position as head of the Pulaski County agency. Mills declined. Rockefeller said when he was appointing Walker to the OEO job that he had been aware of what he described as a "pilgrimage" to see Mills. He said both he and Mills felt that the criticism of Walker was unjustified.

Fisher recalled that Walker was a firebrand, a real revolutionary in the eyes of many. "But Sonny was a stout guy, had a mind of his own," Fisher added, noting that Walker at first wasn't at all sure he wanted the OEO job, "because he didn't want to leave the impression that he was selling out. He didn't want it to look like Rockefeller had bought him, that he had put down the sword and taken up the feather duster."[15]

Here's how Rockefeller appears to Walker in retrospect:

> I think he set a different kind of climate in the state and that's probably his greatest contribution even more than his philanthropic gifts. He set the tone for blacks. For example, he had a commitment to appoint a black to every board and every commission in the state. Winthrop Rockefeller had a commitment to be sure we had black state policemen. He wanted blacks in positions like the Civil Service board that did the testing for state jobs. He wanted blacks on the State Board of Education. Being the wealthy person that he was, he was always called upon to help. He tried to find legitimate ways that he could have confidence that the money would be used for the purpose it was said it would be used. For example, he set up a system whereby he had tried to help the welfare mothers get clothes; and this was his money. And of course he put his own money into supplementing salaries for people in state jobs. Rockefeller paid some of us—including me—a supplemental check in order to get the kind of folk he wanted in state government. Rockefeller attempted to change things in the private sector as well.[16] Now I don't think that he just unloaded his money in any sort of irresponsible way. He tried to find organizations that he felt could be accountable for whatever resources he gave because he always wanted it to go for those things they indicated they were going to use the money for.[17]

Rockefeller commissioned Fisher to take four black ministers to visit principal state agencies and find out from the directors of those agencies what jobs were available, what it took to get those jobs, and how these black leaders could go back home and say, "There are jobs there. This is what you have to do to apply for them. This is what you have to do to qualify, and here are the people you need to see." There had been no access before, and Rockefeller was trying to create that access. He succeeded to a considerable degree, but it took a while. Initially, according to Fisher, "the fruits of that effort were not all that abundant." But as time went on and the tenacity and persistence of Rockefeller had permeated throughout the state on this issue, conditions did improve and many blacks were able to secure positions that would have been unheard of for them during any preceding administration. "He was willing to pay whatever expenses were involved from his own pocket," Fisher explained, "to try to help the black leadership help themselves, to learn how the system worked, to learn where the buttons of power were located so they could push them and try to get their people on board to help run the state and to have access to some of those state jobs."[18]

An article in the *Arkansas Gazette* as Rockefeller was leaving office and as his successor, Dale Bumpers, was moving in as governor, ticked off achievements by Rockefeller in the area of race relations. There had been a dramatic increase in the number of black state employees, from 325 black state employees when he took office in 1967 to some 1,800 in 1971 upon his departure, and with 170 of them holding administrative positions.

After his defeat in an attempt to win a third term as governor, and less than two years before his death, the State Organization for Minority Evolvement presented Rockefeller with a plaque at a banquet at the National Baptist Hotel in Hot Springs. The date was April 24, 1971, and the words on the plaque seemed to capture the meaning of Rockefeller's leadership—publicly and in his private philanthropy as well—for blacks in Arkansas:

> *Governor Winthrop Rockefeller. An inspiration to the young. A symbol of security for the old. Full of love, warmth and compassion. A champion of human rights, brotherhood and dignity who brought the Rockefeller family tradition to Arkansas and sacrificed time, resources, energy and public office for the causes of unity, justice and equality. Thank you for all you have done and are doing to make our state the land of opportunity for all Arkansans. God bless you. The black people of Arkansas.*[19]

CHAPTER

3

Education and Youth

Education was a problem for Winthrop Rockefeller. He never achieved much at all in the classroom, so to speak, and no honor or award throughout his educational career ever mentioned scholarship. A disappointment to his family, he managed to get into Yale but dropped out after a time and never returned to the classroom again, except many years later at Winrock Farms. There, he instituted a reading program for the employees and studied right alongside them. Afterward, he pointed out somewhat ruefully that most of them made more progress than he did.

Dyslexia plagued him all his life. Give him a memorandum and he might or might not read it. If he did, it seemed to take forever, and most things he just didn't bother to read. During the political campaigns—particularly the early ones—when nervous aides were firing off memoranda with abandon, seeking decisions about what they considered to be weighty matters, Rockefeller didn't usually respond. At first, when asked, he would explain to one or the other of them with a chuckle, "You'd be surprised how few of those memos are really important." Only later were they told by Rockefeller's assistant at Winrock, Jane Bartlett, and then by him as well that he read very few of them. However, tell him something and he had a phenomenal capacity for absorbing and retaining the information.

A poignant and most revealing letter was directed to Professor Charles E. Sellers at Loomis Institute from John D. Rockefeller Jr. on July 8, 1929:

"I cannot let the termination of the school year pass without writing to express the appreciation with which Mrs. Rockefeller and I regard the assistance which you rendered Winthrop so patiently and kindly throughout the winter . . . We of course have understood that the school is not in the habit of rendering such outside assistance to the pupils, and are therefore the more appreciative of what Mr. Batchelder arranged for you to do for Winthrop and two or three other boys who had special need."[1] (N. H. Batchelder was headmaster at Loomis.) For perhaps this and other reasons, Rockefeller had great affection for Loomis all his life, and even as a student took on a major responsibility for helping raise funds to support it. He recalled that as the school was carrying on a vigorous endowment campaign among alumni and friends, he concluded that students who would profit from it should take part. "I organized a student campaign," he said, "which has been the source of funds for building a new athletic field, four new tennis courts and a wing on the gymnasium."[2] Rockefeller and his classmates contributed labor to the school as well as money they were able to earn. "Every boy who took part in that work developed a special enthusiasm for Loomis," he said, "and my part as the originator of the campaign was particularly rewarding. I have always retained my interest in Loomis."[3] Rockefeller graduated from Loomis in 1931, and in that year received the school's Batchelder Award for "industry, loyalty and manliness."

Athletic activities were not the highest priority for Rockefeller, even then, but he understood that with the appropriate emphasis, such activities could be an important aspect of the educational process. While most of his gifts in later life did not involve athletics, he made an exception in 1965 and gave Ouachita Baptist University some $50,000 to complete a new field house. The university responded with a glowing resolution from the board of trustees and the naming of the field house for Rockefeller. The fieldhouse was later incorporated into a larger structure and except for a plaque pretty much lost its identity.

The resolution noted that the Rockefeller family for three generations had supported Baptist causes throughout the United States, and that Rockefeller himself—as "the distinguished Arkansas member of this great family, during the past 10 years has supported private higher education in this state in numerous and generous ways."[4] The resolution noted that Rockefeller had encouraged the Rockefeller Brothers Fund (RBF) to invest in Arkansas, which had both enriched and strengthened Ouachita, and then went on to name the new building the Winthrop Rockefeller Field House. Rockefeller—at the dedication—described the facility as "proof, in brick and mortar, that Ouachita is seeking to meet the total educational needs of those whose lives it influences so much." He praised Ouachita for "having the type of educational program covering the whole range of human needs—intellectual, spiritual and physical."[5]

Because Rockefeller performed so poorly in formal education was not to suggest that he did not respect and value it highly. Indeed, he devoted most of his life and a sizable amount of his charitable resources in supporting education at all levels. He tied it in with youth in general, and the programs he provided and opportunities he created were significant. Some 43 percent of all outright gifts by Rockefeller during his lifetime went to education and youth. An arbitrary separation of the two shows that he gave $8,347,719 to education and $233,659 to programs for youth. His interests and involvements varied considerably, reflecting his wide range of experiences and perceived needs that pertained to young people. He was named chairman of a special conference on problems of rural youth in a changing environment, sponsored by the National Committee for Children and Youth, and he employed Elmo Roper and Associates to conduct a study of children in rural environments to learn about attitudes, wants, and needs. "I feel deeply," he said, "that we must anticipate needs and tailor our community activities not only to accommodate youth and its growth but to stimulate it. This is our role, even if it requires our own adjustment to new mores."[6] He was striving to understand and to help shape policy that would benefit youth. As the years went by, more and more he tied opportunities for youth in general with educational opportunity— hence the much greater amounts he gave to support education. Rockefeller provided scholarships and even built the model school from his concern for quality and for educational opportunity and equality that might otherwise not be there for many.

He tied his interest in youth to two other areas of significance in his own life—agriculture and aviation—and created many opportunities for learning in both areas. Rockefeller had developed an interest in aviation early in life, and as a student in the Lincoln School in New York City (he must have been sixteen or seventeen) he arranged for explorer Richard Byrd to come to the school and speak about the admiral's 1927 trans-Atlantic flight. One of his friends in early life was Frank Hawks, who broke the speed record in a 1929 flight from Los Angeles to New York. Hawks knew that American youth must become more interested in aviation and flying, as were European youngsters, as the threat of war mounted. He played an important role in stimulating Rockefeller's lifelong interest in aviation while also turning him on to the Air Youth of America cause. (Later the organization became a part of the National Aeronautic Association.) Rockefeller made contributions for three years—

1939, 1940, and 1941—leading up to World War II. His total gifts to Air Youth of America only amounted to $18,235, but more important than the gifts of money was his leadership. As chairman, he worked to build the organization and to raise funds from others he felt should also help to support it— like Felix du Pont Jr., Henry Luce, William S. Paley, Dr. A. Hamilton Rice, and a number of other widely known personages whom he succeeded in recruiting to support the organization. His letters to them were short and to the point. To Mr. Luce, for example, he sent a descriptive booklet about the organization and stated that until he began his efforts he had not realized the tremendous enthusiasm on the part of youngsters throughout the country for building model airplanes nor how valuable such a youth program could be in connection with juvenile delinquency. He and the other sponsors and organizers foresaw that this interest could be captured in such a way that youngsters who wished to plan careers in aviation would be stimulated and encouraged to pursue such careers. "We have planned our program with the idea that it will be ultimately self-supporting," Rockefeller wrote. "However, in the interim period, the operating and promotion charges will be heavy. We are therefore attempting to raise some funds at present and I am very hopeful that you will be tempted and will send us a check . . ."[7] Many did. This effort—Rockefeller and others explained—must include a long-term program of education to prepare the youth of the nation to fill the many highly technical places brought about by the establishment of new services, as well as the expansion of others. The deep conviction on the part of most, in the assessment of Rockefeller, at least, was that America must make every effort to establish a program of defense that would not only ensure safety from aggression, but likewise establish a strong, lasting peace in the Western Hemisphere.

While Rockefeller expected generous support for such a worthy cause, he also gave himself, as has been noted. But it was not all smooth sailing. Like all the other members of the Rockefeller family, there is no doubt that every strategy known to man was employed to get money from him and even so distinguished an organization as the Flight Safety Foundation of New York—which was a natural place for Rockefeller to provide financial support, with his interest in flying and flight safety—stepped over the line on at least one occasion. When anyone presumed too much, they felt the heat of his anger at their trying to take advantage. Here is a portion of a letter he wrote in August 1959 to Mr. Ansel Talbert of the Flight Safety Foundation:

> I have your lengthy letter of July 22, and only hope that your technical research is handled with greater accuracy than your accounting. During

the past nine years I have contributed seven years, a total amount of something exceeding $13,000. I regret that a contribution was not made in 1957 or 1958, but at no time in sending my contribution have I felt that I have implied an annual responsibility. In case there should be any misunderstanding on this score, I will repeat for the record that I feel no obligation for an annual contribution. Before reading your letter of the 22nd, I had instructed Mrs. Irby [Rockefeller's assistant in his business office] to send a check for $2,000 and, in spite of your letter, the check will still be forthcoming.[8]

He continued to make regular contributions through 1972, the year before he died.

Rockefeller's charitable interests in his early years reflected the influence of his parents, but early on he was searching for his own focus on particular areas of interest. Yet, in that eclectic mix of targets for his philanthropy, he found opportunities to support education and youth, and by the time he reached Arkansas he had zeroed in on a particular set of causes that he stayed with for the remainder of his life. Indeed, his interest was focused, and he formed the Rockwin Fund to help manage his education philanthropy. It was directed by one of his closest friends and education advisors, the late Mary McLeod. Educated at Wellesley and having come with her husband whose work brought him to Arkansas to live, she brought a level of sophistication to Rockefeller's educational philanthropy that was unique to Arkansas—as indeed was she, and of course as was Rockefeller himself. One spate of controversy erupted over the Rockwin Fund in 1968 (when Rockefeller was running for reelection as governor) when the late Wright Patman, a Texas congressman, hammered away on Rockefeller (among others), by proposing that tax-exempt foundations such as the Rockwin Fund donate their receipts to the government during the Vietnam War. Patman was chairman of the House Banking Committee, so he was widely quoted and perhaps his criticism carried some weight, but nothing much came of it. Rockefeller described Patman's criticism as "another political maneuver" and noted that annual reports of all transactions had been filed with the Internal Revenue Service and had never been questioned. He added that "Congressman Patman has been attacking me and my family and others for years."[9]

About $4 million of Rockefeller's gifts to education were in Arkansas, not including gifts specified in his will that will be documented in the chapter devoted to the Rockefeller Trust, which exists to carry out his wishes as expressed and implied in that will.

Rockefeller was awarded a number of honorary degrees and other honors, including doctorates from the University of Arkansas, New York University, Hendrix College, the College of William and Mary, and the University of San Francis Xavier at Sucre, Bolivia. He was made an honorary member of Kappa Delta Pi, a national honorary fraternity in education, and at various points in his life served as a trustee for New York University Medical Center, Vanderbilt University, and Loomis Institute, among many others.

Rockefeller saw the tremendous advantages in reaching people early in life in order to set them on the path to interests in things outside themselves. He always tried to champion agriculture, although it could be—and often was— a comparatively dull area to many kids. But, he found ways to help fund rodeos for high school kids, for example, and believed that could be translated into an interest in horses and cattle and by extension into all areas of agriculture. He went the last mile, so to speak, more than once to demonstrate his support. On one particular occasion, for example, it was noted that he stayed up until 3 A.M. at a rodeo for high schoolers in order to present a saddle and other honors and awards to the winners of various contests. This was during the 1964 campaign for governor. When he finished with the presentation, he called his campaign manager, Eisele, and of course woke him up from a sound sleep. He was reported to have stated, "I am on my second set of pilots, and wondered if there was anywhere else you wished me to go." He chuckled with glee and hung up.[10]

Rockefeller made many smaller gifts to programs for youth along the way, as well as some larger ones. It is safe to say that his heart and his charitable nature got ahead of his objective judgment on occasion, and many of those small gifts he made never even caused a blip on any screen. He virtually wrote the check for one episode of "Agriculture USA," a television broadcast centered on agriculture. This program featured some Arkansas youngsters, including two or three volunteers on his political staff. His plane ferried them to the production studio, and he picked up the tab for all expenses. The program aired in the early morning on a number of stations, but it is doubtful if very many young Arkansans—or older ones, for that matter—were up at 7 A.M. to see it.

He would give money to such established entities as the 4-H Club Foundation, and could feel pretty good that the money would be used as intended. The same went for a number of other such charities, but there were others that could only be described as "doubtful." Someone would grab him by the elbow at a meeting somewhere and extract a promise from Rockefeller —however reluctant—to make a gift. His soft heart was the source of lots of

Rockefeller loved being with young people and found many ways to try to help them up and on to successful futures. Scholarships were one way. "Agriculture USA" was another. He managed to get a group of Arkansas kids on the nationally televised program and went with them to the filming, participated in the briefings, and appeared on the program himself. (Photo courtesy of University of Arkansas, Little Rock, Archives, WR VII Album WR-A-40–41)

difficulties for him and for his staff, whose phones began ringing early the next day, asking for the money. Sometimes, obviously, Rockefeller didn't remember specifically having made the commitment; and of course, the staff was obliged to first determine if a gift was promised, then to sort out the differences in what Rockefeller remembered that he had promised and the new and higher figure that the charity was now asking for. Rockefeller was touched by hard-luck stories. His staff noted that anyone with a crutch had a sure thing if they could just get to Rockefeller and get that crutch into his field of view. The staff tried to protect him. They often succeeded, and Rockefeller was spared a few hundred of the sad stories that might or might not be credible. The names of the organizations seeking support from the charitably inclined were carefully devised to hit home, and they covered the range of human suffering. The list was long and never shortened in the least during all the years that Rockefeller was a benefactor.

One of the comparatively larger gifts in the general area of "youth" included Boy Land of Arkansas. Rockefeller donated a total of $27,168 from 1963 to 1968. This Arkansas program was aimed at providing a safe haven for troubled youth who could be helped through their difficulties and returned to society with value and purpose. Unfortunately, the program faded away after the death of Robert Bitter of Springdale, the man who had put it together and ran it successfully.

Rockefeller contributed $64,106.88 to Boy Scouts of America from 1954 through 1972, and made a gift of $5,812.50 to the Boys Industrial School Foundation of Pine Bluff, a program to help incarcerated teenagers.

Heading the list of gifts to education were three categories that accounted for most of his larger contributions in Arkansas, including the Rockwin Fund (his creation), $2.1 million; the Morrilton Public Schools, $787,000; the Arkansas Foundation of Associated Colleges in Arkansas, $463,000; and the Arkansas Opportunity Fund (his creation), $425,000. The AOF was a leading sponsor of scholarships given through the National Merit Scholarship Corporation, and Rockefeller was its principal supporter in the state.

In 1956 Rockefeller asked for advice from the state Department of Education and Arkansas State Teachers College (now the University of Central Arkansas) about determining the needs of the Morrilton School District, which included his homestead on Petit Jean Mountain. At that time, ASTC (commonly called "Teachers College") was the principal institution preparing students to teach in Arkansas public schools. Rockefeller thought the Morrilton district needed some kind of major shot in the arm to come up to a level where its students could be competitive with students from other pockets of quality in the state and beyond, and he was willing to provide some serious support to make that happen. But what to do?

After thoughtful study and lots of interaction with Rockefeller, a plan was conceived that would take a major chunk of his money but had promise to establish a high standard and plant the seed for continuing after Rockefeller's support came to an end.

So he provided money for the construction of an elementary school ($750,000), and then through the Rockwin Fund he provided a five-year grant of $100,000 annually to enrich the program through increased teacher salaries, a broader curriculum, and other changes to improve quality. Rockefeller wanted those living in the district to help out as well. It was the way he sup-

One of Rockefeller's proudest achievements was creation of Reynolds Elementary School in Morrilton. He built it and endowed it with the idea that it could become a model institution. It has continued to operate at a successful level. (Photo courtesy of University of Arkansas, Little Rock, Archives, WR-A-33, Reynolds Elementary School, 1957)

ported many projects, believing that if it were all his money, public support and pride would be minimal. The people came through. They voted a higher school millage and increased property assessments.

Meanwhile, Rockefeller (through the Rockwin Fund) was the initial donor to the Little Rock School District's Kindergarten Educational Enrichment Program (KEEP), a forerunner of the Headstart program. Mrs. Fred Schmutz, a Little Rock housewife and strong civic activist, was determined to take vigorous and effective action to improve their schools and provide better education for their children, according to *Parade* magazine in 1965. The program won a national award, and Mrs. Schmutz wrote Rockefeller: "We cannot tell you how grateful we are for the contribution you made to us on behalf of these children. The impetus your generous kick-off contribution gave to our drive assured its success."[11]

Rockefeller presented a check at the dedication of the elementary school that he built and endowed at Morrilton. Robert Harris (at left), Sen. J. William Fulbright, and George Reynolds (at right) participated in the program. Reynolds was the son of prominent Arkansas educator John Hugh Reynolds, for whom the school was named. (Photo courtesy of University of Arkansas, Little Rock, Archives, WR-A-33, Reynolds Elementary School, 1957)

While developing a strong program of giving to Arkansas colleges and universities and related programs, Rockefeller kept up his support for some out-of-state institutions, including Vanderbilt University, Columbia University, Cornell, New York University, Rice Institute, the Abby Aldrich Rockefeller Scholarship Fund, and Hockaday School in Dallas. His stepdaughter, Anne, had attended Hockaday and he felt obliged to be supportive. He also was a major supporter of Loomis Institute and Yale University, two institutions where he had been a student.

CHAPTER

4

Culture and the Arts

Win just grew up with beautiful things. He had an appreciation —an innate appreciation—of them.

—ANNE BARTLEY

Winthrop Rockefeller was determined to bring an appreciation for things beautiful to his fellow Arkansans.[1] With his wife, Jeannette, that goal was put on permanent tracks to success. Standing as a kind of memorial to this is the Arkansas Arts Center, a magnificent edifice in Little Rock filled with beautiful art, educational programs, and in particular a mechanism for delivering art throughout Arkansas and making it available to those who otherwise would not see it. It didn't come easy. Rockefeller and his wife had to expend considerable effort just to get the folks who could help make it happen to enroll in the vision. Then they found themselves crisscrossing Arkansas for weeks on end to raise interest—and money—to give the idea a base from which to grow.

A philosophy of giving to worthy causes wasn't well understood in Arkansas. Indeed, Townsend Wolfe, the present director of the Arkansas Arts Center, notes that during that period of time "philanthropy for the people in Arkansas was a brand-new thing."[2]

The first challenge to Mr. and Mrs. Rockefeller was to raise the sights of those with a genuine interest in developing an arts center. The Junior League of Little Rock came to them with a plan to raise $250,000 to develop a "Community Center of Arts and Sciences" in Little Rock. Jeane Hamilton, a key person in the Junior League and a prime mover in the arts center project, arranged with colleagues Carrie Dickinson and Marilyn McHaney to meet with Rockefeller, who invited them to a Sunday lunch with him and Mrs. Rockefeller. She remembered it this way in a 2000 interview published in the *Arkansas Democrat-Gazette:* "We told him we wanted to build a community arts center in Little Rock. I'll never forget this as long as I live. We were sitting there in that living room with that rock fireplace, and he said, 'Well, girls (certainly not politically correct and likely not then either), if we're going to build an arts center let's do it right.' That opened up whole new vistas for us. We made an executive decision—not to build a Little Rock arts center but to make it an Arkansas Arts Center."[3]

"The committee came to discuss the plans with Mrs. Rockefeller and myself," Rockefeller wrote in a 1960 letter to Mr. John Osman at the Fund for Adult Education in White Plains, New York. The committee's hope was to enlist their aid in the fund-raising campaign. "With the experience that Mrs. Rockefeller and I have had in fund-raising and in building," his letter continued, "we felt that their sights were too low and essentially would only produce disappointment."[4] The Rockefellers agreed to help "if they would raise their sights to $750,000, which would include the organization of a statewide campaign," he wrote. Rockefeller wanted them to envision the state as the community and thought that such a plan would have appeal to national foundations. In addition to the efforts of him and Mrs. Rockefeller throughout the state, with excellent response, Rockefeller noted, "On the side I have done a little informal inquiring about the possibility of foundation support, in view of the uniqueness of the concept, and if all goes as I expect we can count on a minimum of $250,000 in foundation support."[5]

Anne Bartley said about the effort, "From the very beginning it was taking art out to everybody—all the rural towns, the black population, white population, wherever. It wasn't just for the wealthy. It was about human dignity and letting people see what humans can create and what they are capable of creating. It was challenging the whole population of Arkansas that this is what humans can do. It is something to strive for, something to learn about, something through which to learn about yourself."[6]

Part of Rockefeller's interest in culture and the arts across the state had to do with his efforts on another front—industrial and economic development. When he assumed the chairmanship of the Arkansas Industrial Development Commission he set about to try to get in place the kinds of things that would help to attract industry to a state that had very little and dim prospects at best for more. It was all a part of his grand vision and he was willing—as the arts center effort illustrates—to put money and, perhaps more important, his leadership into those worthy projects such as the arts center. As chairman of the AIDC, Rockefeller described himself as keenly aware of the important emphasis that potential industrial prospects placed on cultural opportunities for their employees when they were making decisions about plant locations. He knew that art centers were not something very many cities could even begin to establish or manage, and suggested that the Arkansas Arts Center taking form would be a useful tool to the AIDC and to the state as a whole in helping to lure industrial prospects to look over the state. Rockefeller expressed the hope that through the establishment of the arts center there could be workshops for schoolteachers from every Arkansas community; that the arts center could feature exhibitions from the public and private schools of the state; that summer seminars could be instituted for instruction in painting, sculpture, and ceramics; and that circulating exhibitions as well as mobile units containing original art works could travel throughout the state.

The Arkansas Arts Center was opened in 1963, and cost about $1.5 million. Rockefeller had contributed $432,426 through that year and would contribute another $1,603,626 to the arts center before his death, with more to come from the charitable trust afterward. Mrs. Rockefeller continued her involvement also, serving as a trustee and then as president. The program was immediately a statewide one, as the Rockefellers envisioned, thanks in part to the acquisition of an artmobile, which enabled the center to take art from one corner of the state to the other.

Some twenty-eight communities had arts center chapters, and programs in the Little Rock facility offered instruction in drawing, painting, pottery making, sculpture, graphic arts, ceramics, enameling, acting technique, and creative drama. Students ranged in age from preschool to senior citizens. Also, a four-year program of professional courses was offered. Wolfe said that in 1982 the Winthrop Rockefeller Gallery was added to the arts center, and it had no Rockefeller money in it at all. "We did not approach any member of the family, the charitable trust, the foundation. It was a way in which I wanted this community indeed to honor someone who had done so much for us."[7]

Rockefeller never really liked raising money. Perhaps he had been hit up so many times himself that he was reluctant to turn the tables on others. But if he believed in it, if he was passionate about it, he bored in and was more often than not quite successful. So he and Mrs. Rockefeller set out and in twenty-one days visited nineteen different communities and had lunch or dinner to give the pitch for the Arkansas Arts Center. Ms. Hamilton said that with their help, the museum gained wider financial support from community leaders and "then Rockefeller went to the Rockefeller Brothers Foundation, which matched the money raised."[8]

Dorothy Kilgallen, a *New York Times* columnist, reported that "Win is just trying to take culture to the barefoot people of Arkansas."[9] Wolfe was offended by that, and he said it grated on Rockefeller as well. However, in an overly dramatized way and allowing for the view of New Yorkers that Arkansas and perhaps most of the nation west of the Mississippi River was covered wagons end to end, Arkansas remained a comparatively unsophisticated place. Although Rockefeller was generous with his gifts to the project, he tried to downplay that as much as he could because he held fast to the belief that he and Jeannette must convince people that they had to help support the arts center "because it was theirs; it was their responsibility, not his," Wolfe remembers.[10] And, according to Wolfe, "he got people to understand and to reverse their thinking about this place . . . that it wasn't just his toy, but it was theirs . . . and they (the people) began to take ownership and we began to build on it."[11] "Townsend," Rockefeller said more than once to Wolfe, "I want this place to be good. Not only do I want it to be good, I want it to be the best it can possibly be."[12]

Rockefeller got his family involved early on. David Rockefeller donated a Renoir painting for the opening in 1963, and his sister, Abby Mauze, donated a Diego Rivera painting. Other members of the family made substantial gifts as well, as did the Rockefeller Brothers Fund. In an article later in the *New York Times* written by Arkansan Steve Barnes, Ms. Hamilton is quoted as saying "Win was the key man. Without Win, we would have never got the center off the ground."[13]

While stumping the state to raise money and build interest in the arts center, Rockefeller was also writing letters to moneyed friends and acquaintances, such as the one to Col. T. H. Barton, a wealthy and much-celebrated Arkansan who had a home in La Jolla, California. After greeting Barton and thanking him for his good wishes on Rockefeller's recent birthday (he turned 48 on May 1, 1960), Rockefeller told of the meetings he and Mrs. Rockefeller had participated in throughout the state on behalf of the arts center. He wanted Barton to kick in a generous sum, primarily to help get at artmobile to travel over the state, and on one occasion proposed laughingly but with a trace of seriousness that the vehicle could be dubbed the "Bartmobile." Rockefeller said he would be out west on the upcoming Memorial Day and "it occurred to me that if you didn't have other plans and were so inclined, I might once again fly down to La Jolla to visit with you about Mrs. Barton about the Arts Center, its progress, its potential, and the possibility that you both might still be interested in recommending to the Barton Foundation the donation of the Artmobile that we have discussed on several occasions previously."[14]

Barton came through, but with only about $5,000, considerably less than enough to buy an artmobile, and so Rockefeller's contribution to the arts center provided for the balance due on a mobile unit.

By the year 2000 the Arts Center, along with the related Decorative Arts Museum, plus the traveling shows and performances, was attracting some 350,000 visitors a year. The collection of art was valued at $25 million. The arts center membership totaled more than 5,000, and its annual budget was some $4.5 million.

A few days after Rockefeller's death in 1973, the Arkansas Arts Center's *Members Bulletin* had this to say:

> To many people in Arkansas, he meant a great deal, but to art in Arkansas, he meant almost everything. His dedication and wealth carried the main load of the peoples' efforts to build and develop the Arkansas Arts Center, not only the finest institution of its kind in the state, but in the whole United States.
>
> With his wonderful, people-centered generosity, Winthrop Rockefeller spent the monies he committed to art not on building a great personal collection, but on developing the Arts Center; and by doing so, he opened up the possibility for every person in this state to become sensitive to art. No doubt in the long run, a citizenry so involved in art is the greatest collection of them all. Because of Winthrop Rockefeller's commitment to the Arkansas Arts Center, the Board of Trustees decided to dedicate the Center to him. All of us in Arkansas have lost a big, friendly human being who did more for us than anybody in a hundred years. Maybe now is the time to say thank you and pay him back.[15]

While the Arkansas Arts Center was the most obvious beneficiary of Rockefeller's charitable gifts to culture and the arts, it was one of many causes to which he directed resources and his attention.

Principal among those was the Sealantic Fund, which acquired Carter's Grove Plantation near Colonial Williamsburg and opened it to the public in 1964. The fund was established by Rockefeller's father, not as a general grant-making foundation, but as a program that confined its activities to certain special projects, including the preservation of selected historic houses and sites in the lower Hudson River Valley. Carter's Grove, one of the James River Estates, has been described as the most beautiful house in America. It has

This plaque denotes the Winthrop Rockefeller Archaeology Museum, established near Carter's Grove Plantation to display artifacts and tell the story of Martin's Hundred and its administrative center, Wolstenholme Towne. (Photo courtesy of Colonial Williamsburg Foundation)

hosted such guests as George Washington, Thomas Jefferson, and Franklin D. Roosevelt and other prominent personages over three centuries. It was constructed in the 1750s.

Rockefeller, who served as chairman of the board of Colonial Williamsburg for many years, was involved in the acquisition and operation of Carter's Grove, and his gifts from 1964 through 1969 totaled $410,900. The Winthrop Rockefeller Archaeology Museum was established a decade after his death to present exhibits and artifacts recovered from nearby sites of Martin's Hundred and its administrative center, Wolstenholme Towne. In the museum, a modern underground facility, the story is told of how Colonial Williamsburg archaeologists discovered and excavated the site. Parts of weapons, agricultural tools, ceramics, and domestic artifacts on display in the museum illustrate how the settlers lived in the Old World and their strategies for survival in the New World.

Inside the Winthrop Rockefeller Archaeology Museum visitors study artifacts such as this helmet (one of two) recovered from settler life at Martin's Hundred and learn the story of survival in the New World. (Photo courtesy of Colonial Williamsburg Foundation)

Rockefeller's gifts to Williamsburg other than for the Carter's Grove project were comparatively modest, totaling $16,117. (However, the Winthrop Rockefeller Charitable Trust made a substantial gift, which will be discussed in the chapter devoted to the Trust.) The Museum of Modern Art, an important New York location for the showing of fine works by such distinguished artists as Cezanne, Gauguin, and Van Gogh, attracted support from Rockefeller in 1948. He gave $21,750. The center was cofounded by his mother in 1929. The Rehearsal Club in New York was provided $13,336 by Rockefeller from 1947 through 1972. The club provided a residence for young girls in the theater, which included radio, television, concerts, nightclubs, and motion pictures. While in New York, Rockefeller had demonstrated a great deal of interest in theater and participated in various efforts to help strengthen it, but

Rockefeller wasn't particularly enamored of celebrities, although he encountered them all the time throughout his life, but he was intrigued and complimentary of the likes of jazz great Duke Ellington, with whom he was photographed backstage before a performance. Rockefeller was not a jazz aficionado, but he admired trailblazers such as Ellington. (Photo courtesy of University of Arkansas, Little Rock, Archives, WR-A-27.18)

he never gave much money, and continued a pattern of limited financial support after he arrived in Arkansas. His other gifts showed no perceptible pattern of particular interest, ranging from theatrical societies to arts councils and institutes to various libraries. He supported musical aggregations that covered the gamut with the exception of rock and roll and country and western. Included were high school bands, orchestras, and choral societies, and after his major support for the Arkansas Arts Center, he also helped the arts councils in Arkansas and elsewhere with which he had some connection, including festivals, museums, and clubs.

It seems clear that Rockefeller was far more interested in art than in music. That was apparent to all who were around him, but he understood that music deserved support as well. One thing singled out in his will was his interest in the oriental sculpture that was a part of the Eyrie Garden. A home at Seal Harbor known as "The Eyrie" belonging to the Rockefeller family was torn down in 1963, but the extensive gardens remained. Rockefeller's mother had started these gardens after a trip to the Orient. After the home was removed the gardens were opened one morning a week to a limited number of visitors. In his will, Rockefeller said that the garden, of which the sculpture forms an integral part, was worthy of permanent preservation and he recommended that the sculpture be transferred to the Island Foundation of Mount Desert, Maine. Ownership of the sculpture, valued at $130,675, however, was transferred by the trust to the Winthrop Rockefeller Foundation in 1975.

CHAPTER

5

Physical and Mental Health

Winthrop Rockefeller's interest and leadership in health matters was a gradual process that began quite modestly when he was still laboring in the Texas oil fields. He came from a rich tradition of giving to hospitals and health programs, with the pioneering work of his grandfather and further development of the family's interest in health matters carried on by his parents. Nevertheless, he didn't consider matters of health much of a priority in his early years of giving. That changed in 1947, when he became the first chairman of the board of New York University Medical Center, a post in which he served until he moved to Arkansas in 1953.

From the moment he became chairman, Rockefeller was determined to have input, to advance ideas that would help to guide the development of the medical center. "People are seeking health security today just as they are seeking financial security," he said on the occasion of his being named chairman. "Health security, as I understand it," he went on, "means the assurance to the average family that it will have access to the full benefits of modern medical science at a price it can afford. I believe that business and community leaders, working in cooperation with the medical profession, should accept the responsibility for meeting these demands."[1]

He wanted to think big and to enroll others in his vision for what could be. The *New York Times* in April 1950 quotes extensively Rockefeller's formula

Rockefeller was awarded an honorary doctorate by New York University Medical Center for his leadership and effectiveness in helping raise funds for the NYU-Bellevue merger. (Photo courtesy of University of Arkansas, Little Rock, Archives, WR 1.702)

for increasing the nation's health resources by developing throughout the nation a regional plan worked out by New York University–Bellevue Medical Center. According to Rockefeller, the nation was in a critical period in developing national health facilities, and he saw danger in many health programs that he said placed too much emphasis on the decisions of persons "too often partisan or specialized in their approaches." He called for cooperation between professional and laypersons and suggested that from regional groups could be drawn competent professional and laypersons who could provide teams to cope with the nation's health problems. He was quite proud of the regional plan developed by Bellevue and cited results at the new rural medical center at Hunterdon County, New Jersey, as an example of what he was talking about. That center, he said, drew upon the medical center for help in assessing local facilities and also as it developed a building program and techniques for securing community support. Through that teamwork, he said, "a model medical program is underway in this rural area."[2]

At the cornerstone-laying ceremonies for the medical science building on November 7, 1952, Rockefeller expressed his great pride in what had been accomplished. The complex had been in the process of development for five years to house a comprehensive program in medical education, research, and care of the sick. It had a price tag of $32 million, with the medical science building (at $7.5 million) as the second unit in the overall project. Rockefeller described the center as "an operating fact" and in his remarks at the occasion applauded the work of the 1,300 faculty members and 1,200 employees who, "despite cramped ancient buildings, inadequate facilities and other trying conditions, have worked faithfully."[3]

An article in the *Arkansas Democrat* in 1966 quoted board chairman Samuel D. Leidsdorf as saying that it if had not been for Rockefeller's work, devotion, and inspiration, "the New York University Medical Center—one of the outstanding such centers in the world—would never have been achieved."[4] The occasion for the remarks was a program honoring Rockefeller and electing him to the newly created post of honorary chairman of the board. Rockefeller also served on the New York City Board of Hospitals and as a director of the city's Public Health Research Institute. His first gift to NYU–Bellevue was in 1948, when he gave $14,575. Over the next years he would donate a total of $1,094,309.

When he got to Arkansas in 1953, Rockefeller had accumulated a great deal of knowledge and experience pertaining to the delivery of health care, and he proceeded to put all that to work in his adopted state. The University of Arkansas invited him to head the Medical Center Advisory Committee, and he accepted. The committee advised on the scope and activities of the university's new medical center, which occupied its new multi-million-dollar facilities in 1956. But Rockefeller would take the ideas he developed at Bellevue and apply them in a different way in Arkansas, of course on a much smaller scale. To him, scale wasn't nearly as important as the idea itself, and he would work just as hard, just as passionately as he set about to establish a rural health center in one of the poorest counties in Arkansas—Perry—and do so by developing for it a relationship with the University of Arkansas Medical Center that was clearly along the lines he had been involved in while in New York. He had long since learned that if a Rockefeller was seen putting big bucks in a project—however much it was designed to benefit the public—that public wasn't likely to put up a whole lot of money, on the assumption that those "deep pockets" would take care of it. As a part of his planning, he proposed and paid for a statewide survey of rural health needs in Arkansas. It was conducted by the University of Arkansas School of Medicine. The intent was to obtain a better knowledge about the distribution of medical services and facilities throughout the state and to gain some understanding of what would be required for a more efficient and effective coordination of what was already out there. "Furthermore," he advised Gov. Francis Cherry in a 1954 memorandum, "it is anticipated that such a study would be helpful in better defining the role and potentialities of the Medical Center in better serving the Arkansas community."[5] Rockefeller then outlined the advantage of a pilot project, "establishment of a modest clinic in a county which has no medical facilities currently available permitting study of how service could be rendered essentially within the means of that community by the development of the cooperation of the physicians in the surrounding area." He thought Perry County, with its close proximity to the Medical Center, would seem to "recommend itself for this pilot operation."[6]

Rockefeller had expressed to the governor that he had been concerned about "the problem of the distribution of adequate medical care" in Arkansas ever since he arrived, and that this concern was supported by the experience of five years' association with the New York University–Bellevue Medical Center. He saw the same problems here as he had seen in New York, he told the governor, and then gave the governor a report on the status of things as it pertained to a proposed rural health clinic that would serve as a model, perhaps. He had met with Dr. Hayden Nicholson, dean of the College of Medicine, along with several other interested persons, and then a meeting was conducted with the University of Arkansas president, Dr. John Tyler Caldwell, to see how much interest there would be in doing the statewide survey, first of all, and then a review of the problems and opportunities that Rockefeller and the others saw. Rockefeller told *Business Week* in an interview in 1955, "the cost of medicine has gotten to a point where people can't afford to get sick; they can only afford to spend money to keep well."[7] There were no ambulances in Perry County, no hospitals, no clinics, and no doctors licensed by the Arkansas Medical Society. The county population was six thousand.

An article in the *Arkansas Democrat* of January 30, 1955, written by Robert S. McCord, had this to say:

> There is no industry in Perry County. And even if there were, there are no young people left to work at it. Drouth after drouth has ruined the farming, and what dry weather didn't do to the cotton, the boll weevil did. Until recently no one was even vaguely interested in Perry County's problems, except, maybe, the people who live there. It would be a bit ridiculous, therefore, to assume that a man who has a 16-room apartment on Park Avenue, a man who is one of six heirs to the grandest for-

tune every accumulated by one man in the United States, would concern himself with Perry County. But this man has, and certainly it is a strange paradox of our times.[8]

McCord's article went on to point out the vast gifts made by Rockefeller's grandfather and father, and added that "the real paradox here is the fact that Rockefeller money is coming to Perry County, to each of its citizens directly, not to impalpable things like fellowships, foundations and boards. This automatically brings up the question that is often asked: 'What is Rockefeller doing in Arkansas anyway?'" The article continued by acknowledging that the question would not be answered in the article. "In fact," it stated, "as the matter now stands, no one in Arkansas, least of all the citizens of Perry County, really care. They are just pleased that there is a Santa Claus and that he lives on Petit Jean Mountain."[9]

With confirmation of needs and the appropriateness of a pilot project, Rockefeller set about in 1955 to establish the clinic in Perryville, the county seat and the largest town in the county. He had been in Arkansas only two years, but he was already deeply involved in a variety of worthy causes that people knew about and respected. They had confidence that he could get things done. Thus, it was a challenge but one that could be met to have the people of Perry County themselves put up a chunk of the money and a good bit of the labor needed to build the clinic, and then Rockefeller provided the equipment and three years of financial support. Perry County contributed $13,000 and a lot of labor to build the clinic, and then Rockefeller did the rest. He was exceedingly proud of the project, in particular because the folks in the county who could afford virtually nothing nevertheless managed to raise what was, for them, a considerable sum, to help the dream become reality. "Nobody would have guessed that you could have raised that much money in Perry County," Rockefeller told the reporter.[10]

So there it was: a modern brick and concrete building, with nineteen rooms, including two recovery rooms that could accommodate five beds in each, an X-ray room, a laboratory, an operating room, three examining and treatment rooms, a kitchen, three offices, and three toilets. Some two thousand people showed up on July 10, 1955, for the dedication of the clinic. It was the result of "a tremendous amount of dreaming, thinking and need," Rockefeller said at the time.[11] Arkansas government executives, business leaders from throughout the state, residents of Perry County, a doctor from British Honduras, and two young women from India were among the attendees. A colorful and controversial state representative, Paul Van Dalsem, had donated the site, and worked with Rockefeller in development of the plans for the clinic.

Later, they would become bitter political enemies. Van Dalsem reviewed the interest of the Rockefeller family in health and reminded his listeners of the campaign to eradicate hookworm, utilizing as part of the program a health train that passed through many counties of Arkansas, including Perry, in the ultimately successful program that began in 1915. Rockefeller told the audience that the problem the clinic hopefully could help to address was the fact that doctors tended to concentrate in certain localities (he meant in the cities) but they were hard to get out in the rural areas, and he hoped the clinic would reveal some ways in which this distribution problem could be solved. "There will be doubters who will say this cannot work," he said, and "there will be optimists who will expect too much; but here you will have a doctor who will give you first class medical service. And I believe the figures say that one out of every seven people need a doctor at least one time every year."[12]

Dr. Austin Gullett, whose hometown wasn't so far away from Perryville, was the first physician and for a while things went along quite well. Unfortunately, he left a year later to join a bigger medical clinic in nearby Morrilton. Then there was a kind of parade of doctors who came and stayed briefly while they put together another move somewhere else. Even with that, for the early years, clearly the clinic provided service and was a credit to the county, to the community, and to Rockefeller and those others who had dreamed this dream with him. But then his support—as scheduled from the beginning—ended after three years and it was time for the clinic to make it on its own. Actually, it didn't. Not at all the way Rockefeller had intended or hoped it would.

Dr. Ben Hyatt still practices part-time in the clinic, most of which is unused now. Perry County folks go to Morrilton, not so far away, for medical care and particular treatment, and Conway to the east, a city of forty thousand with a first-class hospital, is only about twenty miles distant.

At the time the clinic was built, transportation was more of an issue than it is now. The roads and highways have been greatly improved, the economy of the county is much better, and its population is increasing year by year. Dr. Hyatt has been there about forty years, and is looking toward retirement now. "At one time," he recalled, "I'll bet there were ten people employed here in various capacities. For example, any time anybody came in, a social worker took down kind of a life history of this person, where they were born, what kind of work they did, and so on. All about them. It would be single-spaced, three-quarters of a page of dictation in these people's chart."[13] He said there was also a stenographer, and many other employees, some of them really who were just being provided jobs, in his opinion. As a nonprofit corporation, it had a board of directors, but Dr. Hyatt said all of them have passed away and none was ever replaced. He said many people think that Perry County owns the clinic. "People every now and then will wonder, why doesn't the county do this and that? Why doesn't the county blacktop the driveway? Well, it's not the county's."

So what happens when Dr. Hyatt retires? "I don't know," he said. "I presume that quite possibly some informal arrangement will continue."

Looking back over his forty years at the clinic, has it provided a service that wouldn't be available somewhere else? "Oh, I don't think it has meant just a terrible whole lot to the community," he responded. "I think it has been a service to the community in a way, but in any small town, a lot of the people are accustomed to going to the next larger town to see the doctor or buy their clothing or whatever."[14] Dr. Hyatt sees patients at the clinic nowadays, but much of his medical practice is concentrated in the nursing home nearby.

Rockefeller, after the great start for the rural health clinic, became disappointed and frustrated as the years passed, and others at the University Medical Center and at the clinic itself made decisions with which he was not in agreement. He observed that many of those Perry County citizens who might have been expected to use the health clinic were driving over to Morrilton for their medical care, and as the Conway County Hospital grew, Rockefeller was asked for a gift to help the expansion project along. He gave $50,000 in 1966, and commented that he was delighted to supplement the bond issue. "We will have the kind of hospital we need now," he said, "a need that all citizens of my county have recognized for 10 years." Just ten years before, Rockefeller and others had celebrated the opening of the Perry County clinic.[15] Recalling the late Dr. Henry Mobley, whose medical practice the first doctor at the Perry County clinic had joined after just one year in Perryville, Rockefeller said about the Conway County Hospital, "I know he would be pleased that we are moving ahead with an institution of such excellence."[16]

Rockefeller helped arrange for a $500,000 gift from the Rockefeller Brothers Fund to the Arkansas Baptist Medical Center, announced in January of 1970, part of the hospital's major building-fund campaign. Before then, he had become involved in mental health issues. He hadn't naturally gravitated in his thinking toward mental health issues. It was his wife, Jeannette, passionate about them, who prodded and encouraged and informed and led until he caved in and became a real supporter. In 1963 he was named national campaign chairman of the National Association for Mental Health. "The year 1963 will be a decisive one in the fight against mental illness," Rockefeller said as the announcement was made. "Never before has there been so much interest in mental illness or such a demand for action to combat this grave national problem . . . Medical science must press further the search for more effective methods to treat mental illness."[17]

Jeannette Rockefeller worked tirelessly with her husband and on her own during the years 1956–70 in education, mental health, disabled children, and the arts. She was a philanthropist in her own right and was praised for both her leadership and her charitable giving. (Photo courtesy of University of Arkansas, Little Rock, Archives, WR VII 2.154)

About that time his Rockwin Fund agreed to underwrite the Conway County Association for Mental Health in a guidance clinic in Morrilton for counseling emotionally disturbed children and their families.

Rockefeller's personal gifts to physical and mental health causes amounted to $1,691,557 during his lifetime. Some of his gifts were to alcoholism groups (a health problem of his own that he struggled with throughout his adult life), cancer, heart, crippled children, retarded children, the blind, several mental health organizations, rehabilitation services, programs for tuberculosis treatment and other respiratory diseases, arthritis, rheumatism, polio, cerebral palsy—indeed, the whole gamut of diseases and health problems that afflicted his fellow citizens. He also contributed to the Birth Control Federation of America and other such organizations, which would have been quite a campaign issue, had news of that support reached the public. It would have appeared to his detractors as one of those liberal causes that rich New Yorkers and other privileged classes liked to support because the problems that were so distant from them were a kind of "feel good" outlet for their "generous spirit."

6

Religion

Rockefeller didn't attend church. Back in New York, that might not have been a big deal, at least not after he was grown, but in Bible-belt Arkansas in the 1950s if you didn't attend church you were frowned upon at best, and declared to be "going to hell" at worst. It was complicated, of course, and depended on which denomination you did or did not claim and whether you lived in a rural area or a city and a number of other factors that largely escaped Rockefeller. During his earlier days in Arkansas, it didn't seem to be such a problem. He wasn't visible unless he wanted to be anyway, and so people for the most part didn't really know what he was doing or not doing. But, when he began to inch toward political involvement, the issue began to grow into something serious, at least as far as his growing political staff was concerned. They and others interested in his political success tried to talk him into making an occasional appearance (he had indicated early on that he was a Baptist) but he resisted, offering a half-dozen reasons why he couldn't and, in fact, wouldn't. He said his presence in church might make a stir. He thought that would be disruptive. He knew that any church that landed him in the congregation would be anxious to have his financial support for the range of needs most churches had. His schedule was unpredictable to the extent that he couldn't be regular, and he didn't want to go to church on a piecemeal basis. It may well have been that the staff harping on this was remindful of his early days at home, when the rigidity of his father reached all the way to his bones, and he didn't want all that over again. He seemed to think of himself and the Christian life in a kind of detached way, talking about it (which he rarely did) in a philosophical way that leaned heavily on good works (Baptists argued that good works alone wouldn't get you into Heaven) and showing compassion and sensitivity to others. To some it was a bit surprising that Rockefeller didn't want to become involved, even on a superficial basis, with some convenient congregation of Baptists or others because he might have enjoyed the fellowship and gain from the opportunity to get to know his adopted fellow citizens on a more personal basis. But it was not to be.

On April 17, 1927, shortly before his fifteenth birthday, Rockefeller and his brother David joined the Park Avenue Baptist Church by profession of faith and baptism. (The church is now known as Riverside Church.) This decision came after years of instruction and discipline from his father, including morning prayers and worship (not attended by Mrs. Rockefeller or big sister) and constant reproof when he strayed from the straight and narrow in any way. As he got older he managed to slide organized religion to an ever lower priority until finally it just went off his screen. He continued his support in various ways, but just didn't want to get closely hooked up. He had seen the way churches and other religious organizations shamelessly appealed for financial support to his family in New York, and besides, he just didn't like the constraints on his personal life. So aides pressuring him to be seen at church now and then by claiming it was de rigueur in Arkansas were treated just as they were when wondering aloud if he couldn't lose the cowboy boots. He was urged to start wearing shoes instead. And he might want to abandon that cowman's hat as well, which he seemed to wear everywhere. Exasperated, he finally told them in no uncertain terms, "That's me." He explained patiently but in a final sort of way that he was willing to accept the judgment of the people and if they were willing to base their opinion and support of him on what he wore or whether he went to church, then so be it. This may have been the first experience of his political staff in understanding that this man had a stubborn streak a mile deep and would not, could not be swayed too much in any direction by political considerations. Nevertheless, it was important to Rockefeller to outline to his son in somewhat careful words what he believed about religion. He expressed some ideas in a preliminary "think" session (which was recorded) that would lead to development of *A Letter to My Son*, the mini-book-length work that he wanted Winthrop Paul to have, to know the "truth" about his father. The messy separation and divorce from his son's mother caused Rockefeller concern that he would be described in unflattering terms to his son. Since he and Winthrop

Paul weren't likely to spend a lot of time together in those early years, the picture painted by Bobo would be burned into the brain of his son, Rockefeller reasoned; and that picture would not be flattering, he further reasoned. However, it was never evident that a negative portrait of his father was hammered into the son, or if it was hammered there that it stayed intact. Winthrop Paul appears to have grown up with a good impression of his father, with obvious pride and even a wish to emulate his father in certain ways.

So, as stated earlier, Rockefeller had religion drilled into him and his siblings as he was growing up. It was part of the family culture. From his grandparents to his parents, the transfer of ideas, the sense of duty and commitment, seemed very efficient. However, from the parents to Rockefeller and his brothers and sister, the transfer seemed to lack a little horsepower. Here's what he expressed in the dictating session in which he was crafting a sketch for the letter project: "It seems to me that . . . some specific reference ought to be made to the thinking on a Christian life, whether this life is reflected by one's regular attendance to church or whether this life is based on a combination of that and an attempt throughout one's daily effort to live according to the Golden Rule."[1] Rockefeller curiously seemed to approach the matter as though it were not him and his thinking that would be conveyed to his son, but rather some principles and ideas that might issue from someone else. He went on, "very definitely we ought to indicate our fundamental beliefs in the Christian principles." He said he didn't want to attempt to make a contrast between a person who believed in what he described as "applied religion" versus "a more formal religion." He hoped to give appropriate recognition to the "differences in human beings, in that many people find strength in group activities as reflected in church activities."[2] That was as far as he ever went. During inaugural activities when he took office as governor in 1967, a program was held at Second Baptist Church in Little Rock. As the hymns were being sung, Rockefeller wasn't making a sound but his lips were moving. He seemed to know the words.

Rockefeller's gifts to churches and strongly religious organizations amounted to $81,064 throughout his lifetime. The largest of them recorded was to Pocantico Hills Church in Westchester County in 1967. The $19,625 might have been more family loyalty than out-and-out support for a religious enterprise, because other churches elsewhere did not get any amounts approaching that. Another gift of some size—$16,066—was to a University Religious Conference at UCLA in 1951.

When analyzing all his gifts to all causes, one finds many quite small amounts provided to churches and religious organizations of various kinds. It is not hard to conclude that many times he was responding to someone grab-bing him by the elbow and making the case before Rockefeller could shake the person off or before an aide could intercede. It was unlikely that very many of these gifts were thoughtful and disciplined philanthropic acts.

CHAPTER

7

America's Place in the World

Travels with family in the early years, military service abroad during World War II, his involvement with Colonial Williamsburg, participation in the family businesses, in the Rockefeller Brothers Fund and his experiences with Winrock Farms and Arkansas in general all combined to develop in Winthrop Rockefeller a great interest and concern about America's place in the world.

He would provide almost $1.5 million during his life toward what he believed would advance the cause of America, with more than $1 million of that going to RBF to support the programs in which he and his brothers and sister shared an interest. The view of the Fund was that "we live in one world and that giving patterns should not be narrow or parochial" (to quote his brother David). His contributions to the Fund would begin in 1941 and end in 1955, only a couple of years after he arrived in Arkansas.

Rockefeller had seen some of the problems that left so much of the rest of the world either envious or hostile, and he thought that to concentrate on taking to them a good picture of America and Americans and using the resources of America—both public and private—was the strategy most likely to improve the view and introduce the best that America had to offer to the rest of the world. There is no doubt that he most certainly would have subscribed to the views stated long after his death by RBF in its program guidelines, adopted in 1984 and restated in its 1987 guidelines, that the objective was to improve the well-being of all people through support of efforts in the United States and abroad that "contribute ideas, develop leaders and encourage institutions in the transition to global interdependence and that counter world trends of resource depletion, militarization, protectionism and isolation."[1]

Rockefeller's more personal focus in his later life on America's place in the world concentrated on education, military affairs, agriculture, health, and culture. He was especially proud of Colonial Williamsburg, and while he did not contribute large amounts of money during his lifetime (although a considerable sum was provided from his assets in the Winthrop Rockefeller Trust after his death), he served as its chairman for many years and helped to preserve and expand the magnificent restoration. In 1957, he and Mrs. Rockefeller participated in presenting to Queen Elizabeth II and Prince Phillip on behalf of the people of the United States a collection of papers from the British Headquarters compiled during the Revolutionary War. Colonial Williamsburg first presented the papers to President Eisenhower, who subsequently presented the 107 volumes to Her Majesty on behalf of the people of Great Britain. President Eisenhower wrote Rockefeller afterward how gratified he was by the action of Colonial Williamsburg in presenting to him the British Headquarters Papers, so that he in turn could give them on behalf of the America people to Her Majesty and the British people.

Winrock Farms was on the world stage as far as cattle breeding and research was concerned, and this was just what Rockefeller intended. From its inception Winrock served to provide education, expertise, and guidance to the many persons who came in contact with it. Rockefeller was especially proud of the quality of the operation, from the scientific to the utterly practical, and the farm's contributions to development of better beef cattle was widely known and appreciated. His annual cattle sale at the farm attracted buyers and interested participants from throughout the world who needed fine Santa Gertrudis breeding stock that could help build a foundation herd of these "big red cows" originally developed into a breed by the King Ranch in Texas. Representatives of the King Ranch were regular buyers at the sale, as was Rockefeller at their sales in Texas. To some degree, Rockefeller buying King Ranch stock at high prices and King Ranch doing the same thing at the Winrock cattle sale was a bit of public relations, probably, but it was a source of amazement to those who watched prices of $40,000 to $50,000 being paid for outstanding bulls. Winrock had intern programs for youth and other opportunities for young and old alike to gain knowledge and experience, and it pleased him to see the acceptance and continuing development of the livestock and the science surrounding it he so carefully husbanded at the farm.

The Rockefellers entertained Queen Elizabeth and Prince Phillip at ceremonies in Williamsburg and also in Washington in October 1957. (Photo courtesy of University of Arkansas, Little Rock, Archives, WR VII 6.324)

From that operation evolved the Winrock International Livestock Research and Training Center in 1975, established in response to Rockefeller's request in his will that trustees of his estate be venturesome and innovative in creating and supporting institutions that would help people help themselves. A decade later, a larger entity was created from combining with Winrock two other organizations also rooted in the philanthropic tradition of the Rockefeller family. One was the Agricultural Development Council, which grew from an organization founded by Winthrop's eldest brother, John. It was designed to stimulate and support economic training related to human welfare in rural Asia. The other was the International Agricultural Development Service, created with initial support from the Rockefeller Foundation. Its aim was to provide services to developing countries that wanted to strengthen their agricultural research and development programs. Together, they became the Winrock International Institute for Agricultural Development. The Winthrop Rockefeller Trust put more than $85 million into it during its first decade of existence, while it was headquartered atop Petit Jean Mountain in Arkansas. Its mission was and is to reduce poverty and hunger through sustainable agricultural and rural development in Asia, Africa, the Middle East, Latin America, the Caribbean, and the United States.

One of Rockefeller's consistent world interests was youth and education in China, and he contributed $30,200 to the Yale-In-China program from 1937 through 1972. The program was founded in 1901 and until the 1950s maintained a middle school, a hospital, a medical school, and a nursing school in Changsha, Hunan Province. It also provided scholarship aid for Chinese students in the United States and had a supportive relationship to New Asia College in Kowloon, Hong Kong. Retreating Japanese troops burned the buildings, but the program continued on. Rockefeller failed to make contributions in 1959 and 1960. He got a letter from the director of the program that opened by praising his generous contributions through the previous years and suggesting that "there are doubtless good reasons why you have felt obliged to withhold your previous support this current year." The letter went on to describe the human predicament of Chinese young men and women uprooted and with limited opportunities for earning a living yet eager for an education in a free environment. "It may be," the letter from Sidney Lovett went on, "that in earlier communications we have failed to represent our present association with the New Asia College in Hong Kong with sufficient clarity and cogency . . ."[2]

It was the kind of letter Rockefeller would throw down on his desk in frustration, the kind that sometimes caused him to respond negatively. This time he simply resumed his annual contribution, and that continued until the last year of his life.

He also gave to the American International Association and such other entities defined as contributing to America's place in the world, such as the Common Council for American Unity and the Middle East Institute. The Common Council was an outgrowth of work begun by the federal government during World War I. It became an independent agency in 1921, and used the foreign language press and radio to help immigrants become effective citizens. Smaller gifts went to the American Association for the United Nations, American Colony Charities Association of New York, Arkansas Commission for Radio Free Europe, Center for Information Pro Deo, Committee for the United Nations, Crusade for Freedom (Arkansas Division), Finnish Relief Fund, Friends of Turkey, Moral Rearmament, People to People, Radio Free Europe, and the United Committee for the United Nations.

Rockefeller was always interested in learning about other cultures and other languages, and he continued to encourage understanding and interest

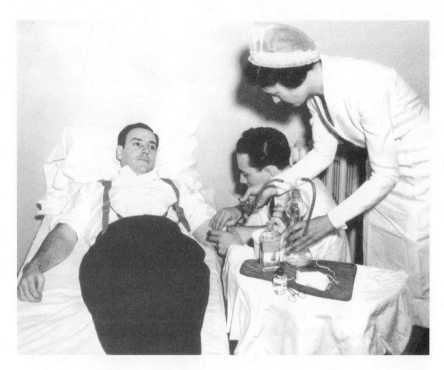

Rockefeller cared what went on in the world, even from an early age. In November 1940, not long before he enlisted in the infantry, he donated blood for Britain's wounded in the war America would soon enter. (Photo courtesy of University of Arkansas, Little Rock, Archives, WR-A-5)

on the part of his fellow Americans. He taught himself to speak French passably well, less effectively in some other languages as well. While he was learning and encouraging others to learn in this country, he was also cultivating friendships with world leaders, and the guest list at Winrock Farms through the years was a veritable "Who's Who" of international figures who were in one way or the other involved in decisions that would affect the world in some way.

Perhaps because it was so close to him, so "at home," so to speak, Rockefeller never tired of talking about Winrock Farms and was always trying to find ways to share that information and expertise, not only in Arkansas, but throughout the world. To some degree, and for a time after his death, Winrock International continued that initiative.

With Socony-Mobil during the late 1930s, Rockefeller worked with the foreign trade department with particular emphasis on the Middle East, to

As chairman of IBEC Housing, Rockefeller wanted to see first hand the situations and lives of some of those the program was designed to help. Here he visits one of the low-cost homes in Puerto Rico. (Photo courtesy of University of Arkansas, Little Rock, Archives, WR VII 1.721)

which he traveled several times. This certainly broadened and deepened his understanding of the world, and he was cognizant of the growing dangers as war clouds loomed. In November 1940, he volunteered to donate a pint of blood for wounded British soldiers, and before long he joined the military. In early 1941, nearly eleven months before Pearl Harbor, Rockefeller enlisted as a private in the army and was assigned to the Twenty-sixth Regiment of the First Infantry Division. He reached the grade of sergeant and applied and was accepted to Officers Candidate School, graduating as a second lieutenant in January 1942. He became a machine-gun instructor at the Infantry School at Fort Benning, Georgia, and was promoted to first lieutenant in June of that year. He was transferred to the 305th Infantry Regiment of the Seventy-seventh Division at Fort Jackson, South Carolina, and was assigned as H Company commander. He was commissioned captain in 1942 and was promoted to major the next year. Rockefeller's division made the assault landings

Rockefeller aided in providing low-cost housing to the poor in a number of places in Latin America as chairman of the International Basic Economy Corporation. He visited an elementary school in Puerto Rico as part of a survey in that part of the world. (Photo courtesy of University of Arkansas, Little Rock, Archives, WR VII 1–723)

on Guam, Leyte, and Okinawa. During the invasion of Okinawa, a Japanese kamikaze carrying two 500-pound bombs hit the troop transport *Henrico*. Rockefeller was the senior army officer left alive, and assumed command (although wounded) until relieved the following day. He had suffered flash burns and was hospitalized for six weeks. He later contracted infectious hepatitis, and after V-J Day was evacuated to a hospital in the United States. There, still in the hospital, he was requested by Secretary of War Robert P. Patterson to make a nationwide survey of veterans' adjustment problems and report his findings to the War Department. After a six-month study, Rockefeller recommended specific action to be taken by the federal government, individuals, and organizations to coordinate and make more effective veterans' activities on all levels.

During his service, Rockefeller was awarded the Bronze Star with Oak Leaf Cluster, Purple Heart, American Defense, American Theater, Asiatic Pacific

Bob Hope interviewed Rockefeller during a fund-raising event at Fort Benning, Georgia, in March 1972, to establish an infantry museum there. (Photo courtesy of University of Arkansas, Little Rock, Archives, WR VII 1.967)

Bob Hope's humor caused Rockefeller and his friends to break up in laughter at a benefit for the Fort Benning Infantry Museum in 1972. (Photo courtesy of University of Arkansas, Little Rock, Archives, WR VII 1–1102)

Theater, and Victory and Philippine Liberation ribbons. Later, he served in the Seventy-seventh Division Reserve in New York City.

Rockefeller became chairman of the board of the IBEC Housing Corporation, affiliate of International Basic Economy Corporation, which had been set up under the leadership of his brother Nelson to help improve living standards in developing areas abroad through joint business enterprises. IBEC Housing was established to help meet the demand for low-cost housing, and Rockefeller never tired of talking about the many thousands of units built and describing the method of building that employed poured-in-place concrete. Among other places, there were major projects in Puerto Rico, Peru, and Chile.

In 1971, Rockefeller and nineteen others met to exchange ideas for raising $6 million to build an infantry museum at Fort Benning, Georgia. Rockefeller was supportive both in money and leadership and served as chairman of the National Infantry Museum Development Program. He saw the museum as a recognition of the valor of the GIs and "a monument to the patriotism of the United States," adding that "we are appealing to those who are aware of the sacrifice."[3] He supported other military and veterans' services as

Rockefeller was wounded during World War II and received the Purple Heart, among other decorations. He always seemed to have a special feeling for wounded soldiers and visited at length with these at Fort Benning. He played a significant role in establishing an infantry museum there. (Photo courtesy of University of Arkansas, Little Rock, Archives, WR VII 1.967)

well, including the Seventy-seventh Division Association, the American Veterans Committee, the National War Fund, Inc., the Pacific War Memorial in New York, the USO Defense Fund in New York, and the USO of New York City.

He stayed interested and supportive through the remaining years of his life, but less so as his memories of World War II dimmed.

8

The Winthrop Rockefeller Foundation

The Rockwin Fund—which Rockefeller created to distribute funds (mostly in Arkansas) for educational purposes at all levels—had already grown too constricted as he broadened his philanthropic interests in the latter stage of his life. So it was a natural evolution to an entity that more fully represented his views and interests when the Rockwin Fund became the Winthrop Rockefeller Foundation in December 1974, not long after his death. A thoughtful and sensitive process took place as the transition was accomplished, led by the late Mary McLeod, who had been Rockefeller's closest advisor on educational matters for many years and who had built the Rockwin Fund to the powerful educational philanthropy it was at the time of Rockefeller's death. Also playing a key role in the transition was Henry McHenry, who was at the time an employee in the regional office of the U.S. Department of Labor in Dallas, with a keen insight and an objective approach to the process that was needed. The governor at that time, Dale Bumpers (who had defeated Rockefeller's third-term bid in 1970), was interested in helping the process work out successfully, and he interceded to get McHenry back to Arkansas on a "loan" basis. McHenry, a native of Ouachita County in south Arkansas, knew a great deal on his own about the disadvantages of growing up black in Arkansas and the disparity in educational opportunity that in essence left deep ruts across the landscape of Arkansas that were quite difficult to negotiate for many Arkansans.

Bumpers believed that the successful establishment of the Winthrop Rockefeller Foundation "would benefit all of Arkansas," McHenry said.[1] McLeod spent a considerable time, according to McHenry, explaining the history of Winthrop Rockefeller and what he was trying to do as governor and for the state of Arkansas. "She gave me hundreds of names of persons from all over the state who had had contact with the Rockwin Fund or with Governor Rockefeller." McHenry's first assignment, he recalled, was to compile a list to interview and meanwhile to get on with the creation of a working document. He set up small sessions with groups of them and gathered information that would be helpful in establishing a blueprint for the foundation in the name of Rockefeller. McHenry said gathering the folks together was easy. "I just explained that Governor Rockefeller left a significant amount of money in a trust and he wanted to form a foundation that would continue the things that he did in Arkansas with the money he left. If we can put it together, we will have an Arkansas-based foundation that will distribute the resources to carry out in Arkansas primarily what the governor wanted to do in his political career and that he wanted to do that made him come to Arkansas in the first place."[2] There were problems. McHenry said many of them came with projects. "They all had stories about what the governor had promised to do for them. So we had to sift through a lot. That was one of the reasons it took a while to get down to how they saw the governor's overall effect on the state. Many of the persons who came were thinking, 'How can I make it look as if what I want to happen with the money is something the governor wanted?'"[3] McHenry discovered that he wasn't a writer, and Tom Wahman from the Rockefeller offices in New York came down to shape the ideas into policy and help to develop all the needed materials for the transition.

The trustees of the Winthrop Rockefeller Charitable Trust took a very active position, according to McHenry, who said, "If we transfer funds to this new foundation, we want an initial board of directors that is small, that is diverse, that would have some connection with the governor while he was governor, but also would have some feel for what is best for Arkansas."[4]

The foundation was large by Arkansas standards and set a pattern of giving that served as a kind of blueprint for other charitable organizations in Arkansas. Clearly the most visible evidence of Rockefeller's philanthropy, it concentrated on a broad range of causes throughout Arkansas, as it attempted to be faithful to Rockefeller's stated wish in his will to "be innovative and venturesome in supporting charitable projects." Tom McRae, the first president of the foundation, and the board took to heart the admonition in Rockefeller's will that "they should not feel that they need to be conservative . . . and will apply the full resources of the trust towards the realization of significant charitable ends."[5]

The Winthrop Rockefeller Charitable Trust—established in the will—began making substantial grants to the foundation in 1974, and by the year 2000 the trust had distributed $36,996,452 to the foundation, with some funds remaining to transfer to it. Meanwhile, the foundation continued to grow its assets on its own so that it not only had distributed some $66 million by the close of 2000, but had also built an asset base of $165 million. Of those distributions by the foundation, some $7.8 million was in program-related investments, which included loans, equity investments, and loan guarantees. Of the $7.8 million, some $2 million in Program Related Investment (PRI) loans has been forgiven.

The foundation began its work with an attempt to be as faithful as it could be to what Governor Rockefeller would have wanted. His track record was examined, and the interests he had expressed were all taken into account —mostly by McRae—and shared with the board as they began grant making. Many of the grants were small ones and later on the foundation began to conclude that lots of small grants just made correspondingly small blips on the screen, whereas larger, if fewer, grants might make a more significant difference.

The Rockwin Fund had been dependent upon annual cash contributions from Rockefeller, and that totaled $2.1 million from 1956 until 1973. Meanwhile, Rockefeller was providing substantial funds to the Arkansas Opportunity Fund, a sponsor of scholarships given through the National Merit Scholarship Corporation. Rockefeller, as principal donor to the Fund, contributed some $425,339 from 1956 through 1972, shortly before his death. But with the creation of the foundation, Rockefeller's philanthropy was continuing to evolve, to broaden. McRae stated that "instead of traditional giving, we wish to actively demonstrate ways to make the system work. We are willing to take risks. We want people to have a stronger voice in the decisions that affect their lives. Significant resources will be concentrated upon the problems of economic and community development. Through better utilization of existing mediums and the creation of new income generating mechanisms, we hope to achieve a more equitable distribution of economic resources within Arkansas."[6]

The foundation in its first year authorized $459,294 in grants. Included were $100,000 to the state of Arkansas to enable the governor's Economic

Development Study Commission to conduct a comprehensive analysis of factors affecting the growth and development of Arkansas. A total of $50,447 went to the National Merit Scholarship Corporation as a continuation of Rockefeller's support of outstanding Arkansas students, and $9,000 went to the Arkansas Community Foundation to cover initial expenses of organizing a statewide community foundation. Well over $2 million would be granted by the foundation to the ACF in the next few years. Another program supported in a major way by the foundation in that initial year of grant making was $62,306 to the National Community Education Association, the first of three annual grants, to develop a rural community education model that would use local school districts as catalysts to sustain and develop the quality of life for rural Arkansas. Early on, the grand vision was somewhat colored by the reality of the landscape on which the foundation hoped to make its mark. McRae said a disappointment was the reluctance of potential grantees to make a serious commitment to improvement within their institutions, stating rather bluntly, "We have received fewer good projects than we had hoped." He opined that it was not likely the trend would change and that the foundation had concluded it "should be more aggressive in stimulating and developing good projects." In the years to follow, it would have some success and some failures as well with that more aggressive approach to grant making. McRae had identified the problem with the foundation's grant making from the very beginning. Projects submitted were a mixed bag, at best, and as McRae and the board pushed forward they began to seek out and encourage projects that more closely conformed to the mandate they believed they had from Rockefeller and projects with a better chance of genuinely making a difference. The foundation moved into controversial areas fairly quickly, and it is safe to say that the original Republican Party that had supported Rockefeller throughout his public life was appalled at some of the things the foundation did. For example, the foundation provided $50,000 to the NAACP Legal Defense Fund to support employment litigation in Arkansas in order to bring about a more equitable distribution of income among Arkansas residents, by upgrading the employment status of minorities and women already working and by creating substantially more jobs for other minorities and women. McRae observed in a 2000 interview that "we had a remarkable number of grants that focused on minority and disadvantaged issues, and that sort of stood out"[7] as he reviewed all the grants that had been made through the twenty-five years. "Some probably made some people mad, but like the grant to the NAACP fund to pursue employment discrimination, it really changed a great deal and eliminated disparity where you had blacks and whites doing the same job but at tremendously different pay scales."

Clearly, though, based on Rockefeller's own direct gifts during his lifetime, concentrating the foundation's resources to a considerable extent on efforts to bring about a greater degree of racial equality was right on the mark. Like Rockefeller had done himself, it was going against the Arkansas grain. Blacks simply had never made as much money as whites, identical jobs notwithstanding, and trying to change that very much meant changing the mentality of people who had grown up in, and lived in, such an environment all their lives. Progress was sure to be very, very slow. In the beginning, when no one even knew about the foundation for the most part, one could see the foundation reaching for things to fund. One grant of $25,000 in 1976 went to the Beebe branch of Arkansas State University to develop a dairy goat management program that would provide an opportunity for the minimum resource farmer to supplement his income. In a grant a few years later the foundation sought to weigh in on the opportunity for increased swine production and better management of the market with a swine cooperative. Both those grants didn't seem to lead to any more interest on the part of the foundation as it turned its attention toward youth and other issues. For example, efforts to foster language development and creativity in young children through improvisational drama was the basis of a $37,165 grant to the University of Arkansas at Little Rock. Included in that was a field testing program to evaluate the effect of language enrichment "through action dramatics of the language, social, and moral development of disadvantaged children."[8] How effective were these programs, really? It is virtually impossible to measure, but the foundation message was getting out there that it wanted to reach beyond conventional education and standard and existing programs to work with enterprising and creative people at the local level to improve lives at all levels and ages.

The foundation was already concentrating careful attention on rural life in Arkansas and the whole range of disadvantages that weighed on children who were growing up in that environment. Another grant of $93,000—the second of three—went to the National Community Education Association to develop a model for community education that would use local school districts as catalysts to sustain and develop the quality of life in rural Arkansas, and $30,259 to the University of Arkansas for Medical Sciences to (1) improve the capacity of smaller Arkansas communities to retain physicians and (2) develop within the College of Medicine a curriculum that would be more effective in preparing students for practice in small communities. McRae commented that the foundation made a determined effort to find out what it took to get doctors to stay in small towns in rural places, and credited the program with leading to initiatives that are still ongoing at the medical center oriented to meeting the health needs of rural Arkansans. "That was some pretty ground-breaking stuff," he said, "that started a process that's really prospered."[9] Actually, Rockefeller himself had already broken that ground when he moved to meet the health needs of rural Arkansans by establishing a clinic in Perryville not too many years after he arrived in Arkansas.

The foundation continued to change, to evolve, and by 1977 was beginning to focus on projects that would give people a better grasp of public issues and societal problems. The idea was to make possible an improved community awareness of issues and the problems that prevent educational, governmental, and corporate institutions from meeting the public's expectations. The foundation funded a seminar of opinion leaders and a series of seminars for journalists, the publication of a book that included a series of interviews discussing problems faced by public education. "We hope to stimulate dialogue that will lead people to consider whether or not they are satisfied with this (the state's) investment in education," McRae stated.[10] It is worth noting at this juncture that the foundation's image was beginning to change. In its first days, most of the public imagined it as somewhat more conservative than it turned out to be. Members of the board—some of whom were from out of state—were more liberal than conservative, and as the years passed the foundation seemed to become even more liberal.

Grant totals were going up every year and by 1977 had reached more than a half-million dollars. The public was really beginning to notice, now. A little more than $58,000 was granted to the Community Council of Central Arkansas to plan and implement coordination of services provided to children and adolescents by twelve participating agencies in Pulaski County (the seat of government in Arkansas). The seminar program for journalists on current issues and events was staged at Arkansas College. Also, a grant went to the Arkansas Community Foundation to continue the process of providing resources for the organization and development of the community foundation to serve the philanthropic and charitable needs of the state. The third year of a three-year grant to the community education project was funded.

Sharpening its focus even more, in 1978 the foundation made grants totaling almost $700,000 that concentrated on encouraging new ideas and constructive change to deal with the fact that "Arkansas is poor in economic terms." It continued through its grant making to initiate projects that provided information and a better understanding of significant public issues, and included support for a program of workshops for inmates of the state's prisons "intended to help participating inmates develop self-confidence and improve communicative skills."[11] Rockefeller as governor had done all he possibly could to bring the prison system into the twentieth century—or at least, the late nineteenth—with limited success. Whether the foundation's program to move further forward with efforts to recognize inmates as human beings capable of changing was again one of those things that was exceedingly difficult to measure. Indeed, there doesn't seem to be much evidence that the foundation even tried to measure results in most grant follow-ups, possibly because so many of them were for things that would be ongoing and simply had no specific end point. It appeared then as now that recidivism rates weren't changing all that much. Craftmaking among low- to moderate-income Arkansans in north-central Arkansas was supported, and the foundation continued its efforts to get health care to rural citizens through a program to make available a specialized health-care system to patients and families involved in advanced/terminal stages of cancer or other terminal illnesses and to create a more realistic public attitude toward death and dying. Still concentrating its focus on rural Arkansas, the foundation provided funds to Heifer Project International to assist in implementing a rural agricultural economic development project in southwest Arkansas to increase the supplemental income of small farmers interested in cooperative feeder pig production and provided support to Human Service Providers of Arkansas, which aimed to improve the human service delivery system in Arkansas by acting as an advocate and by providing direct technical assistance.

In 1979 for the first time the foundation's authorized grants exceeded $1 million, amounting to $1,156,277. By now there was certainly no dearth of proposals. Close attention was being paid by organizations throughout the state who wanted help with their projects. In addition to initiating projects to conform to the sense of Rockefeller's philosophy and goals, the foundation found itself sifting through many, many projects and deciding among them on an almost daily basis.

Among projects funded in that year were these: Arkansas Advocates for Children and Families, to establish the grantee as a permanent organization to work for the protection, education, and well-being of children in Arkansas through advocating various approaches for strengthening families; Arkansas Business Development Corporation (ABDC) to finance a feasibility study for a Regional Minority Purchasing Council in Arkansas; ABDC to develop and implement an Arkansas Regional Minority Purchasing Council; Arkansas Community Foundation, final funding for a five-year organizational and development program for a community foundation to serve the philanthropic and charitable needs of the state of Arkansas; Arkansas Consumer Research, to implement a program to improve public access and accountability of state boards and commissions through training for public members; Arkansas Issues Program, to initiate a variety of projects administered by WRF to provide people with information and a better understanding of significant public issues in society; Arkansas State University for the Mid-South Writing Project, which was to establish and operate a program to re-train teachers of high school English and composition in northeastern Arkansas; ARVAC Rural Industries, to increase the supplemental income of low-income craftspeople in seven northwestern Arkansas counties by improving marketing and management capabilities; Criminal Justice Institute (CJI) to enable it to open an office to offer mediation services to inmates in the Arkansas Prison System; Arkansas Department of Education, to initiate a comprehensive in-service training program for teachers, emphasizing teaching to an objective, to be adopted and maintained on a permanent basis by the state; Arkansas Department of Health, to produce and initiate an extensive media campaign to make the public aware of the sexually transmitted disease epidemic in Arkansas and to create the understanding necessary to allow the department to combat such diseases effectively; Human Services Providers Association, to improve human services delivered by private, nonprofit agencies through advocacy, management improvement, and information exchange; NAACP Legal Defense Fund, to provide financial assistance in support of employment-related race and sex discrimination cases in Arkansas; National Endowment for the Humanities, through Winrock International, to develop a documentary film on Arkansas agriculture; National Endowment for the Humanities, to support a family farm conference; National Merit Scholarship Corporation support for four-year scholarships for outstanding Arkansas students; Natural and Cultural Heritage Department (Arkansas), to develop a classification system, conduct an inventory, and establish an information management system that would set priorities and identify Arkansas land of natural and aesthetic value, and to assist in the maintenance of the diversity of ecological and natural areas within the state; $100,000 to establish a fund for the development of minority businesses in the state of Arkansas; Save the Children (Arkansas Delta Project), a second-year program to develop a process of community-based, integrated rural development in Lee, Phillips, and St. Francis Counties (all in the eastern Arkansas Delta) to focus upon human resource development, social infrastructure improvement, and economic growth; University of Arkansas for Medical Sciences (UAMS), to address the problem of low-birth-weight infants by improving infant-parent relationships in the hospital, providing support for the infant and parent in the home, and improving the continuity of clinic-based care. All these grants may have seemed on a superficial level to be all over the map, but underneath, the core of virtually all of them was the late benefactor's wish to find ways to improve opportunities for blacks, to upgrade their quality of life, and to help them understand how to access services to which they were entitled.

In 1980 the foundation awarded $1,300,216 in grants, including one that was a departure from the pattern of grant making in the past. This was $750,000 in the form of an interest-free loan to the Nature Conservancy. This loan, coupled with money from the state, made possible the purchase and preservation of more than six thousand acres of one of the few remaining tracts of bottomland hardwoods in the southern United States.

Other grants in 1980 included the following: Second-year funding to advance the cause of minority business enterprise through increased opportunity to do business with established corporations; Arkansas Department of Energy, to plan, design, and construct up to three methane-generating facilities, which were expected to have broad potential application within the state; $35,500 to introduce and implement over a three-year period a comprehensive community education, advocacy, legal, and technical assistance program for black landowners and small family farmers in a forty-two-county region of Arkansas; Heifer Project International, to assist HPI in providing management assistance to a rural feeder pig cooperative with the idea of increasing the supplemental income of limited-resource farmers; $100,000 to provide an allotment of funds to be used for loans to finance and develop minority businesses in Arkansas; Save the Children, to assist with the third year of community-based integrated rural development in the Arkansas Delta; the University of Arkansas minority engineering project, to deal with the socioeconomic, cultural, and academic problems "that make it difficult for minority students to succeed in predominantly white institutions"; the University of Arkansas, to develop for Arkansas rural school districts a model secondary-education program to offer curriculum opportunities not generally available to small rural school districts.

In 1981 McRae observed that "we granted $250,000 to the Nature Conservancy to begin a long-term program of protecting and preserving Arkansas' unique natural heritage. If the project goes as planned, the foundation will contribute a total of $1,150,000 over three years—the largest grant for a single purpose we have ever made. And," he added, "our funds will be matched by at least $1 million from other sources."[12] Thirty-seven other grants to specific projects totaled $1,455,752, including the Arkansas Civil Liberties Foundation, to organize poor and working women in Arkansas around issues of concern to their quality of life; the Arkansas Delta Housing Development Corporation, to conduct a comprehensive housing needs assessment and to increase the grantees' Land Bank Fund for executing long-term land options on four housing development sites in remote delta communities; Boy Scouts of America, south-central region, to provide awareness, education, and opportunity in the medical and health professions for teenagers with emphasis on minority, rural, and handicapped Arkansas youth; University of Arkansas at Little Rock School of Law to increase the number of black lawyers in the state, having in mind that lawyers usually are community and governmental leaders and role models as well as practitioners.

The foundation was continuing to look at existing entities with track records as prospective grantees to be more likely to assure a successful outcome. For example, during 1982 a total of $1,148,648 was authorized, and included grants to UAMS, to implement the first year of a three-year curriculum development project to establish a new and permanent division within the College of Medicine to be called the Division of Medical Humanities; the University of Arkansas, to fund the third year of a transition/retention program for minority students in the field of engineering; United Methodist Church, to initiate a statewide effort to end violence against women and children; Southern Coalition for Educational Equity, to provide a training model for producing skilled, highly motivated members of the work force in Arkansas, to engage the idea that while Arkansas needed skilled workers it nevertheless suffered from high unemployment rates; Arkansas Family Planning Council, to provide an innovative approach to the reduction of the present extremely high incidence of adolescent pregnancy "which is detrimental to the health and future life of mothers and children and tends to perpetuate the welfare cycle";[13] Arkansas Land and Farm Development Corporation, to provide legal and technical assistance to small rural landowners who were in danger of losing their land because of tax sales, adverse possession, partition sales, and other similar means; Central Arkansas Legal Services, to implement the second year of a three-year project to empower low-income persons and groups in an eight-county service area through preventive law/community development activities.

The foundation was refining its policies. McRae explained that as the foundation looked at the state's problems the conclusion was reached that a focus on projects in economic development and education would be essential "if we are to change the systems that keep Arkansas at the bottom of most indicators of economic, social and educational well-being."[14]

He noted that the foundation can represent the alternative point of view or can play the role of honest broker between differing factions on critical public issues. "The resources that WRF has to spend can directly affect only a few Arkansans. However, through positive example, encouragement of leadership and public education on crucial issues we can foster an environment that invites people to take control of their lives."[15]

In 1983 the foundation authorized grants totaling $2,043,321 as it refined the emphasis of its policy to an even sharper focus on economic development and education. Noting that the per capita income of Arkansans was at or near the bottom of most indicators of poverty, McRae observed that "if this is to change we must develop strategies for economic development that are realistic." He said these strategies must take into account who lives in Arkansas, the strengths and weaknesses of each population segment and region, and what is possible in view of the economic and technological changes taking place in the United States and in the world. "Because of our diversity in geography and agricultural and industrial potential," McRae continued, "such a plan will have to be multifaceted and should provide opportunity for all our residents."[16]

According to data cited by McRae, some 300,000 of the 2.3 million population were illiterate, and 45 percent of Arkansans over the age of twenty-five did not have a high school diploma and only 9 percent had a college degree. Sophisticated technologies or large industrial plants are most likely to locate in the Arkansas River Valley or in northwest Arkansas, and thus most citizens of the state will benefit little from policies concentrating on attracting these kinds of industries. "If we are to break the cycles of poverty that keep Arkansas at the bottom of most economic indicators we must develop strategies that address the economic needs of all regions of the state and concurrently improve the level of education and capacity of the work force,"[17] he wrote in 1983. Saying the foundation will encourage any project that will make a significant difference in Arkansas's economy, he explained that the foundation is particularly interested in small-scale enterprise in rural places . . . where many of our most needy citizens live. These small-scale enterprises in rural places required a great deal of research to establish whether existing entities or those formed to qualify as a grantee from the foundation could actually measure up, could be effective. It was not always the case that needed research was completed, and somewhere along the line guesses and opinion were put in place to move projects along toward funding.

As stated earlier, there was a tendency as well to fund larger enterprises through existing organizations with a good chance of success. Among grants made in 1983 were Arkansas Advocates for Children and Families, to fund a project designed to address the problems and issues related to school dropouts, suspensions, and expulsions; Arkansas Delta Housing Development

Corporation, to implement a program to establish the Arkansas Delta Housing Development Corporation Land Bank and to conduct a housing need study and strategy development project; Arkansas Department of Higher Education, to publish a pamphlet for junior high and high school students on college attendance and steps necessary to prepare for college; Arkansas Family Planning Council; Arkansas Land and Farm Development Corporation, to continue its effort to assist black landowners and family farmers in land retention and family farm development by providing community education programs and technical assistance; College Station Community Development Fund, Inc., to fund a development program for College Station (essentially a black community), to include organization of a fund, securing and developing of a forty-acre tract, establishing a land bank, planning and implementing a housing rehabilitation program, securing funding for a sanitary sewer, and small business start-up assistance; Criminal Justice Ministries, to develop a model of a countywide organization that brings together the power and commitment of diverse religious institutions to meet the needs of incarcerated offenders, ex-offenders, families of offenders, and victims of crime; Historic Preservation Alliance of Arkansas, to support the creation of a pilot program in small-town, central business revitalization (the Arkansas Main Street Program); Manpower Demonstration Research Corporation, to determine the long-term effectiveness and impact of the state's policy to increase the flow of welfare recipients to unsubsidized employment by means of a mandatory job search/community work experience program; $350,000 to Nature Conservancy, to ensure protection for Arkansas's remaining natural heritage by establishing a model land conservation program, to protect Arkansas's rarest and most threatened land systems, and to provide a national model for protection of unique natural areas; Southeast Arkansas Educational Cooperative, to demonstrate and document as a basis for future public funding that multi-county education service units can contribute to local school district improvement, to show that these service units represent a cost-effective means of pooling resources and delivering higher quality educational services; Southwest Arkansas Educational Cooperative, to demonstrate cost, labor, and program effectiveness through multi-school district cooperation in providing educational services and programs; United Methodist Church, to provide training and technical assistance to programs and individuals whose purpose is to end violence against women and children; University of Arkansas, to develop information that demonstrates how water rules and laws affect the sustained availability of groundwater and the economic well-being of groundwater users and to convey this information to lawmakers, administrators, and

water managers; $459,299 to the University of Arkansas at Little Rock
(UALR), nine grants for the following: (1) to plan a model education program
for mathematically gifted elementary and secondary students that incorporates
an innovative, enriched, and accelerated curriculum not available in traditional programs; (2) to implement a model education program for mathematically gifted students with programming for elementary students, secondary
students, and math teachers; (3) to increase the number of black lawyers in
Arkansas; (4) to ensure the quality of and expand Engineering Technology's
outreach program to provide access to a four-year high-technology program
outside the Little Rock area; (5) to sustain the core staff of the Local Government Institute so that it can provide timely, in-depth research reports and
short-term research projects on demand to state and local officials and public
interest groups; (6) to identify, catalog, interpret, and preserve Indian picto-
graphs found in the Arkansas River Valley; (7) to provide unique learning
experiences for gifted students, which are not available in traditional elementary and secondary programs; (8) to provide and distribute one thousand
copies of *Arkansas Issues '83* (a publication of the foundation); and (9) to provide partial financing for the 1984 UALR North American Conference on
Prehistoric Rock Art; UAMS, to continue the development of the new Division
of Medical Humanities within the College of Medicine; and Wilowe Institute,
to empower people to improve their lives and their communities through
leadership development.

Forty-one grants amounting to $1,647,814 were awarded in 1984. Thirty-
two discretionary grants totaling $29,515 were made, and $105,160 was
expended for *Arkansas Issues* projects—tax reform, the environment, state
legislature, and water and land use.

McRae, observing that the foundation marked its tenth anniversary in
December 1984, described policy shifts toward many new programs, including a process to result in formal requests for proposals from local school districts as well as regional service centers throughout the state. The foundation
had begun working directly with communities to introduce them to new con-
cepts for capital retention and job creation. While working to be good stewards of the endowment and good citizens of our state, McRae said, "we keep in
mind the direction of the man whose generosity made our activities possible
—Governor Winthrop Rockefeller—who said, 'Be innovative.'"[18]

Meadowcreek, in north-central Arkansas, was one of the grantees in 1984
that sounded real good at first but turned out to be something less than that.
The idea was to help create a nationally recognized education center that offers
Arkansas students and faculty opportunities to explore alternative approaches

to agriculture and related disciplines. The foundation board even met there once, staying overnight in rooms without flush toilets (a composting system instead) and meeting in a space that was cooled by nature rather than air conditioning. It worked out pretty well, but later on a debt load on Meadowcreek that the foundation had not known about caused serious problems. Another grant that year was to Philander Smith College, a mostly black private institution, to launch a comprehensive development and recruitment program designed to provide a broader economic base for the college. Other grants included one to UAMS (which had become a favorite grantee for several years running), to further develop the new Division of Medical Humanities within the College of Medicine; the Cornucopia Project, to identify at least one area in Arkansas to receive support and technical assistance as it develops its local economy; Southern Arkansas University, to continue technical assistance to small-income and subsistence-level farmers who are primarily engaged in beef, pork, and sheep production in southwestern Arkansas; the Southern Coalition for Educational Equity, to support the second year of an experimental jobs-training program targeted at minorities and single heads of households; Manpower Demonstration Research Corporation, to conduct an evaluation of the Arkansas Department of Human Services' Welfare-to-Work Demonstration Program; UALR, to launch the Land Stewardship Project in Arkansas, to heighten local awareness that soil and water management is essentially an ethical proposition; Voter Education Project, Inc., to increase the level and quality of black voter participation in the political process through voter education/registration and get-out-the-vote activities; Delta Foundation, Inc., to stimulate economic development in the Arkansas Delta by providing training and technical assistance to established or emerging community leaders, community-based organizations, and local entrepreneurs; UALR, to provide scholarships to the School of Law for black students; Arkansas Family Planning Council, to fund a community-involvement approach to addressing the adolescent pregnancy problem through schools, churches, and community organizations; $250,000 to the Arkansas Nature Conservancy, for the acquisition and preservation of rare and scientifically important lands under the model Arkansas Land Conservation Program; United Methodist Church, to provide training to nonprofit organizations so that they will develop the consciousness and skills necessary to work against racism and for social justice within their communities.

A total of $1,856,784 in grants was disseminated during 1985 in the areas of economic development, education, public policy and advocacy, leadership development, and community empowerment. Among the grants was one to

"Project Vote," a program funded by the Winthrop Rockefeller Foundation, sought to increase citizen participation in the voting process through the registration of citizens to vote. This effort in 1985 took place in Pine Bluff. Throughout his life in Arkansas, Rockefeller worked hard to clean up the election process and see that all citizens were registered to vote and then that they voted. (Photo courtesy of Winthrop Rockefeller Foundation)

Arkansas Able, to increase employment opportunities for Arkansans fifty-five years of age and older. Grants also went to Arkansas Delta Housing Development, to expand the organization's reach and programming, and to continue sponsorship of the Farmers Home Administration self-help housing programs; Arkansas Human Development Corporation, to demonstrate an effective model for career development training combining public and private efforts aimed at unemployed and underemployed single heads of households; Arkansas Land and Farm Development Corporation, to promote the stability of small farmers using such tools as advocacy, incorporation, tax laws, and a demonstration farm; Main Street Arkansas, to continue the support of a pilot program for the revitalization of the central business districts in small towns in Arkansas; Pulaski Heights Presbyterian Church, to establish neighborhood church-based farmers' markets in central Arkansas (this one greatly offended

Main Street Little Rock organizers who had included a farmer's market in their effort to attract visitors to a moribund downtown), to encourage crop diversification and growing season expansion for increasing the income of small farmers, and to coordinate and provide technical assistance to a statewide network of neighborhood farmers' markets; Southern Arkansas University, to assist low-income and subsistence-level farmers in twelve southwest Arkansas counties; Philander Smith College, to support the comprehensive marketing program designed to recruit and retain students and increase the endowment; Sheridan School District, to develop the capacity of people in the district to plan effectively and to make and implement the decisions necessary for school improvement; UALR, to provide more support for its model education program for mathematically gifted students and more support to UALR as well to help black law students; $196,488 to the Arkansas Education Television Network (AETN) Foundation, to produce a series of four television documentaries for public television on contemporary public policy issues that will affect Arkansas's future; the Voter Education Project, to increase the level of black voter participation in the political process through voter education and get-out-the-vote activities and more money (this time some $300,000) to the Arkansas Nature Conservancy to acquire and preserve rare and scientifically important lands.

Combining the years 1986 and 1987 in its report, the foundation announced that a development bank project, Southern Development Bancorporation (SDB), was going to be taken on by the foundation, that Shorebank Corporation of Chicago would provide needed financing and technical assistance, and that a total of $11.3 million had been raised to support the development of the project and the capitalization of the bank and its nonprofit affiliate. This was really McRae's baby, the biggest idea he had advanced since he'd been at the foundation helm. He worked very hard on it, and while the board wasn't altogether reluctant to get their arms around it, McRae had to do some selling to some of them to get it approved. "In an attempt to address rural economic development needs," he explained, "the foundation has been chosen to focus on a decentralized, multifaceted approach emphasizing small-scale enterprises. Capital is a necessity for this type of development, but so is management training and assistance." Investors included private and corporate foundations, businesses, and individuals from Arkansas and elsewhere. "This is the most ambitious economic development project ever undertaken by the foundation, and it is an example of the kind of philanthropic, business, and governmental cooperation necessary to secure Arkansas' future," he noted.[19] The foundation also announced that it was working with communities throughout the state to build their local economies by helping them to honestly assess their strengths, providing support for their leaders, and locating opportunities to market local products in Arkansas. McRae said the survival of the family farmer was critical to the well-being of rural Arkansas, and that the foundation supported groups that worked to keep the farmer on the land through crop diversification, income supplementation, cooperative marketing of farm products, and other innovative methods.

As the foundation's asset base grew, it was increasing its grant totals significantly. For example, in 1986 the grant total was $5,690,349 and included $2,850,000 to Southern Development Bancorporation for capitalization and start-up costs of the bank holding company established for the purpose of conducting rural economic development activities in Arkansas, plus $1 million to capitalize the rural economic development affiliates of the SDB. Other grants included these: Arkansas Conference of Churches and Synagogues, to provide referrals, assistance, and a hotline for farm families under stress; Arkansas Land and Farm Development Corporation, to promote income-generating alternatives for small farmers; Delta Improvement Corporation, to provide technical assistance to aid the development of rural, low-income communities in eastern Arkansas; Ozark Institute, to strengthen and diversify the small farm economy of the Ozarks through development of local markets, pick-your-own crops, and technical assistance mechanisms for farmers; Presbytery of Arkansas, to expand the Home Grown Marketing Project model of income enhancement for small farmers; Regenerative Agriculture Project, to develop regenerative economic development tools in Arkansas communities and identify on-farm research and demonstration sites; Southern Arkansas University, to assist low-income and subsistence-level farmers in the development of new production and marketing alternatives for agricultural products; UALR, to support the Arkansas Land Stewardship Project's soil and groundwater protection efforts; Urban League of Arkansas, to conduct a comprehensive study of the economic, social and political status of blacks in Arkansas; Arkansas Advocates for Children and Families, to establish and evaluate two model HIPPY (Home Instruction Program for Preschool Youngsters) projects in rural Arkansas.

In 1987, a total of $2,024,480 was awarded, in economic development, civic affairs, education, and community incentive programs, including $250,000 more to Southern Development Bancorporation for additional start-up costs; Arkansas Land and Farm Development Corporation, to continue the Crop Conservation and Land Retention Project for the benefit of black landowners; Heifer Project International, to complete the sustainable agriculture education trial and establish a test plot for draft animal power; Lee County School District, to design and implement, with the collaboration of parents and the community, a school-improvement program focusing on academic achievement; and the Literacy Council of Jefferson County, to continue a reading program for illiterate mothers that includes enriched experiences for their preschool children.

The foundation made grants totaling $4,305,256 in 1988, primarily in the areas of civic affairs, economic development, and education, with a reduced emphasis on community incentives, and included among grantees the Arkansas Coalition for the Handicapped, to prepare a report that would inform the public about issues affecting handicapped citizens in Arkansas and press for reforms in service delivery; Arkansas Community Foundation, to provide technical assistance, to develop a volunteer program, and to increase the asset base of ACF; Arkansas Institute for Social Justice, to empower black and low-income residents of Pine Bluff to effectively organize for improvements in city services, community participation, and leadership development; $250,000 to the Arkansas Enterprise Group, to support its systematic delivery of services to local residents to improve their capacity to increase the volume of local small business and self-employment activity; Arkansas Land and Farm Development Corporation, to continue addressing problems faced by limited-resource and black family farmers in their bid to remain productive citizens in a very competitive farm economy; Ozark Regional Land Trust, to systematize the development of the small farm economy of the Ozarks using sustainable, ecologically sound, regenerative methods of agriculture while addressing the basic needs for technical assistance, alternative financing, and market coordination; Save the Children Federation, to establish a system to bring into the family day-care network nontraditional providers in east and southeast Arkansas; Women's Project, to put into place a system to get women into nontraditional, higher-paying employment and careers; Arkansas Advocates for Children and Families, to establish a successful international model for preschool education of disadvantaged children and to develop a comprehensive state plan for early childhood education; $30,000 to Kiwanis Activities of Little Rock, to establish an alternative to out-of-school suspension of at-risk students who would benefit from an intensive academic remediation and counseling program; Little Rock School District, to restructure the seventh and eighth grades to provide at-risk students with the support needed for an effective transition between elementary and high school; $155,000 to the Sheridan School District, to aid a consortium of two universities and nine school districts working as partners to bring institutional change in both schools and colleges of education; UAMS, to support a collaborative, statewide effort among secondary schools, undergraduate institutions, UAMS, and the Area Health Education Centers aimed at improving minority medical student recruitment and retention; $102,884 to the Arkansas School Reform Study, a longitudinal study examining implementation of Arkansas's school reforms and their effects on students, teachers, and administrators; $22,800 for the study "Water For Arkansas' Future," a project to inform Arkansans about the water crisis in Arkansas and the need to develop a state water plan to protect the state's water resources; $1,000,000 to the Arkansas Enterprise Group, to establish and operate the "Good Faith Fund" and to capitalize Southern Ventures, Inc.; $900,000 to the Arkansas Repertory Theatre, to help finance the final renovation, construction, and equipping of a multi-use theater and performing arts facility on Main Street in Little Rock.

The foundation continued its effort to try to help kids through various programs already organized for that purpose and to support empowerment programs for blacks in various locations around the state. Among grants totaling $2,268,443 in 1989 were these: Arkansas Advocates for Children and Families, to provide information and alternatives to decrease the dependency of the juvenile courts on secure confinement for hard-to-manage youth; Arkansas Community Foundation, to provide technical assistance for an at-risk youth program, to increase the asset base, and to narrow the information gap between funders and fund-seekers by providing a bi-monthly newsletter about funding sources; Arkansas Institute for Social Justice, to empower black and low-income residents of Pine Bluff to effectively organize for improvements in the areas of city services, community participation, and leadership development; $250,000 to Arkansas Enterprise Group to improve their capacity to increase the volume of local small business and self-employment activity; Delta Community Development Corporation, to address causes and conditions of chronic economic depression and under- and unemployment in eastern Arkansas; Southern Growth Policy Board, to network small- and medium-sized Arkansas manufacturers to test the concept of using technical and community colleges to be not only training grounds for new technology, but also a base for its diffusion into the small business sector; Henderson State University, to increase the recruitment and retention of black students in the university's graduate programs; Kiwanis Activities of Little Rock, to continue funding of an alternative to out-of-school suspension for at-risk students who would benefit from an intensive academic remediation and counseling program; Planned Parenthood of Arkansas, to assist school districts in meeting the school standards requiring health and sexuality education; UAMS, to support

A group hug was part of the program funded by the Winthrop Rockefeller Foundation to develop local leadership. Throughout Arkansas, grants were made to groups enrolling in the program. In each case, the training cycle ended with trainers in the center and the trainees clasping them tightly, building common ground for later communication. (Photo courtesy of Winthrop Rockefeller Foundation)

a collaborative, statewide effort among secondary schools, undergraduate institutions, UAMS, and the Area Health Education Centers aimed at improving minority medical student recruitment and retention; Black Community Developers Program, to create an ongoing statewide network and support system to battle the exploding crisis of crack cocaine addiction in Arkansas, especially in the black community.

It was clear and had been for several years through an examination of grants made that the foundation considered the difficulties, the disenfranchisement, the lack of education and employment opportunities and so on, that blacks needed special help and lots of it to help bring about some form of equality. McRae had said earlier and it was obvious to all concerned that the amounts distributed by the foundation were minuscule when measured against the problems, but it was an attempt to provide leadership along with funds and hopefully attract the interest of others who shared this philosophy.

And many shared the foundation's philosophy, had created organizations and efforts of various kinds, but all suffered from a lack of funds to really make things happen and the foundation's grants, however generous, were just a drop in the bucket.

For 1990, a total of $3,128,759 was granted, including the following: Arkansas Community Foundation, to produce a film about the achievements of the Little Rock Nine, to increase the asset base of ACF, and to narrow the information gap between funders and fundseekers; Arkansas Institute for Social Justice, to empower black and low-income residents of Pine Bluff to effectively organize for improvements in city services, community participation, and leadership development; Ozark Recycling Enterprise, to provide quality information to local governments and community and service organizations and to increase public awareness of the benefits of recycling and source reduction; to UALR School of Law, a continuation of the foundation's grants to provide fellowships to black scholars; Arkansas College, to provide free or low-cost assistance in business operations and economic development to small business owners through consultation, training, and active participation with regional economic development agencies; $250,000 to Arkansas Enterprise Group, to support the systematic delivery of services to local residents for increasing self-employment activity and the number of local small businesses; Delta Community Development Corporation, to address causes and conditions of chronic economic depression and underemployment and unemployment in eastern Arkansas; Ozark Regional Land Trust, to systematize the development of the small farm economy of the Ozarks; Arkansas Aviation Historical Society, to support development of a comprehensive plan for the establishment of an aerospace education center; $30,000 to Kiwanis Activities of Little Rock to establish an alternative to out-of-school suspension for at-risk students who would benefit from an intensive academic remediation and counseling program; UAMS, to improve minority medical student recruitment and retention; Philander Smith College, to support the creation of a long-range plan for capital development and capital campaign activities; and $21,270 in an *Arkansas Issues* study of philanthropy in Arkansas and strategies or structures for stimulating more philanthropic giving for the state. The foundation needed more help, and it wasn't getting it to any serious extent from other prospective funders.

In 1991, the foundation made grants totaling $2,312,115, including the following: $250,000 to Southern Ventures (SV), to leverage a $3.2 million investment in SV's capital pool for venture capital loans in rural Arkansas; Arkansas Coalition Against Violence to Women and Children, to build the organizational capacity of the coalition so it would become self-sustaining and organizationally sound; continuation of the fellowship program at UALR School of Law for black law students; UA Foundation, to design, develop, implement, document, and evaluate Training Community Organizations for Change, a leadership and organizational development training program; Acorn Housing Corporation, to promote affordable homeownership opportunities and neighborhood revitalization; Arkansas Land and Farm Development Corporation (ALFDC), to expand and stabilize its resource base by increasing membership, reducing dependency on project grant funds, and bolstering middle management capacity; Delta Community Development Corporation, to address causes and conditions of chronic economic depression and underemployment and unemployment in eastern Arkansas; Urban League of Greater Little Rock, to develop the Homebuyers' Institute to address problems faced by low- and moderate-income persons who want to become homeowners; Arkansas Education Renewal Consortium, to help selected Arkansas schools address the educational and developmental needs of children in middle-grade schools; Philander Smith College, to establish a fast-track, year-round evening program to allow full-time working students time to complete their college degree requirements.

In 1992, President Mahlon Martin described the foundation as continuing to believe that long-lasting improvement in the quality of life happens person by person, organization by organization, and community by community. "We also believe," he went on, "that our overriding themes of equity and capacity building ensure that all Arkansans share in an improved quality of life."[20]

The foundation's awards in 1992 totaled $2,627,710, including the following: Arkansas Humanities Council, to create and manage a planning grant program to help community groups that want to renovate structures for socially beneficial purposes; UALR Law School, for the ongoing fellowship program for black students; $150,000 to various entities for housing initiatives over the state, oriented to establishing self-help housing information clearinghouses and housing plans, promoting homeownership for people with low and moderate incomes; $591,303 to community development corporations over the state—community-based nonprofits engaged in economic development activities that target low-income populations; $875,580 to educational improvement initiatives, including improving teaching, and to help break the intergenerational cycle of undereducation and poverty of public housing residents; $111,907 to public policy initiatives, including a grant to the Arkansas Department of Health to plan and develop a proposal to improve recruitment and retention of primary health-care providers in rural Arkansas.

In 1993, Martin described the goals of the foundation for the 1990s as (1) to encourage the development of Arkansas's ability to provide an equitable, quality education for all children; (2) to strengthen the capacity of local communities to break the cycle of poverty by supporting projects that promote local economic development; and (3) to nurture strong, broad-based grassroots leadership through the development of community-based organizations. Martin added that the foundation's goal of local capacity building meant supporting local citizens as they work to remove barriers to change in their communities. "Building local capacity," he said, "may include providing access to training, technical assistance or current information. In some communities, we may partner with an organization to support an inclusive planning process or to test a new program or strategy."[21] By now, the foundation has moved beyond the mandates of Rockefeller, but was still thematically tied in with what he had tried to do in his life with his own gifts. He wanted local people to help themselves and provided funds for that purpose, but he did not have the research capacity developed to search out and fund programs that had a chance of success, so he didn't do very many. The foundation was taking that on down the road and, under the strong management structure that Martin provided, was achieving success and following up on funded programs to be sure they were reporting properly and measuring up to expectations.

The foundation's grants in 1993 totaled $4,768,137, including the following: $1,085,996 in the area of civic affairs; $1,541,256 in the area of economic development (including $207,068 to Delta Community Development Corporation [CDC] to establish a partnership combining the skills and resources of Delta CDC with those of approximately one hundred African American churches in the Delta focusing on programs to develop people and communities); $1,259,823 in education; $400,396 in public policy; and $96,000 in community incentive grants.

In 1994, the foundation's grants totaled $5,515,747, broken down broadly this way: $1,394,271 to civic affairs; $1,531,282 to economic development; $1,289,043 to education; $477,698 in public policy grants; $87,523 in community incentive programs; and $13,400 in discretionary grants. Among grants were these: Arkansas Community Foundation, to provide long-term support and leverage for ACF's fund-raising efforts; Arkansas Humanities Council, to expand a planning grant program to help community groups that want to renovate structures for socially beneficial purposes; Boy Scouts of America, to recruit and train additional volunteer leaders and organize at least twenty-five new Scout units per year for four years in unserved neighborhoods in Little Rock and Pine Bluff; Arkansas Delta Housing Development Corporation, to test a comprehensive system designed to attack the major barriers to low- and very-low-income homeownership in the Arkansas Delta; Arkansas Economic Corporation to improve the economic well-being of small-acreage, limited resource farm families by promoting cooperative marketing development and rural entrepreneurship; an additional grant of $182,623 to Delta Community Development Corporation to support the partnership combining the skills and talents of Delta CDC with African American churches in the Delta; Shirley Community Service and Development Corporation, to develop shiitake mushroom growers in north-central Arkansas as part of a sustainable industry that used local resources; $270,000 in "Break the Mold" programs, described by Martin as "our attempt in the educational program area to change the way teacher education is handled in Arkansas." The partnerships involved Arkansas universities and public schools to improve education by preparing teachers and schools for the twenty-first century. The focus of the partnerships was to reform teacher education and renew current teachers through comprehensive student teaching experiences and staff development.

A total of $5,710,328 was granted in 1995, the year the second president of the foundation, Mahlon Martin, died.

Among the grants in 1995 were these: Boy Scouts of America, to recruit and train additional volunteer leaders and organize at least twenty-five new Scout units per year for four years in unserved neighborhoods in Little Rock and Pine Bluff; Arkansas Community Foundation to provide long-term support and leverage for ACF's fund-raising efforts; Non-Profit Resources, Inc., to develop NPR organizational capacity; $130,627 to Delta Community Development Corporation (final year of the grant), to establish a partnership to combine the skills and talents of Delta CDC with African American churches in the Delta area; Arkansas Rural Development Commission, to support an economic development planning grant program for small towns as a project of the Office of Rural Advocacy; UAMS, to increase the numbers of, and improve the academic competitiveness of, minority students enrolled in and graduating from UAMS health professional colleges; Arkansas Advocates for Children and Families, to study the impact on juveniles of recently enacted laws that allow prosecutors to charge juveniles as adults.

A total of $5,266,823 was granted in 1996, in the following broad areas: civic affairs; economic development; education; public policy; community incentives; discretionary grants; and education minigrants. Among the grants in 1996 were the following: Arkansas Gay and Lesbian Task Force, to implement an organizational development plan; Delta Community Development

Corporation, to implement an organizational development plan; Arkansas Delta Housing, to implement an organizational development plan; Southwest Arkansas Community Development Corporation, to implement an organizational development plan; Arkansas Community Foundation, to provide long-term support and leverage for ACF's fund-raising efforts; Boy Scouts of America, to recruit and train additional volunteer leaders and organize at least twenty-five new Scout units in unserved neighborhoods in Little Rock and Pine Bluff; Training Community Organizations for Change, to conduct a year-long training program for teams of leaders from community-based organizations in Arkansas; Arkansas Association of Community Development Corporations, to support a comprehensive technical assistance delivery system for community development corporations in Arkansas; Arkansas Delta Housing Development Corporation, to test a comprehensive system designed to attack the major barriers to homeownership for low-income people in the Arkansas Delta region; Arkansas Economic Corporation, to improve the economic well-being of small-acreage, limited-resource farm families by promoting coopera-tive marketing development and rural entrepreneurship; Arkansas Land and Farm Development Corporation, to encourage youth to explore farming and agriculture-related jobs as career options through the Youth Enterprise in Agriculture Project; Arkansas Low-Income Housing Coalition, to work for decent, safe, and affordable housing by empowering low-income Arkansans in their efforts to obtain affordable housing; Arkansas Rural Development Com-mission to support an economic development planning grant program for small towns as a program of the Office of Rural Advocacy; Shirley Community Service and Development Corporation to develop shiitake mushroom production in north-central Arkansas, as a sustainable industry that uses local resources.

Dr. Sybil Hampton became president of the foundation in October 1996, and the decision was made that no new grants would be awarded in 1997, because the staff believed it was highly important to spend that year exploring the state, examining internal operations, reflecting on the foundation's work, and most significantly, reevaluating WRF's role as a philanthropic organization in Arkansas.

"A large part of what we spent the first six months doing, was thinking about internal systems," she explained. "That led to the request in December 1996 to the board to take time in 1997 and only do the continuing grants because we should not only look at new internal systems and decide what our capacity was and should be, but also give me an opportunity to go around the state and get a sense of who was doing what, our grantees as well as others."[22]

Dr. Sybil Hampton became the third president of the Winthrop Rockefeller Foundation, embracing the vision of Rockefeller and leading in the creation and implementation of programs related to that vision. (Photo courtesy of Winthrop Rockefeller Foundation)

Grants were continued in 1997 in the broad areas of civic affairs, economic development, education, and public policy, and totaled $2,928,722.

A total of $3,446,481 was awarded in 1998, including a grant of $1,500,000 to Enterprise Corporation of the Delta, and $525,111 to the Arkansas Community Foundation. Other grants targeted the foundation's proactive stance about rural youth and the intention to address the needs of small, rural Arkansas communities and their young people. The Rural Community Jump-Start Technology Initiative was "our considered response to the Jonesboro tragedy," Hampton said. (The tragedy involved two students who opened fire on students and teachers at Jonesboro High School, killing several.) All the targeted communities had populations of 10,000 or less. The program was to serve as a mechanism for linking young people and adults as they began to plan for the future of their communities in the knowledge-based society. Hampton said that success in the new millennium "will require people to work cooperatively as they build economically viable and just communities. Our youth in rural areas will be called upon to provide leadership that builds on collaborative, not competitive, models . . . to give participating youth an opportunity to learn how to provide leadership in new ways."[23]

In 1999, the twenty-fifth year of the foundation, grants made totaled $3,024,591, and included the following: $1,150,000 to the Enterprise Corporation of the Delta; Arkansas Arts Center and Arts Center Foundation, and the Arkansas Arts Council; Arkansas Community Foundation; Arkansas Humanities Council; Arkansas Land and Farm Development Corporation; Fort Smith Symphony; New Horizon Church and Its Ministries; Wildwood Center for the Performing Arts, and Winrock International.

In viewing the foundation's work in its first quarter-century, Hampton said changes were indicated in emphasis and management as the asset base had continued to grow and as the process of careful, thoughtful grant making became ever more demanding. "At the end of 2000 we had a three-year strategic plan developed," she said. "The board came to terms with our vision, our values, our program areas." She explained that the vision is that Arkansas is a state where economic, racial, and social justice is universally valued and practiced. "The mission of the foundation," Hampton explained, "is to improve the lives of Arkansans. The foundation uses resources to build and sustain strong communities for all Arkansans, by supporting and strengthening organizations which serve them."[24] She cited economic development and an emphasis on empowering individuals and institutions to improve the standard of living and economic viability of low-income communities. She described a goal of the foundation as a program enabling all—children and adults alike—to develop fully their capacities to improve themselves and contribute to the educational, cultural, economic, and social vitality of their communities. In the area of economic, racial, and social justice, she said, the foundation seeks to "engage institutions and individuals in the struggle for pervasive justice in the lives of all Arkansans and their communities."[25]

Nancy Delamar, vice president and state director of the Nature Conservancy, Arkansas Field Office, said about the support the foundation had given,

> At the end of the grant period we were able to say that based on acres protected we had leveraged the foundation's dollars ten to one. Now that original million has been leveraged maybe 100 times. We've protected

everything from big huge, ancient trees that five people can't even get their arms around, to a tiny little plant that grows in a limestone glade in the Ozarks. We've been involved in the protection of 100,000 acres in counties all over Arkansas. It so beautifully fulfills what must have been Winthrop Rockefeller's dream for what a foundation like that could do for Arkansas.[26]

CHAPTER

9

The Winthrop Rockefeller Charitable Trust

"I give the bulk of my estate to charity."[1] Those words, in the will of Winthrop Rockefeller, gave the guidance which the Winthrop Rockefeller Charitable Trust, set up with the remainder of his assets, has attempted to follow in the years since his death in 1973. During those some eighteen years, the trust has distributed almost $150 million to various charities in which Rockefeller had shown an interest during his life (and some that he hadn't) but which seemed to conform to his wishes about what was to be done with his remaining wealth. Presently, the trustees are Marion Burton, the co-trustee in charge of the Trust office; Robert Shults, a Little Rock attorney; Win Rockefeller, son of the late Winthrop Rockefeller and the state's lieutenant governor; Donal O'Brien, a New York attorney; and William Dietel of Flint Hill, Virginia, retired president of the Rockefeller Brothers Fund.

In his will, he asked the trustees to be innovative and venturesome in supporting charitable projects. The trust and subsequently the Winthrop Rockefeller Foundation—which the trust funded from Rockefeller's assets—took that admonition to heart. "They should not feel that they need to be conservative in the use of principal," Rockefeller's will stated in regard to the trustees. "It is my hope," the will continued, "that they will apply the full resources of the trust towards the realization of significant charitable ends." Rockefeller noted that although he had provided that the trust run until the death of the last to die of the descendants of his father, John D. Rockefeller Jr., living at the time of Winthrop's death, "I have done so simply to give the Trustees maximum flexibility in carrying out my charitable objectives."[2]

Rockefeller attempted to provide lots of latitude to the trust, giving discretion in the distribution of his assets and even laying out a scenario in which the trust might reach the point where it deemed it advisable to close down entirely. "I expressly authorize and empower the Trustees, in their sole and absolute discretion, to terminate the trust at any time, if they feel that by doing so the best charitable use will be made of the trust property, and I wish them to know that it is not my desire to extend the life of the trust for an undue period of time."[3] Nevertheless, the trustees have since appeared to operate on the basis that the trust would continue indefinitely. It had a principal base remaining of roughly $100 million at the end of 2001.

Rockefeller wanted Winrock Farms proper to constitute a part of his residual estate and be a substantial part of the assets held in the trust, stating, "I have devoted a significant part of my life to the establishment and expansion of Winrock Farms, and I would like to see the farm operations continued, to the extent possible, for the benefit of charitable purposes." He cautioned the trustees that if they disposed of certain farm properties, to do so "in a fashion which respects the integrity of Winrock Farms and particularly the integrity of the Winrock Farms operations in and around Petit Jean Mountain."[4] Subsequently, Winthrop Paul Rockefeller was able to purchase the farm proper from the estate, and its operation has continued uninterrupted since.

Rockefeller speculated in the will whether it would be possible to give, or make available, to the University of Arkansas, or to Hendrix College, or some other educational institution, some part or all of the farm properties for use in its agricultural, animal husbandry, or other programs. "It may be," he stated, "that a part of Winrock Farms would lend itself to a model farm project fitting within the programs of the university, and other parts might lend themselves to a research, cultural or educational center, such as a public affairs center."

He continued that he didn't expect that all of the assets of the trust would be devoted to Winrock Farms, and thus "I ask the Trustees, in applying the income and principal of the trust, to give sympathetic consideration to those charities with which I have been most closely associated during my life." Rockefeller listed several entities that had been the subject of his interest— including the Arkansas Arts Center, the Arkansas Opportunity Fund, and the Rockwin Fund, which became the Winthrop Rockefeller Foundation. About the Arts Center, he suggested that some of the paintings owned by him might be given or loaned to the Arts Center.

He identified several educational institutions with which he had been associated, including Loomis Institute and Vanderbilt and Yale Universities. "It is my desire that they receive support from the trust to the extent the Trustees deem appropriate," he wrote. Rockefeller described his "deep interest" in the Colonial Williamsburg Foundation, Rockefeller Brothers Fund, Inc., and Rockefeller Family Fund, "and it is my wish that these organizations might be given support."

The trust subsequently gave $3.8 million to the Arts Center Foundation and $210,890 to the Arts Center directly; $9.5 million to Colonial Williamsburg; $500,000 to Vanderbilt University; and $300,000 to Yale University.

As of 2001, the trust had not distributed anything to the Rockefeller Brothers Fund or the Rockefeller Family Fund. Rockefeller himself gave no more to RBF after 1955, and he never made a gift at all to the Family Fund.

The major beneficiary of the trust's disbursements has been Winrock International. Almost $80 million has been distributed there. Trustee Burton referred to the will in discussing Winrock International and said the creation of Winrock International Agricultural Development Institute yielded initially a good institution that worked worldwide. "The organization was set up to leverage the money that it got from the trust through contracts and grants for development programs throughout the world," he pointed out. "It's unfortunate," Burton continued, "that it is not going to continue to headquarter in Arkansas."[5] Indeed, some months after the interview, Winrock International took its headquarters to Washington, D.C.

The trust's total distributions through 2001 totaled more than $147 million. Burton said he thinks that "one of the most important things the trust has done is to demonstrate to other wealthy people in Arkansas what they can do with their assets after their deaths."

After the grants to Winrock International, which began in 1976 and continued through 2001, totaling $79,912,152, the other major distributions, ranked by amounts, include the following: the Winthrop Rockefeller Foundation, $40,042,432; Colonial Williamsburg, $9,500,000. Of the total, $1 million has been distributed to the Abby Aldrich Rockefeller Folk Art Center, in four payments in 1990 and 1991. The folk art center—named in honor of Winthrop's mother—is located at Williamsburg. The balance—$8,500,000—went to the Carter's Grove Restoration. Payments were made beginning in 1977 and continued through 1990. In a letter to Carl Humelsine, then president of Colonial Williamsburg, David Rockefeller—one of the

Winthrop Rockefeller Trust trustees at the time and Winthrop's younger brother —wrote that the trustees were making a grant of $1 million and had considered the foundation's request for additional support in connection with the restoration of Carter's Grove and that "in recognition of Win's particular interest in this project, the Trustees have decided in principle to make a further grant of $2 million" to help with the Carter's Grove project. There was this caveat. "As Win's estate continues to be in administration, however, and as the Trustees cannot determine now the total amount which will ultimately pass to the trust, this additional commitment in principle is necessarily subject to the availability of funds. The continuing complexities of Win's estate also render uncertain the timing of any additional trust grant to Colonial Williamsburg. Nevertheless, the Trustees hope that this expression of their intention to contribute further will be helpful to the project." The letter was dated July 19, 1977.[6]

Funds also went to the Arkansas Arts Center and Arts Center Foundation, $4,043,404.80. Payments were made from 1976 through 1988, and included (in 1984) the sum of $150,000 for restoration of the Terry Mansion, which is part of the arts center complex. As part of the grant, the trust provided $1,000,000 on a 2 for 1 matching basis, but not enough was collected by the arts center for the match before the deadline of January 1, 1986. The trustees in February 1988 approved additional grants including the unpaid balance on the original matching grant.

Contributions to the Arkansas Aerospace Education Center totaled $1,716,609. In the late 1970s the Arkansas Aviation Historical Society was established to promote an awareness and appreciation for expanding technologies in the aviation and aerospace industries and their enormous impact on the citizenry. An Arkansas Aviation Hall of Fame was established (Winthrop Rockefeller was inducted posthumously) and long-range goals included the establishment of an aviation-aerospace museum and expanding educational and tourism opportunities.

In 1995, the Aerospace Education Center (AEC) opened, and well over a million people have visited it since then. After providing $60,000 for a feasibility study in 1990, the trust made a challenge grant of $500,000 in that same year, then began making gifts regularly as the program continued to develop. It was a follow-up, in a sense, to Rockefeller's interest dating back to the 1930s in establishing and helping to fund Air Youth of America, to acquaint and interest young Americans in flying and the future of aviation. The AEC program includes an IMAX theater that attracts many school children, teacher in-service programs, and summer camps for kids. Through AEC an Airframe Interior Modification Certification program was enlarged at Pulaski Technical College to assist the work force in acquiring the skills required for employment at local industries, such as Raytheon Aircraft and Desault-Falcon Jet. In the mid-1960s, Rockefeller decided to acquire a Falcon jet, which was flown from France to Little Rock "green"—devoid of interior avionics. Rockefeller wanted all that technical work to be done in Little Rock, if at all possible. This was not the way it was ordinarily done, Rockefeller quickly learned. An arrangement had been established with Central Airmotive in Burbank, California, to finish out the Falcons. (Rockefeller's was one of the first in the United States.) A visit by Burton (who was also one of Rockefeller's pilots, later his chief pilot) and another representative of Rockefeller to those in charge earned the rejoinder from the New York office "that's got to be stupid! They can't do that airplane. They'll ruin it!"[7] Rockefeller was not convinced. He saw to it that his plane was outfitted in Little Rock after all. It was done beautifully and well, and the plane went on to set new speed records and won the Great Air Show award. Without question, Rockefeller got the airplane completion business started in Arkansas and it continues to be successful to this day. "I don't know of anybody else who would have taken that kind of risk with that kind of investment," Burton commented.

A commitment of $2 million to Philander Smith College is pending. This primarily black, Methodist-supported private college, is in Little Rock. Rockefeller had contributed more than $53,000 during his life, and in 2000 the trust committed $2 million over five years for library books in the college's Library and Technology Center, with the conditions that the center is constructed along the lines of the proposed building, and that before each installment of the payment the college certifies that it is able to house the books it plans to purchase. Dr. Trudie Reed, president, in her communication with the trust had noted that Rockefeller had always been generous with his time and influence on behalf of the college, and "I understand he wanted to help in more ways than the college knew how to accept."[8] (Rockefeller had been invited out to the campus in the sixties, long before Dr. Reed had become involved, and described himself afterward as unimpressed at what could be accomplished with gifts of money but nothing much else.) She added that the project "has the potential to transform this college for the next century."[9] According to Dr. Reed, "Our students will no longer have to leave this campus to study at other nearby libraries. Because of this generous gift, our students will be able to study at Philander Smith College."[10] The college had received other substantial gifts and was prepared to go forward with the 49,404-square-foot library.

The National Rural Center received $1,950,000. Rockefeller had a deep and continuing interest in rural affairs from fairly early in life, and had made a particular study of rural youth in a changing environment to help him focus his thinking on what could and should be done to improve the lot of those whose lives were not centered in the cities of America. From the beginnings of Winrock Farms, he created opportunities for Arkansans and others to learn and share in the knowledge about cattle in particular as the research continued with highly trained professionals and excellent facilities that were a part of Winrock. A few years after his death, an organization—the National Rural Center (NRC)—was formed, which likely would have attracted his interest because it seemed to conform to his own thinking about rural America, and perhaps was a natural target for support from the Winthrop Rockefeller Trust in 1976. The NRC set about to develop policy that would affect rural areas, including research, evaluation, and monitoring of legislation that addressed rural issues. An example of the findings of the NRC was that economic development is not an automatic consequence of massive federally funded waterway projects, and project jobs "do not automatically go to local residents." The report was based on a study of the Tennessee-Tombigbee Waterway Construction Project, a 253-mile waterway to connect the Tennessee and Tombigbee Rivers. The NRC also concerned itself with matters of health and helped develop data and information for the law permitting Medicare and Medicaid payments to rural primary-care health clinics for nurse practitioners and physician assistants. Rockefeller had concentrated a lot of attention on rural health. Other aspects of the NRC focus were such things as rural development in general, small farms, rural justice, and rural education.[11]

The Arkansas Center for Health Improvement (ACHI) was granted $1,820,000. The gift in four installments went to the University of Arkansas Medical Center Foundation, to be used exclusively by ACHI. An effort was being made to raise matching funds, but the agreement was not to hold ACHI to the larger match requirement. ACHI was established as an independent and nonpartisan organization to improve the health of Arkansans through policy research, professional education, program development, and public advocacy. Some 70 percent of its funding comes from public and private sources. It has been boring in on problems unlikely to improve until root causes are determined that make Arkansans less healthy than other Americans and until programs, education, and services are defined to alter behaviors and improve health in the state.

TCU (Texas Christian University) Ranch Management was awarded $1,050,000. The gift required that a match of $2.1 million in a three-year time frame from 1988 be raised before the trust provided the $1 million-plus. This requirement was met for the gift intended to strengthen the Ranch Management School at Texas Christian University. Winthrop Paul had completed the program himself to help prepare for the challenges of operating Winrock Farms. He later became a trustee.

Hendrix College received $1 million. An outstanding—if small—liberal arts college in Conway, the institution was mentioned in the will and in 1988 the trust distributed the funds in two installments of $500,000 each to provide scholarships. Dr. Joe Hatcher, president at that time, said that the additional funds from the trust made it possible for students regardless of financial capacity, if otherwise eligible, to study at Hendrix, and provided merit awards for a limited number of students. Hatcher noted that some 55 percent of Hendrix students were receiving need-based financial aid.

Rockefeller in his lifetime had given a considerable amount of money to Loomis Institute, as discussed elsewhere. The gift of $698,500 was to cover the outstanding balance on his pledges.

The Rockefeller Brothers Fund played a key role in establishing Worldwatch Institute, awarded $645,000, and when the organization planned to prepare an annual report measuring worldwide progress, or lack thereof, toward the creation of a sustainable global society, RBF expressed the hope that the trust would make a gift to help support it. The trust was advised that the project had special merit. The report, which the trust helped to fund, included sections on such topics as agricultural production and food security, population stabilization, energy efficiency, and desert reclamation.

The Arkansas Department of Parks and Tourism received $475,900. In 1976 the trust provided $95,000 for improvements to the Arkansas Museum of Automobiles property on Petit Jean Mountain, and $380,000 in 2000 to establish a fly-in campground near the Petit Jean Airport. Both the museum and the airport had been given to the state of Arkansas by Rockefeller.

Other distributions from the trust include the following: Arkansas Cattlemen's Association; American Farmland Trust; American Heart Association, San Francisco Chapter; Arkansas Governor's Mansion Association; Arkansas State Council on Economic Education; Perry County Public Library; Center for Community Change; Central Arkansas Library System; Citizen's Participation Project; Close-Up Foundation; College of the Ozarks; Infantry Museum Association; National Audubon Society; Nature Conservancy; Rockefeller University; Rural Housing Allowance; Society of New York Hospital; United Fund of Pulaski County; University of Arkansas Foundation; Vanderbilt University; Yale University, and YMCA of Metropolitan Little Rock.

10

Building Arkansas

A friend of the Rockefeller family recalls standing at the Little Rock airport with others as Rockefeller was returning from New York, where he had undergone medical treatment for cancer, and where he learned that nothing more could be done. These were the last days of his life. He was thin, but had grown a large beard, which had turned mostly white. As he got off his jet at the flying service, a child was heard to call out that he looked like Santa Claus. Perhaps he was regarded that way by many through the years, but the respect and appreciation for him was a deeper feeling and was directly based on his generous and consistent efforts to improve Arkansas with his wealth, leadership, and arguments against inferiority and hopelessness and a sharing of the vision that lives could be better, communities could be better, Arkansas could be better.

Rockefeller changed Arkansas. It isn't too much to say he did. An objective look at the state before him and after he was gone demonstrates that. Industrial and economic development became a fact of life; educational opportunity was broadened; blacks found greater opportunities and more information and thus more access to their local and state governments and to the nonmenial jobs to be found there; the election process was cleaned up; brutality was ended at the state's prisons; access to better health care was assured; good art was accessible throughout the state; and perhaps as important as anything else, he changed the state's politics. Before him it was a controlled system where moneyed inter-ests elected public officials who would do their bidding and help them con-tinue to add to their fortunes. Rockefeller ended that by the very fact of his election, and without access to him or influence over government, the good old boys faded into the background and that made room for the Democratic Party to clean itself up as it had not been for decades. Once progress was made and good people were back in charge of the party, they could put a Dale Bumpers into office and after him other progressive and effective public offi-cials who saw beyond their own self-interest to the public need and the public good. In a way, you could say that Rockefeller—by winning public office—had sowed the seeds of his own political destruction at the hands of a revitalized political party that could put an obscure lawyer from Charleston into the governor's chair.

Dreary though the Arkansas landscape could often be in 1953, it was a challenge and a cause for excitement in Rockefeller, and he never lost that enthusiasm for making things happen, for "selling" his fellow citizens on what was possible, and for generously proving from his own pocketbook and per-sonal involvement how changes could be made. Pride had not come all that easily to Rockefeller. There was his holding up admirably under the rigors of hard work in the Texas oil fields. He had proven himself able and certainly up to the task in the infantry, and his taking over of the troop ship *Henrico* after a kamikaze attack had won him justifiable praise. And there was the Greater New York Fund, which he in effect headed (although he didn't have the title) to a successful conclusion. But in his eyes and that of his family he had yet to prove himself. They had witnessed a whole range of things involving him in which neither he nor they could take pride. There was the café society publicity that was nothing less than an embarrassment; there were his educational failures, his inability to settle into the family enterprises, his chafing at the need to be a "Rockefeller" in New York. Here, in Arkansas, he would turn the page. He did it, and it is poignant and so sad that mostly his family was no longer interested in what he was doing. They had seen and heard enough. He was finding it dif-ficult to attract their attention in a positive way, particularly his father. He did persuade his brothers on separate occasions to come to Arkansas and have a look as he was building Winrock, but his father would not come. This was a real heartbreaker for Rockefeller, because he wanted to show he had indeed turned that page. It was no use. When he made the film about the building of the farm, it was mainly to show his father what he had accomplished.

For the first ten years or so, he would work with the people of Arkansas as Rockefeller the private citizen; then he would seek and win the governorship in order to take additional steps of leadership. He was fought every step of the way by anyone who thought they could get an angle on him from legislators to the governor to other political opponents of every stripe. He answered every charge as best he could as he pressed doggedly on. Arkansas was comparatively undeveloped, unspoiled, and populated with people who were, Rockefeller readily acknowledged from almost the very beginning, badly in need of a shot of optimism, even a kick in the pants, in order to get things going. Rockefeller delivered both.

As stated earlier, even though he arrived with some successes in his background, when he had punched a button in New York, it was doubtful if a light ever came on, at least not readily. In Arkansas, though, things weren't like that. He really could make a difference and almost before he set down his suitcase he was getting involved. He contributed $50,000 to an expansion program for Arkansas Baptist Hospital and simultaneously accepted a role on the committee to urge others to support the program as well. He headed the Medical Center Advisory Committee for the University of Arkansas, to advise on the scope and activities of the new medical center. He financed studies of various kinds to get a clearer understanding of attitudes as he set about to change Arkansas with his leadership and his philanthropy. One study he paid for was to ascertain public perception of the medical center and its role in the state. Another was to better understand rural health needs in Arkansas. He funded several studies of water resources and management in the state. Water was a very big issue with Rockefeller. He had experienced the difficulty of not having enough water, once he began building his farm atop Petit Jean Mountain. He did what most could not; he financed the construction of a system to pump water up the mountain from Petit Jean River down below, pouring the water into irrigation ponds and thus making possible the further development he had in mind. During the years to come he would involve others in examining the issue of water for the state of Arkansas. He employed a groundwater geologist, Dr. Leslie E. Mack of Fayetteville, to help develop studies and recommend policy where applicable. As soon as he was elected governor, Rockefeller turned up the heat as best he could in regard to water. He hosted a national conference on interstate water problems at Winrock Farms, with special emphasis on the legal aspects of water rights, and he talked about the "extraordinary legal problems that could tie up cases in the courts for years to come."[1] Noting the increases in population and industrial water needs, Rockefeller reminded everyone who would listen that as chairman of the AIDC he had started a water management project to gather information and make it available, and he was proud to report that "all agencies involved in

Critics of Rockefeller tried to attack him on the basis of his wealth by ascribing a negative quality to it. No different was James "Uncle Mac" MacKrell, who entered the Republican primary for governor in 1970 with the claim of the high moral ground and the promise that he could explain how to be "Richernrockyfela." Rockefeller bested Uncle Mac by an overwhelming majority to win the nomination again. (Photo courtesy of University of Central Arkansas Archives)

water" were working as a unit, and that water management decisions would be made on a professional rather than a political basis.

At the very beginning of his first term as governor, he was warning that Arkansas must come to grips with the problems of water conservation and pollution "before we find ourselves in the same situation as other industrial states that are paying a high premium for solving pollution and other water problems."[2] It was not all in vain, but all the studies and findings and other data that Rockefeller either gathered or caused to be developed did not and have not appreciably changed the situation very much in Arkansas. Indeed, the warnings could be issued today without changing one word from what

Rockefeller was saying more than thirty years ago. Yet, logical and knowl-edgeable planning, Dr. Mack advised Rockefeller, was absolutely essential if Arkansas prepared for future social and technological advances.

A month after Rockefeller won election as the state's first Republican governor since 1874, *Time* magazine stated in the December 2, 1966 issue:

> For its economic and social transformation, Arkansas owes much to a transplanted Yankee whose surname—connoting vast wealth, liberal Republicanism and cosmopolitan interests—once seemed as alien to the state as fine champagne. Winthrop Rockefeller has not only devoted his time and fortune over the last 13 years to improving the quality of life in Arkansas. He has also succeeded almost single-handedly in renovating its political structure.[3]

That was an accurate observation. For the nine years Rockefeller served as chairman of the Arkansas Industrial Development Commission he worked closely with communities throughout the state to help bring six hundred new industrial plants to Arkansas, creating ninety thousand new jobs and a payroll of $270 million. Not only did he give of his time and leadership, and use his influence and connections throughout the United States and the world to help build Arkansas, he also gave a great deal of money to particular entities he believed could make a difference.

The first year after he arrived in Arkansas, he made a gift of $47,100 to the Arkansas Publicity and Parks Commission, and through the years following he gave a total of $464,768 to that agency alone. From 1955 on, he contributed $70,000 to the AIDC. In fact, he contributed a total of $1,506,000 to the state of Arkansas through these and various other entitites. He loaned his airplanes and met other expenses on behalf of Arkansas, primarily in its quest for industry, amounting to $785,385 throughout the years, which ended with his death. As he became more involved in politics he saw the tremendous problems with voter fraud and manipulation, and looked upon that as a serious impediment to progress in Arkansas. He funded the Election Research Council first, then the Election Laws Institute, to investigate and document voter irregularities and propose ways to clean up the election process. He put some $120,000 into the effort and it clearly paid off in many ways. Thanks to the bright light he shined on the process, elections were cleaned up considerably (although some of his associates were jailed in the process, and others were threatened with bodily harm if they didn't leave things alone), voting machines were purchased by several counties, and in general there was a statewide improvement in the entire voting process.

Rockefeller distributed many gifts to many organizations in Arkansas that could be included under a "building Arkansas" title, many of them listed under chapter headings that pertain to them more specifically, and all are documented in Appendix A. Among those not listed in other chapters were these, ranging in size of gift from a few dollars to $20,000 or more: 4-H Club Foundation; American Association of University Women, Arkansas chapter; American Legion in Arkansas; American Red Cross in Arkansas; Arkansas Audubon Society; Arkansas Bar Association; Arkansas Barrel Racing Association; Arkansas Basin Association; Arkansas for a Revised Constitution; Arkansas Junior Chamber of Commerce; Arkansas Science Fair Association; Arkansas State Council on Economic Education; Arkansas Travel Council; Arkansas Wildlife Federation; Associated Industries of Arkansas; Boys Industrial School Foundation, Pine Bluff; Camp Mitchell, Morrilton; Civil Air Patrol, Little Rock; Community Chest of Greater Little Rock; Community Concert Association; Conference on Controlled Environment and Food Technology; Cummins Prison Chapel Fund; Farm and Ranch Youth Center Club; Governmental Efficiency Study Commission; Governor's Youth Council; Junior Chamber of Commerce; Junior Deputy Sheriffs' Association; Junior League of Little Rock; Kiwanis Club; Little Rock Friends of the Library; Little Rock Air Force Base Youth Activities; Little Rock Boys' Club; Little Rock Fire Department; Little Rock Hadassah; Little Rock Police Department; Morrilton Baseball Club; Morrilton Chamber of Commerce Industrial Site Fund; Morrilton High School Library Fund; Morrilton Little League Baseball; Museum of Science and Natural History; Negro Florence Crittenton Home, Little Rock; Optimist Club of Greater Little Rock; Order of American Firemen, Little Rock; Salvation Army, Little Rock; Tucker Prison Chapel Fund; United Fund, Little Rock; United Fund of Pulaski County; University of Arkansas, Underground Water Recharge Project; YMCA, Little Rock.

Can you find a pattern in that giving? It is very difficult to do, and while his overall goals had to do with economic development, racial equality, culture and the arts, and physical and mental health, he was an easy touch for hundreds of other organizations and entities who were able to reach him. Saying "no" was a hard thing for him to do, and in more than one year he exceeded the limits set for his charitable giving. That parade of people and the flow of letters requesting money from Rockefeller began very, very early and continued until his death. As the child observed at the airport, the attitude of many Arkansans seemed to be that indeed Winthrop Rockefeller was Santa Claus and each person wanted a little something, maybe a whole lot of something.

Billy Apple, an accountant in Rockefeller's personal office, said the requests came in a constant stream. He remembered one man's letter early in

Rockefeller's time in Arkansas, asking for a Buick Electra. But it didn't stop there. The man also listed all the accessories he wanted on the automobile. Yet, Apple said, Rockefeller didn't complain about giving (although he didn't do that) and even when offended by someone's brash request, he would try to approach it reasonably and consider if it was worthwhile and if it was, the person would likely get a favorable response.

The late Harry Ashmore, executive editor of the *Arkansas Gazette* and a Pulitzer Prize winner for his editorials about the desegregation of Little Rock Central High School, commented to *Time* in March 1957 about Rockefeller, that "we thought he had come down here just to sit on his tail. We soon found out different."[4] Rockefeller, who always described himself as a catalyst, could lead to changes in attitude and commitment because he had the horsepower in terms of name and prestige, and because he had money to put into worthy causes himself, to set the example, if nothing else. The industrial development program he led is illustrative. When Gov. Orval Faubus appointed Rockefeller to the Arkansas Industrial Development Commission, the members elected him chairman and almost the first decision Rockefeller made was to ignore a legislative recommendation to hire someone at $8,000 a year to run the program. Instead, Rockefeller hired two outstanding professionals in the field at $20,000 and $12,000 (good salaries in those days) and continued on assembling a nonpolitical staff who could work with him on a serious industrial recruitment program. When the money appropriated was all gone (and it didn't take long) Rockefeller buttonholed those he had recruited to form an advisory panel and asked them to kick in $100 each. They did. He put in $5,000 (the first of many gifts from his own pocket) and then proceeded to travel over the state raising more funds, rounding up another $200,000 in the process as he continued to invest himself. He got the cities involved and organized to be attractive to industrial prospects and more than anything else, Rockefeller convinced them that industrial development was possible. They hadn't believed it before, but now they did. And it paid off handsomely.

Cultural and educational opportunities were also created under Rockefeller's leadership, and when the state missed out on some high-tech industry because there was limited cultural and educational opportunity for the employees, Rockefeller used that to push and push to get more and more in the state. He and Mrs. Rockefeller would lead in the development of the Arkansas Arts Center, now a showplace of quality and culture in Little Rock that serves the entire state.

As Rockefeller entered his tenth year as a citizen of Arkansas, he was hailed by *Middle South News,* a publication of the Middle South Utilities System, as "the No. 1 salesman of and for the Middle South state of Arkansas."

Rockefeller receives from Gov. Orval E. Faubus a certificate for "great work as leader of AIDC" during a presentation at the capitol. Also participating is W. M. Campbell of Forrest City, one of the commissioners. Rockefeller served as chairman and led the state in attracting some six hundred new plants employing about ninety thousand people during his tenure. (Photo courtesy of University of Arkansas, Little Rock, Archives, WR VII 6.13)

The magazine credited Rockefeller's person-to-person selling as a major factor in bringing an increasing number of industries to the state, and praised the professionalism of the AIDC.[5] Rockefeller explained that "our major contribution to the industrial development has been made through assembling basic and accurate facts concerning our communities and presenting these in an orderly, believable and understandable manner."[6]

Rockefeller was involved in many other things while he was building a stronger industrial base in Arkansas, and in part his efforts had provided—and would continue to provide—leadership and example for others who might follow his lead and invest in comparatively risky ventures that would help Arkansas. For example, Rockefeller built the eighteen-story Tower Building in downtown Little Rock when the skyline otherwise was squatty and undistinguished. He was not daunted by observations that it was likely to bomb and

The family car was one of the automobiles (a 1916 Crane-Simplex) that came from New York to Petit Jean Mountain after Rockefeller built the Museum of Automobiles as a tourist attraction. He later gave the collection of automobiles and the entire complex to the state of Arkansas. (Photo courtesy of University of Arkansas, Little Rock, Archives, WR VII 6.614)

that Little Rock was not ready to support such a "skyscraper" office complex and so on. Rockefeller located his own business offices in the building, a fine restaurant located above his offices, and the building was soon filled with businesses and professional people who were only too glad to occupy such quality space at such a distinguished address.

He got interested in low-cost housing, to some degree a consequence of his work with the International Basic Economy Corporation in Central and South America. He established Winrock Enterprises—described as an Arkansas investment in new ideas—to engage in land development and low-cost residential construction, manufacturing, and development of commercial property for rental purposes. It too was successful. Rockefeller invested considerable funds in the development of Petit Jean Airport and later gave it to the state of Arkansas. He also built the Museum of Automobiles atop Petit Jean Mountain to house his collection of old cars and try to stimulate more tourism and help the economy on the mountain, and that too was later given to the state.

Ten years into his life in Arkansas, Rockefeller stated for the daily *Arkansas Democrat* his philosophy about things that seemed to illuminate his efforts through the remaining decade of his life. He said, "If you have an interest in people, you are never satisfied even with your ultimate objective. You always work a little harder for something more. I hope I never lose that enthusiasm until the day I die."[7] In his obituary issued from Palm Springs, California, where he died, was this statement:

"Reluctantly, he entered a hospital here February 9 [1973], troubled with a deepening chest congestion, but even then taking with him a briefcase filled with work that he never was able to complete." He died thirteen days later.[8]

APPENDIX A

Winthrop Rockefeller
Charitable Contributions, 1934–1973

1934

Community Chest, Houston, TX	$10.00
Larger Parish of Northeast Harbor	$30.00
Loomis Institute	$50.00
Riverside Church	$30.00
Union Church (Pocantico Hills)	$30.00
TOTAL	$150.00

1935

Community Chest, Houston, TX	$25.00
Loomis Institute	$50.00
Mount Desert Larger Parish	$30.00
Riverside Church	$30.00
Union Church (Pocantico Hills)	$30.00
TOTAL	$165.00

1936

Loomis Institute	$50.00
Mount Desert Larger Parish	$30.00
Riverside Church	$30.00
Union Church (Pocantico Hills)	$30.00
University of Texas	$345.00
TOTAL	$485.00

1937

American Red Cross	$5.00
Big Brothers Movement	$20.00
Loomis Institute	$50.00
Mount Desert Larger Parish	$30.00
Riverside Church	$30.00
Union Church (Pocantico Hills)	$30.00
University of Texas	$465.00
Yale in China Association	$25.00
Yale University Alumni Fund	$25.00
TOTAL	$680.00

1938

American Red Cross	$5.00
Big Brothers Movement	$40.00
Community Chest, Philadelphia, PA	$5.00
Greater New York Fund	$75.00
Grosvenor House, NY	$40.00
Loomis Institute	$50.00
Mount Desert Larger Parish	$50.00
Riverside Church	$50.00
Temple of Religion, NY	$100.00
Travelers' Aid Society	$25.00
Union Baptist Church, NY	$10.00
Union Church (Pocantico Hills)	$50.00
United Hospital Fund	$25.00
University of Texas	$700.00
Yale in China Association	$25.00
Yale University Alumni Fund	$25.00
TOTAL	$1,275.00

1939

Air Youth of America	$7,600.00
American Red Cross	$5.00
Big Brothers Movement	$40.00
Birth Control Federation of America	$25.00
Boys' Clubs of America	$50.00
Girl Scouts of America	$50.00
Greater New York Fund	$50.00
Lambs Club, NY	$120.00
Loomis Institute	$100.00
Mount Desert Larger Parish	$50.00
New York Tuberculosis Fund	$5.00
Riverside Church	$50.00
State Charities Aid, NY	$25.00
Travelers' Aid Society	$25.00
Union Church (Pocantico Hills)	$50.00

University of Texas	$500.00
Winona Parents Association (Denmark, ME)	$25.00
Yale in China Association	$25.00
Yale University Alumni Fund	$25.00
Youth Consultation Service	$25.00
TOTAL	**$8,845.00**

1940

Air Youth of America	$5,135.00
American Red Cross	$1,000.00
Big Brothers Movement	$50.00
Birth Control Federation of America	$25.00
Church Mission of Help, NY	$25.00
Colored Orphan Asylum, NY	$10.00
Elmsford Community House, NY	$75.00
Finnish Relief Fund, NY	$500.00
Friends of Turkey, NY	$25.00
Governor Dummer School, South Byfield, MA	$50.00
Greater New York Fund	$140.00
Henry Street Visiting Nurse Service, NY	$25.00
Mount Desert Larger Parish	$50.00
National Urban League	$100.00
New York Association for the Blind	$25.00
New York Tuberculosis and Health Association	$5.00
Riverside Church	$50.00
Salvation Army, NY	$75.00
Seeing Eye	$5.00
Society of the New York Hospital	$25.00
St. Philip's Church, NY	$10.00
Stage Relief Fund, NY	$35.00
State Charities Aid Association	$25.00
Temple of Religion, NY	$50.00
Travelers' Aid Society	$25.00
United Hospital Fund	$25.00
University of Texas	$300.00
Yale Club of New York City	$10.00
Yale in China Association	$25.00
Yale University Alumni Fund	$25.00
YMCA, NY	$25.00
TOTAL	**$7,950.00**

1941

Air Youth of America	$5,500.00
Church of Clinton Prison, TX	$10.00
Greater New York Fund	$25.00
Mount Desert Larger Parish	$75.00
Rockefeller Brothers Fund	$1,000.00
University of Texas	$200.00
Yale University Alumni Fund	$10.00
TOTAL	**$6,820.00**

1942

Boys' Clubs of America	$20.00
Union Church (Pocantico Hills)	$125.00
TOTAL	**$145.00**

1943

National Aeronautical Association	$10,000.00
National War Fund	$25,000.00
Rockefeller Brothers Fund	$63,812.50
TOTAL	**$98,812.50**

1944

Loomis Alumni Association Fund	$1,000.00
National War Fund	$25,000.00
Riverdale Children's Association	$1,000.00
Rockefeller Brothers Fund	$96,875.00
Yale University	$600.00
TOTAL	**$124,475.00**

1945

American Veterans Committee	$1,000.00
Governor Alfred Smith Memorial Fund, NY	$250.00
Loomis Alumni Association Fund	$6,000.00
National Aeronautical Association	$5,000.00
National War Fund	$25,498.21
Negro College Fund, NY	$10,040.63
Rockefeller Brothers Fund	$53,400.00
Seventy-seventh Infantry Division Association	$70.00
Yale University	$300.00
TOTAL	**$101,558.84**

1946

Columbia University	$5.00
General Theodore Roosevelt Jr. Library Fund, NY	$100.00
Historical Society of the Tarrytowns	$500.00
Legion of Women Veterans, NY	$1,000.00
Loomis Institute	$26,267.50
Riverdale Children's Association	$1,000.00
Rockefeller Brothers Fund	$69,125.00
Seventy-seventh Infantry Division Association	$27,764.59
Yale University	$100.00
TOTAL	**$125,862.09**

1947

305th Infantry Division Association	$20.00
American International Association for Economic and Social Development	$25,962.50
American Veterans Committee	$2,500.00

Collegiate Chorale	$50.00
Columbia University	$1,500.00
Disabled American Veterans	$105.00
Greater New York Fund	$50.00
Irvington House	$10.00
Jackson Hole Preserve	$25,293.75
Loomis Institute	$1,000.00
Military Order of the Purple Heart	$5.00
National Urban League	$10,075.55
National Variety Artists	$100.00
New York University	$40,000.00
Piney Woods Country Life School	$5.00
Professional Children's School, NY	$50.00
Public Education Association	$5,000.00
Rehearsal Club	$500.00
Riverdale Children's Association	$1,000.00
Rockefeller Brothers Fund	$25,593.75
Seeing Eye	$100.00
Seventy-seventh Infantry Division Association	$1,127.60
Spelman College	$9,568.75
Urban League, White Plains, NY	$50.00
Yale Club Scholarship Fund	$110.00
Yale in China Association	$10,100.00
Yale University	$9,668.75
TOTAL	**$169,545.65**

1948

American Veteran, Halloran Hospital, NY	$20.00
American Veterans Committee	$6,000.00
C.A.R.E., NY	$100.00
College City of New York	$36.00
Common Council for American Unity	$1,000.00
Disabled American Veterans	$60.00
Federal Hall Memorial Associates, NY	$250.00
Four Chaplains Memorial Fund, NY	$1,000.00
Greater New York Fund	$250.00
Irvington House	$10.00
Loomis Institute	$1,087.50
Museum of Modern Art, NY	$21,750.00
Musicians' Emergency Fund, NY	$150.00
National Urban League	$19,398.01
National Variety Artists	$100.00
Negro Actors Guild of America	$25.00
New York Tuberculosis and Health Association	$10.00
New York University, Bellevue Medical Center	$14,575.00
Old Newsboys Goodfellow Club	$100.00
Pacific War Memorial, NY	$7,287.50
Pocantico Hills Veterans Association, Tarrytown, NY	$25.00

Public Education Association	$5,348.08
Rehearsal Club	$500.00
Riverdale Children's Association	$1,000.00
Rockefeller Brothers Fund	$71,072.00
Salvation Army, NY	$250.00
Sealantic Fund	$217.50
Seeing Eye	$200.00
Seventy-seventh Infantry Division Association	$10.00
Seventy-seventh Infantry Division Association	$3,540.77
St. Paul's Polytechnic Institute, Lawrenceville, VA	$1,000.00
United Hospital Fund	$50.00
Urban League, White Plains, NY	$50.00
Yale Club Library Fund	$5.00
Yale Club Scholarship Fund	$10.00
Yale in China Association	$500.00
Yale University	$7,856.25
TOTAL	**$164,843.61**

1949

American Red Cross	$25.00
American Youth Hostels, NY	$5,053.12
Bayway Community Center	$5,000.00
Catholic War Veterans	$24.00
Children's Medical Center, Boston, MA	$24.38
Common Council for American Unity	$14,957.50
Cornell University	$20,268.75
Disabled American Veterans	$60.00
Flight Safety Foundation	$1,500.00
General Theological Seminary, NY	$1,000.00
Greater New York Fund	$250.00
Heart Association/Fund	$250.00
Irvington House	$10.00
Loomis Institute	$1,000.00
National Urban League	$27,921.22
National Variety Artists	$100.00
Negro Actors Guild of America	$25.00
New York City Police and Fire Departments, Welfare Fund	$7.20
New York Tuberculosis and Health Association	$5.00
New York University, Bellevue Medical Center	$27,294.46
Public Education Association	$5,104.47
Rehearsal Club	$500.00
Rice (William M.) Institute, Houston, TX	$20,081.25
Riverdale Children's Association	$1,000.00
Rockefeller Brothers Fund	$61,037.13
Roosevelt Hospital, NY	$500.00
Salvation Army, NY	$250.00

Seeing Eye	$100.00
Seventy-seventh Infantry Division Association	$3,234.15
Storer College, Harper's Ferry, WVA	$10.00
Trudeau Sanitarium	$250.00
Union Church (Pocantico Hills)	$50.00
Urban League, White Plains, NY	$50.00
VFW	$5.00
Yale Club Library Fund	$10.00
Yale Club Scholarship Fund	$10.00
Yale in China Association	$500.00
Yale University	$1,000.00
TOTAL	**$198,467.63**

1950

American International Association, NY	$26,243.75
American Red Cross	$275.00
Catholic War Veterans	$48.00
Cerebral Palsy Society of New York	$500.00
Common Council for American Unity	$15,000.00
Disabled American Veterans	$160.00
Flight Safety Foundation	$1,500.00
Friars' Club	$50.00
Greater New York Fund	$250.00
Hospitalized Veterans Music Service	$50.00
Irvington House	$20.00
Loomis Institute	$10,934.50
National Amputation Association/ Foundation	$50.00
National Foundation for Infantile Paralysis, NY	$97.72
National Urban League	$20,646.48
National Variety Artists	$100.00
Negro Actors Guild of America	$25.00
New York City Police and Fire Departments, Welfare Fund	$7.20
New York Pioneer Club for Underprivileged Children	$500.00
New York University, Bellevue Medical Center	$30,546.07
Public Education Association	$1,030.00
Quaker Emergency Readjustment Center, NY	$500.00
Rehearsal Club	$500.00
Riverdale Children's Association	$1,000.00
Rockefeller Brothers Fund	$70,700.00
Seeing Eye	$100.00
Seventy-seventh Infantry Division Association	$5,117.00
Union Church (Pocantico Hills)	$8.00
United Hospital Fund	$1,050.00
VFW	$100.00

Washington, D.C., Mosque Foundation	$5,000.00
Yale Club Library Fund	$25.00
Yale Club Scholarship Fund	$12.00
Yale in China Association	$1,000.00
Yale University	$11,000.00
TOTAL	**$204,145.72**

1951

Al Jolson's Servicemen's Free Canteen, Brooklyn	$100.00
American International Association for Economic and Social Development	$10,000.00
American Legion	$36.00
American National Theater and Academy, NY	$171.20
American Red Cross	$75.00
Arthritis and Rheumatic Foundation	$120.00
Bayway Community Center	$1,250.00
Children's Village	$13.10
Common Council for American Unity	$10,000.00
Disabled American Veterans	$250.00
Dobbs Ferry HighSchool Scholarship Fund, NY	$25.00
Flight Safety Foundation	$1,500.00
Free Milk Fund for Babies	$100.00
Greater New York Fund	$500.00
Historical Society of the Tarrytowns	$25.00
Hunterdon Medical Center, Flemington, NJ	$26,184.38
Industrial Relations Counselors, NY	$702.89
Irvington House	$300.00
Lenox Hill Hospital, NY	$100.00
Lenox Hill Neighborhood Association	$50.00
Lexington School for the Deaf	$250.00
Loomis Institute	$9,900.00
National Amputation Association/ Foundation	$50.00
National Urban League	$23,266.59
National Variety Artists	$100.00
Negro Actors Guild of America	$25.00
Neighborhood Children's Center, NY	$30.40
New Rochelle Hospital, New Rochelle, NY	$9,900.00
New York City Cancer Committee	$2,300.00
New York Tuberculosis and Health Association	$5.00
New York University, Bellevue Medical Center	$54,967.20
Public Education Association	$4,965.00
Rehearsal Club	$500.00
Riverdale Children's Association	$1,000.00

Rockefeller Brothers Fund	$75,262.50
Salvation Army, NY	$250.00
Seeing Eye	$100.00
Seventy-seventh Infantry Division Association	$3,905.95
Soldiers', Sailors', and Airmen's Club, NY	$250.00
Spence-Chapin Adoption Service, NY	$100.00
St. Faith's House	$100.00
Trudeau Sanitarium	$250.00
United Hospital Fund	$500.00
United Negro College Fund	$26,184.38
University Religious Conference, UCLA	$1,066.70
USO of New York City	$26,184.38
Yale Club of New York City	$47.00
Yale in China Association	$1,000.00
Yale University	$27,184.38
TOTAL	**$321,147.05**

1952

American Colony Charities Association, NY	$500.00
American Red Cross	$50.00
American Women's Voluntary/ Volunteer Services	$100.00
Big Brothers of America	$500.00
Center of Information Pro Deo, NY	$5,000.00
Child Placing and Adoption Service, NY	$100.00
Children's Village	$56.00
College of Wooster, Ohio	$5,000.00
Columbia University	$100.00
Common Council for American Unity	$10,051.56
Cornell University	$5,575.00
Damon Runyan Cancer Fund, NY	$110.00
Disabled American Veterans	$5.00
Father Duffy Catholic War Veterans, NY	$25.00
Flight Safety Foundation	$1,500.00
Free Milk Fund for Babies	$100.00
Greater New York Fund	$300.00
Heart Association/Fund	$100.00
Herald Tribune Fresh Air Fund, NY	$10.00
Historical Society of the Tarrytowns	$25.00
Hospitalized Veterans Emergency Fund	$100.00
Industrial Relations Counselors, NY	$19.90
Irvington House	$200.00
Lenox Hill Hospital, NY	$100.00
Lenox Hill Neighborhood Association	$250.00
Loomis Institute	$31,892.18

National Amputation Association/ Foundation	$50.00
National Hospital for Speech Disorders	$500.00
National Urban League	$125,910.75
National Variety Artists	$100.00
Negro Actors Guild of America	$25.00
New York University, Bellevue Medical Center	$107,385.70
Overseas Press Club of America, NY	$5,000.00
Public Education Association	$5,741.25
Rehearsal Club	$591.20
Riverdale Children's Association	$1,000.00
Robert B. Patterson Memorial Fund, NY	$500.00
Rockefeller Brothers Fund	$104,640.62
Scarborough School, NY	$76.00
Seeing Eye	$100.00
Seventy-seventh Infantry Division Association	$2,982.35
St. Charles School and Community Center, NY	$2,500.00
St. Paul's Polytechnic Institute, Lawrenceville, VA	$1,000.00
Thayer Academy, Braintree, MA	$2,931.25
United Hospital Fund	$500.00
University Religious Conference, UCLA	$15,000.00
USO of New York City Defense Fund	$10,237.50
Virginia Council on Health and Medical Care	$3,000.00
Yale Club Scholarship Fund	$37.00
Yale in China Association	$1,000.00
Yale University	$54,718.75
TOTAL	**$507,297.01**

1953

305th Infantry Division Association	$17.00
American Museum of Health, NY	$2,500.00
American Red Cross	$250.00
Arkansas AM&N	$26,312.50
Arkansas Association for the Crippled	$2,000.00
Arkansas Baptist Hospital	$52,625.00
Arkansas Tuberculosis Association	$10.00
Arthritis and Rheumatic Foundation	$200.00
Boys' Clubs of America	$25.00
Boys' Industrial School Foundation, Pine Bluff, AR	$5,812.50
Common Council for American Unity	$5,337.50
Community Chest	$15,750.00
Damon Runyan Cancer Fund, NY	$384.40
Daughters of the American Revolution, Arkansas Chapter	$236.00

Disabled American Veterans	$25.00	United Hospital Fund	$500.00
Dunbar Junior College	$25,625.00	United Negro College Fund	$500.00
Eastern State Hospital, Williamsburg, VA	$5,237.50	University of Arkansas, Fayetteville	$33,125.00
Flight Safety Foundation	$2,625.00	USO of New York City	$10,700.00
Fort Roots Veterans Hospital	$915.55	Yale Club of New York City	$32.00
Foster Parents for War Children, NY	$250.00	Yale in China Association	$1,000.00
Grand Street Boys' Association, NY	$5.00	Yale University	$5,550.00
Greater Little Rock Community Council/Fund	$60.00	**TOTAL**	**$595,794.37**

1954

Greater New York Fund	$300.00
Hospitalized Veterans Emergency Fund	$100.00
Irvington House	$192.00
Junior League of Little Rock	$500.00
Kiwanis Club Activities	$75.00
League of Women Voters	$50.00
Little Rock Boys' Club	$250.00
Little Rock Junior College	$26,250.00
Little Rock Schools	$23.00
Loomis Alumni Association Fund	$1,000.00
Loomis Institute	$107,000.00
National Amputation Association/ Foundation	$50.00
National Urban League	$20,383.71
National Variety Artists	$150.00
National Wildlife Association/ Federation/Foundation	$5.00
Negro Actors Guild of America	$25.00
Negro Florence Crittenton Home, Little Rock, AR	$500.00
New York Hospital, Westchester Division	$5,337.50
New York University, Bellevue Medical Center	$107,414.11
New York University Parents Association	$61.60
Newspaper Guild	$150.00
Public Education Association	$1,000.00
Pulaski County Tuberculosis Association	$2,000.00
Pulaski Heights Lions Club Youth Center	$300.00
Rehearsal Club	$500.00
Riverdale Children's Association	$1,000.00
Rockefeller Brothers Fund	$106,375.00
Salvation Army, NY	$250.00
Seeing Eye	$100.00
Shrine Circus	$30.00
Soldiers', Sailors', and Airmen's Club, NY	$100.00
St. Vincent Infirmary	$16,012.50
Trudeau Sanitarium	$250.00
Union Church (Pocantico Hills)	$50.00
United Cerebral Palsy of New York City	$400.00

305th Infantry Division Association	$67.00
American Red Cross	$250.00
American Red Cross	$2,500.00
American Women's Voluntary/ Volunteer Services	$250.00
Arkansas State Forestry and Parks Commission	$47,100.00
Arkansas AM&N	$25,000.00
Arkansas Association for the Crippled	$1,000.00
Arkansas Mental Health Society	$25.00
Bayway Community Center	$5,446.87
Boy Scouts of America	$50.00
Charitable Expenses (Travel)	$13,724.88
College of the Ozarks	$5,000.00
Common Council for American Unity	$5,418.75
Community Chest	$15,741.00
Conway County Fair Association	$100.00
Conway County Special Road Fund	$18,513.37
Disabled American Veterans	$30.00
Flight Safety Foundation	$1,000.00
Fourth of July Celebration Fund, Little Rock, AR	$10.00
Hospitalized Veterans Emergency Fund	$100.00
Junior League of Little Rock	$500.00
Kiwanis Club Activities	$50.00
League of Women Voters	$50.00
Little Rock Boys' Club	$250.00
Little Rock Public Library	$727.50
Little Rock Schools	$500.00
Loomis Alumni Association Fund	$1,000.00
Loomis Institute	$100,250.00
Loomis School, Psychiatry Fund	$2,000.00
Morrilton Little League Baseball	$275.00
National Council of Negro Women, DC	$250.00
National Hospital for Speech Disorders	$500.00
National Trust for Historic Preservation	$1,000.00
National Urban League	$25,287.50
Negro Florence Crittenton Home, Little Rock, AR	$500.00
New York University, Bellevue Medical Center	$105,812.50

New York University Parents Association	$100.00
Newspaper Guild	$150.00
Philander Smith College	$1,000.00
Polio Fund	$50.00
Public Education Association	$1,000.00
Pulaski County Tuberculosis Association	$500.00
Rehearsal Club	$500.00
Riverdale Children's Association	$1,000.00
Rockefeller Brothers Fund	$103,431.25
Scholarship Trust Fund, Little Rock, AR	$1,000.00
Seeing Eye	$100.00
Seventy-seventh Infantry Division Association	$500.00
Shrine Circus	$36.00
Society of the Silurians, NY	$500.00
Soldiers', Sailors', and Airmen's Club, NY	$100.00
Soroptimists Club, Little Rock, AR	$228.50
St. Charles School and Community Center, NY	$1,000.00
St. Faith's House	$100.00
Union Church (Pocantico Hills)	$50.00
United Negro College Fund	$500.00
University of Arkansas, Fayetteville	$5,000.00
University of Arkansas, Fayetteville	$8,000.00
University of Arkansas, Fayetteville	$31,717.50
University of Arkansas Medical School	$3,000.00
Urban League of Greater Little Rock	$1,165.00
USO of New York City Defense Fund	$5,418.75
West Parish Memorial Foundation	$1,000.00
Williamsburg Area Memorial Community Center	$1,000.00
Yale Club of New York City	$22.00
Yale University Alumni Fund	$1,000.00
TOTAL	**$549,448.37**

1955

305th Infantry Division Association	$17.00
Al Hassan Temple, DOKK Charity Benefit	$25.00
American Association for the United Nations	$150.00
American Red Cross, Conway County Chapter	$100.00
American Red Cross, Disaster Fund	$15.00
American Red Cross, Pulaski County Chapter	$2,500.00
Arkansas Foundation of Associated Colleges	$70,134.37
Arkansas Industrial Development Foundation	$5,000.00
Arkansas Junior Chamber of Commerce	$175.00
Arkansas Negro Farmers Association	$100.00
Arkansas State Forestry and Parks Association	$576.50
Arkansas State Horseshow Benefit	$100.00
Arkansas State Hospital Auxiliary	$25.00
Big Brothers of America	$100.00
Boy Scouts of America, Pope District	$500.00
Charitable Expenses (Travel)	$23,452.41
Christian Record Benevolent Association for the Blind	$25.00
Civil Air Patrol	$220.09
Common Council for American Unity	$1,000.00
Community Chest of Pulaski County	$16,838.76
Conway County Fair Association	$100.00
Conway County Special Road Fund	$750.00
Conway County Special Road Fund	$44,717.05
Conway County Tuberculosis Association	$10.00
Disabled American Veterans	$20.00
Flight Safety Foundation	$2,703.74
Fort Roots Veterans Hospital	$159.95
Friends of the Library Association	$50.00
Grand Street Boys' Association	$5.00
Institute for Studies in Social Cooperation	$10,392.08
Jack Kriendler Memorial Fund	$100.00
Kiwanis Boys' Camp	$50.00
Lions Club Sight Conservation Fund	$5.00
Little Rock Boys' Club	$250.00
Loomis Alumni Association	$1,000.00
Loomis-Chaffee Development Fund	$56,441.25
Margaret S. Lewisohn Memorial Fund	$1,000.00
Mental Health Society of Pulaski County	$2.00
Military Order of the Purple Heart	$10.00
Morrilton Baseball Club	$100.00
Morrilton Chamber of Commerce Industrial Site Fund	$500.00
Morrilton Girl Scouts	$50.00
Morrilton Lions Club	$5.00
National Civil Service League	$5,000.00
National Council of Negro Women	$250.00
National Hospital for Speech Disorders	$100.00
National Negro Agriculture Agents Association	$50.00
National Trust for Historic Preservation	$1,000.00
National Urban League	$23,529.05
National Wildlife Federation	$5.00
Negro Actors Guild of America	$25.00

Negro Boy Scouts	$100.00
Negro Florence Crittenton Home, Little Rock, AR	$500.00
Negro Scout Troop #214	$75.00
New York University, Bellevue Medical Center	$115,272.50
Public Education Association	$1,000.00
Pulaski County Tuberculosis Association	$500.00
Rehearsal Club	$500.00
Riverdale Children's Association	$1,000.00
Rockefeller Brothers Fund	$101,900.00
Seeing Eye	$100.00
Seventy-seventh Infantry Division Association	$20.00
Shrine Circus Fund	$54.00
Soldiers', Sailors', and Airmen's Club, NY	$100.00
Southern Regional Council	$100.00
Southwest Council of Student Christian Associations	$100.00
St. Faith's House	$100.00
Sweet Briar College	$11,275.00
Union Church (Pocantico Hills)	$50.00
United Negro College Fund	$500.00
University of Arkansas, Fayetteville	$2,083.34
University of Arkansas, Fayetteville	$5,689.39
University of Arkansas, Fayetteville	$6,175.00
University of Arkansas, Fayetteville	$25,575.00
Urban League of Greater Little Rock	$1,000.00
USO of New York City Defense Fund	$5,107.05
Veterans of Foreign Wars Christmas Fund	$25.00
Virginia 305th Anniversary Commission	$3,500.00
Water Commission of the State of Arkansas	$500.00
Yale Alumni Fund	$1,000.00
Yale Club of New York City	$22.00
Yale in China Association	$1,000.00
YWCA	$25,678.50
TOTAL	**$580,036.03**

1956

305th Infantry Division Association	$17.00
Al Hassan Temple #136	$50.00
American Cancer Society	$100.00
American Red Cross	$125.00
American Red Cross, Pulaski County Chapter	$3,500.00
Arkansas Association of Negro Farmers	$150.00
Arkansas Basin Association	$150.00
Arkansas Council on Human Relations	$500.00
Arkansas Federation of the Blind	$50.00

Arkansas Foundation of Associated Colleges	$50,943.75
Arkansas Junior Chamber of Commerce	$100.00
Arkansas Opportunity Fund	$7,750.00
Arkansas State Publicity and Parks Commission	$32,876.00
Boy Scouts of America	$500.00
Boys' and Girls' Anti-Cigarette League	$100.00
Charitable Expenses (Travel)	$26,696.21
Christian Record Benevolent Association	$25.00
Colonial Williamsburg, Inc.	$10,190.00
Common Council for American Unity	$1,000.00
Conway County Tuberculosis Association	$100.00
Disabled American Veterans	$10.00
Eastern State Hospital	$10,124.00
Flight Safety Foundation	$2,500.00
Freedoms Foundation at Valley Forge	$50.00
Friends of the Library	$50.00
Greater Little Rock Campaign for the 48 States	$18.75
Greater Little Rock Community Council	$100.00
Hospitalized Veterans Service	$250.00
Jack Kriendler Memorial Fund	$100.00
Kiwanis Benefit, Crippled Children	$52.50
Little Rock Boys' Club	$250.00
Little Rock Fire Department Charity Fund	$5.00
Loomis School	$115,611.67
Margaret S. Lewisohn Memorial Fund	$1,000.00
Morrilton Junior Chamber of Commerce	$85.00
Morrilton School District #32	$17,875.00
National Urban League	$31,643.03
National Wildlife Federation	$5.00
Negro Florence Crittenton Home, Little Rock, AR	$500.00
New York University, Bellevue Medical Center	$101,650.00
Philander Smith College	$1,000.00
Pulaski County Audubon Society	$25.00
Pulaski County Community Chest and Council	$17,574.08
Pulaski County Mental Health Society	$2.00
Pulaski County Tuberculosis Association	$250.00
Rehearsal Club	$500.00
Rockwin Fund	$183,438.36
Seeing Eye	$100.00

Seventy-seventh Infantry Division Association	$17.00
Shrine Circus Benefit	$60.00
Sisters of the Good Shepherd, Hot Springs, AR	$50.00
Soldiers', Sailors', and Airmen's Club, NY	$100.00
Stuyvesant Community Center	$500.00
Union Church (Pocantico Hills)	$2,000.00
United Negro College Fund	$500.00
University of Arkansas, Fayetteville	$20,000.00
U.S. Junior Chamber of Commerce, Operation Library	$1,000.00
USO of New York City	$5,495.83
Veterans of Foreign Wars Benefit Fund	$30.00
Virginia Society for the Preservation of Public Schools	$1,400.00
Yale Alumni Fund	$1,000.00
Yale Club of New York City	$27.00
Yale in China Association	$1,000.00
TOTAL	**$652,872.18**

1957

305th Infantry Division Association	$17.00
A.M.E. Church	$10.00
Al Hassan Temple, Shrine Crippled Children's Benefit	$25.00
American Red Cross	$125.00
American Red Cross	$1,000.00
Arkansas Children's Hospital	$10.00
Arkansas Industrial Development Commission	$15.92
Arkansas Opportunity Fund	$14,375.00
Arkansas State Publicity and Parks Commission	$6,750.00
Bottoms Baptist Orphanage	$50.00
Boy Scouts of America	$25.00
Boys' Clubs of America	$100.00
Charitable Expenses (Travel)	$32,400.25
Christian Record for the Blind	$25.00
Common Council for American Unity	$1,000.00
Conway County Fair Association	$50.00
Fort Smith Senior High Band	$500.00
Girl Scouts of America	$25.00
Kiwanis Club, Crippled Children's Benefit	$50.00
Lonoke Tuberculosis Association	$10.00
Loomis School, Psychiatry Fund	$1,000.00
March of Dimes	$50.00
Mary Knoll Sisters Motherhouse	$100.00
Mid-South Public Relations Bureau	$15.00
Morrilton Boys' Baseball Program	$100.00

Morrilton School District #32	$351,368.95
National New Farmers of America	$250.00
National Wildlife Federation	$5.00
Order of American Firemen, Benefit	$25.00
Rehearsal Club	$500.00
Rockwin Fund	$143,812.50
Seventy-seventh Infantry Division Association	$12.00
Shrine Circus Benefit	$18.00
St. Boniface Church, Bigelow, AR	$100.00
United Committee for the United Nations	$20.00
United Negro College Fund	$500.00
University of Arkansas Medical School	$2,897.87
U.S. Savings Bond Drive	$1,229.53
Williamsburg Restoration, Inc.	$20.75
Yale Club of New York City	$27.00
TOTAL	**$558,614.77**

1958

305th Infantry Division Association	$17.00
A.I.D. Foundation	$5,300.00
A.M.E. Church	$10.00
Al Hassan Temple	$25.00
American Assembly	$1,000.00
American Cancer Society	$100.00
American Red Cross	$50.00
American Red Cross	$125.00
Arkansas Association for Crippled Children	$100.00
Arkansas Bar Association	$50.00
Arkansas Basin Association	$150.00
Arkansas Children's Hospital	$10.00
Arkansas Foundation of Associated Colleges	$500.00
Arkansas Foundation of Associated Colleges	$33,308.34
Arkansas Lighthouse for the Blind	$10.00
Arkansas Opportunity Fund	$20,700.00
Arkansas State Publicity and Parks Commission	$47,666.47
Arkansas Tuberculosis Association	$100.00
Association for the Preservation of Virginia Antiques	$1.00
Boy Scouts of America	$25.00
Boy Scouts of America	$25.00
Charitable Expenses (Travel)	$26,040.85
Chicago Chamber of Commerce	$714.54
Christian Rural Overseas Program	$25.00
Civitan Club, Children's Colony	$25.00
Colonial Williamsburg, Inc.	$74.20
Community Chest, Little Rock, AR	$15,253.91

Conway County Fair Association	$50.00
Conway County Special Road Fund	$11,440.79
Conway County Tuberculosis Association	$100.00
Episcopal Diocese of Arkansas, Scholarship Fund	$1,000.00
Industrial Relations Counselors	$75.87
Jack Kriendler Memorial Fund	$100.00
Jamestown, Williamsburg, Yorktown Commission	$41.36
Junior League of Little Rock	$30.00
Kiwanis Club Benefit	$52.50
Little Rock Fire Department, Benefit	$25.00
Lonoke County Tuberculosis Association	$10.00
Loomis School	$109,455.04
March of Dimes	$50.00
Morrilton Girl Scouts	$50.00
Morrilton Junior Chamber of Commerce	$90.00
Morrilton PTA	$5.00
Morrilton Rotary Club	$55.00
Morrilton School Building Fund	$150,486.51
Morrilton School Enrichment Fund	$116,560.53
National Urban League	$50,183.33
National Wildlife Federation	$5.00
New York University, Bellevue Medical Center	$103,766.66
Old Newsboys Goodfellow Club	$100.00
Pulaski County Tuberculosis Association	$250.00
Red Cross	$1,000.00
Rehearsal Club	$500.00
Rockefeller Institute for Medical Research	$20,800.00
Rockwin Fund	$55,693.21
Seeing Eye	$100.00
Shepherd of the Hills Home	$30.00
Shorter College	$15.00
Shrine Circus Fund	$30.00
Soldiers', Sailors', and Airmen's Club, NY	$100.00
Third Marine Division Association	$86.35
U.S. Savings Bond Drive	$1,767.97
Union Rescue Mission	$100.00
United Negro College Fund	$500.00
Urban League, Little Rock, AR	$2,500.00
Urban League, Omaha, NE	$477.25
Urban League, Seattle, WA	$673.86
Yale Alumni Fund	$1,000.00
Yale Club	$27.00
Yale in China Fund	$1,000.00

Youth, Inc.	$15.00
TOTAL	**$781,804.54**

1959

305th Infantry Division Association	$17.00
A.M.E. Church	$10.00
American Assembly	$1,000.00
American Cancer Society	$100.00
American Red Cross	$50.00
American Red Cross	$125.00
American Red Cross	$1,000.00
Arkansas Association for the Crippled	$100.00
Arkansas Athletic Association	$5.00
Arkansas Bar Association	$50.00
Arkansas Basin Association	$150.00
Arkansas Children's Hospital	$10.00
Arkansas Foundation of Associated Colleges	$500.00
Arkansas Foundation of Associated Colleges	$15,293.33
Arkansas Industrial Development Foundation	$3,892.81
Arkansas Junior Deputy Sheriffs' Association	$100.00
Arkansas Lighthouse for the Blind	$25.00
Arkansas Opportunity Fund	$22,325.00
Arkansas State Hospital	$48.15
Arkansas State Publicity and Parks Commission	$2,750.00
Arkansas State Science Building	$50.00
Arkansas Tuberculosis Association	$100.00
Arts Council, Performing Arts Division	$1,000.00
Association for the Preservation of Virginia Antiques	$1.00
Boy Scouts of America	$10.00
Boy Scouts of America	$50.00
Boys' Clubs of America, Arkansas Chapter	$50.00
Browning School, Theater Benefit	$20.80
Charitable Expenses (Travel)	$47,472.79
Community Center of Arts and Sciences	$16.60
Community Chest of Pulaski County	$13,800.00
Conway County Emergency Polio Drive	$50.00
Conway County Fair Association	$50.00
Crusade for Freedom, Arkansas Division	$428.66
Fine Arts Museum	$34.32
Flight Safety Foundation	$2,000.00
Jack Kriendler Memorial Fund	$100.00
Kiwanis Activities, Charity Benefit	$37.50

Little Rock Air Force Base, Youth Activities Program	$250.00
Little Rock University	$10,000.00
Lonoke County Tuberculosis Association	$10.00
Loomis Alumni Fund	$1,000.00
Loomis School	$103,389.82
Mary Knoll Sisters	$100.00
Morrilton Adelaide Club	$50.00
Morrilton Junior Chamber of Commerce	$90.00
Morrilton School District, Enrichment Fund	$105,000.00
Morrilton Youth Center	$200.00
National Urban League	$22,150.85
National Wildlife Federation	$5.00
New York University, Bellevue Medical Center	$144,156.25
Order of American Firemen, Little Rock Fire Department	$25.00
Pulaski County Tuberculosis Association	$250.00
Regents/University of California, H. M. Allbright Lectureship Committee	$500.00
Rehearsal Club	$624.80
Rockwin Fund	$29,030.34
Seventy-seventh Infantry Division Association	$5.00
Shepherd of the Hills Home	$30.00
Shorter College	$5.00
Soldiers', Sailors', and Airmen's Club, NY	$100.00
Southeastern Louisiana College	$1,250.00
Southwest Foundations Conference	$234.40
United Negro College Fund	$500.00
University of Colorado	$1,500.00
Urban League of Greater Little Rock	$2,569.05
U.S. Savings Bond Drive	$944.45
Yale Alumni Fund	$1,000.00
Yale Club of New York City	$5.00
Yale University	$100.00
Youth, Inc.	$10.00
TOTAL	**$537,907.92**

1960

305th Infantry Division Association	$17.00
A.M.E. Church	$5.00
American Cancer Society	$25.00
American Red Cross	$50.00
American Red Cross	$125.00
American Red Cross	$1,000.00
Arkansas Arts Center	$7,681.49
Arkansas Association for the Crippled	$50.00

Arkansas Basin Development	$150.00
Arkansas Children's Hospital	$10.00
Arkansas Enterprises for the Blind	$500.00
Arkansas Foundation of Associated Colleges	$500.00
Arkansas Foundation of Associated Colleges	$15,554.88
Arkansas Industrial Development Foundation	$1,383.07
Arkansas Junior Deputy Sheriffs' Association	$100.00
Arkansas Lighthouse for the Blind	$25.00
Arkansas Opportunity Fund	$15,757.01
Arkansas Science Fair Association	$50.00
Arkansas State Hospital Physical Therapy Department	$50.00
Arkansas State Publicity and Parks Commission	$2,954.77
B. S. Barron Memorial Fund	$200.00
Baucum Memorial Fund	$25.00
Boy Scouts of America	$25.00
Boy Scouts of America, Quapaw Area Council	$985.00
Boys' Clubs of America	$25.00
Browning School	$10,102.40
Christian Record Benevolent Society for the Blind	$25.00
Christian Rural Overseas Program	$25.00
Columbia University	$1,000.00
Conway County Fair Association	$50.00
Council of Jewish Women	$10.00
Elks Club, Crippled Children's Benefit Show	$15.00
Father Flanagan's Boys' Home	$10.00
First Methodist Church	$25.00
Flight Safety Foundation	$1,000.00
Freedoms Foundation at Valley Forge	$50.00
Jack Kriendler Memorial Fund	$100.00
Kansas Heart Association	$25.00
Kiwanis Club, Benefit Show	$45.00
Lakeside Methodist Church	$25.00
Lila Motley Cancer Foundation	$250.00
Little Rock Boys' Club	$50.00
Little Rock Junior Chamber of Commerce	$75.00
Lonoke County Tuberculosis Association	$10.00
Loomis School	$110,011.38
Morrilton School District #32	$9,000.00
National Association for Mental Health	$2,904.83
National Council of Negro Women	$125.00
National Urban League	$20,489.63

New York University Medical Center	$97,706.25
Order of American Firemen, Little Rock Chapter	$25.00
Police Library Fund, Gene Smith Memorial	$1,000.00
Pulaski County Tuberculosis Association	$250.00
Ramon Magsaysay Award Foundation	$439.95
Rehearsal Club	$500.00
Rockwin Fund	$170,543.27
Shepherd of the Hills Home	$30.00
Shrine Circus, Crippled Children's Benefit	$30.00
Soldiers', Sailors', and Airmen's Club, NY	$100.00
Travel for Charities	$40,553.23
Trinity Episcopal Church	$275.00
U.S. Savings Bond Drive	$1,163.18
U.S.S. *Little Rock* Launching Fund	$25.00
United Fund	$10,000.00
United Negro College Fund	$500.00
Urban League of Greater Little Rock	$2,517.50
U.S. Committee for the United Nations	$50.00
Yale University, Class of 1935	$4,000.00
Yale University, Scholarship and Library Fund	$22.00
TOTAL	**$532,401.84**

1961

305th Infantry Division Association	$15.00
307th Infantry Post, #307	$50.00
American Association for the United Nations	$50.00
American Heart Association, Arkansas Branch	$25.00
American Red Cross	$50.00
American Red Cross	$125.00
Arkansas Arts Center	$1,289.36
Arkansas Association for the Crippled	$100.00
Arkansas Children's Hospital	$10.00
Arkansas Foundation of Associated Colleges	$500.00
Arkansas Foundation of Associated Colleges	$10,837.50
Arkansas Industrial Development Foundation	$7,260.11
Arkansas Junior Deputy Sheriffs' Association	$200.00
Arkansas Lighthouse for the Blind	$25.00
Arkansas Opportunity Fund	$21,152.40
Arkansas Parks Commission	$56.48
Arkansas Science Fair Association	$50.00

Arkansas State Hospital	$60.00
Arkansas State Publicity and Parks Commission	$41,756.83
Arthritis and Rheumatic Foundation	$500.00
Arts Council of Greater Little Rock	$250.00
Bayway Community Center	$100.00
Big Brothers of America	$100.00
Boy Scouts of America	$25.00
Boy Scouts of America, Quapaw Area Council	$210.00
Boys' Clubs of America	$25.00
CAP Composite Squadron, Youth Booster Program	$25.00
Christian Record Benevolent Society	$25.00
Colonial Williamsburg, Inc.	$707.22
Columbia University, American Assembly	$1,000.00
Conway County Community Service	$20.00
Conway County Tuberculosis Association	$200.00
Council of Jewish Women, Charity Benefit	$10.00
Disabled American Veterans	$10.00
Father Flanagan's Boys' Home	$10.00
Flight Safety Foundation	$1,000.00
Hartford Heart Association	$25.00
Hockaday School	$50,875.00
Hospitalized Veterans Association	$100.00
Jack Kriendler Memorial Fund	$100.00
Kiwanis Activities	$45.00
Little Rock Fire Department, Charity Fund	$25.00
Little Rock Police Department, Charity Football Game	$25.00
Loomis School	$107,101.38
Metroplan Memorial Fund	$100.00
Morrilton Public School District	$25,000.00
National Association for Mental Health	$1,608.34
National Conference of Christians and Jews	$100.00
National Fund for Medical Education	$500.00
National Urban League	$22,629.66
Perryville Schools	$1,472.19
Pulaski County Tuberculosis Association	$250.00
Ramon Magsaysay Award Foundation	$254.73
Rehearsal Club	$500.00
Rockwin Fund	$69,774.80
Seventh Day Adventist	$10.00
Seventy-seventh Infantry Division Association	$1,054.00
Shepherd of the Hills Home	$30.00
Shorter College	$5.00

Soldiers', Sailors', and Airmen's Club, NY	$100.00
Southwestern Clinic and Research Institute	$28,328.13
St. Vincent Orphan Home	$10.00
Third Marine Division Association	$100.00
Travel for Charities	$33,278.06
Trinity Lutheran Church	$25.00
U.S. Savings Bond Drive	$625.00
Union Church (Pocantico Hills)	$25.00
United Fund of Pulaski County	$15,496.88
United Negro College Fund	$500.00
Urban League of Greater Little Rock	$2,529.35
U.S. Committee for the United Nations	$50.00
USO of New York City	$2,500.00
Waterbury Girls' Club	$1,000.00
Yale Alumni Association	$1,000.00
Yale Club of New York City, Scholarship Fund	$17.00
Yale in China Association	$1,000.00
Yale University, D.K.E. Chapter Capital Fund Drive	$250.00
YMCA	$500.00
TOTAL	**$456,749.42**

1962

305th Infantry Division Association	$17.00
American Red Cross	$50.00
American Red Cross	$125.00
Arkansas Arts Center	$42,671.11
Arkansas Association for Mental Health	$752.38
Arkansas Association for the Crippled	$100.00
Arkansas Baptist College	$25.00
Arkansas Children's Hospital	$25.00
Arkansas Council on Human Relations	$25.00
Arkansas Foundation of Associated Colleges	$500.00
Arkansas Industrial Development Foundation	$1,086.15
Arkansas Junior Deputy Sheriffs' Association	$200.00
Arkansas Lighthouse for the Blind	$25.00
Arkansas Opportunity Fund	$22,953.00
Arkansas Science Fair Association	$50.00
Arkansas State Hospital	$245.00
Arkansas State Publicity and Parks Commission	$2,500.00
Arthritis and Rheumatic Foundation, Arkansas Chapter	$500.00
Asthmatic Children's Foundation	$10.00
Big Brothers of America	$100.00
Boy Scouts of America	$100.00

Boy Scouts of America	$100.00
Boys' Clubs of America	$25.00
Christian Record for the Blind	$25.00
Colonial Williamsburg, Inc.	$481.77
Columbia University, American Assembly	$1,000.00
Conway County Community Service Association	$50.00
Conway County Fair Association	$50.00
Conway County Special Fund	$310.12
Conway County Tuberculosis Association	$100.00
Disabled American Veterans	$15.00
Father Flanagan's Boys' Home	$10.00
Flight Safety Foundation	$1,000.00
Girl Scouts of America	$50.00
Graduate Institute of Technology	$34.15
Graduate Research Center of the Southwest	$1,000.00
Henderson Methodist Church, Women's Society of Christian Service	$410.95
Hospitalized Veterans Association	$100.00
Jack Kriendler Memorial Fund	$100.00
Kiwanis Activities Benefit	$45.00
Little Rock Boys' Club, Women's Auxiliary	$50.00
Little Rock Fire Department, Charity Benefit	$25.00
Little Rock Parade of Harmony	$10.00
Little Rock Police Department, Benefit Fund	$25.00
Lonoke County Tuberculosis Association	$10.00
Loomis School	$2,113.25
Middle East Institute	$28.55
National Association for Mental Health	$1,104.16
National Conference of Christians and Jews	$100.00
National Fund for Medical Education	$500.00
National Urban League	$21,157.71
National Wildlife Federation	$5.00
New York City USO Committee	$2,000.00
North Little Rock Firemen's Charity Benefit	$10.00
Ouachita Baptist College	$500.00
Ouachita Girl Scout Council	$25.00
Ouachita Girl Scout Council	$50.00
Pulaski County Tuberculosis Association	$500.00
Rehearsal Club	$620.00
Rockwin Fund	$56,697.00
Seventh Day Adventist	$10.00

Seventy-seventh Infantry Division Association	$20.00
Shepherd of the Hills Home	$30.00
Shrine Circus Benefit Fund	$36.00
Soldiers', Sailors', and Airmen's Club, NY	$100.00
Timbo Public Schools	$50.00
Travel for Charities	$28,177.76
United Negro College Fund	$500.00
University of Arkansas, Endowment and Trust	$250.00
Urban League of Greater Little Rock	$2,525.00
U.S. Committee for the United Nations	$50.00
Vanderbilt University	$53.65
Yale in China Association	$1,000.00
Yale University Alumni Fund	$1,000.00
Yale University Library and Scholarship Fund	$17.00
YMCA	$500.00
TOTAL	**$196,816.71**

1963

305th Infantry Division Association	$17.00
Abby Aldrich Rockefeller Scholarship Fund	$26,189.72
Airplane Expense—portion used for charities	$41,508.81
A.M.E. Church	$5.00
American National Cattlemen's Association Fund	$100.00
American Red Cross	$50.00
American Red Cross	$100.00
American Red Cross	$100.00
Arkansas Arts Center	$380,785.20
Arkansas Association for Mental Health	$2,172.77
Arkansas Association for the Crippled	$15.00
Arkansas Association for the Crippled	$100.00
Arkansas Children's Hospital	$25.00
Arkansas Commission Radio Free Europe	$100.00
Arkansas Council on Human Relations	$2,525.00
Arkansas Foundation of Associated Colleges	$500.00
Arkansas Foundation of Associated Colleges	$37,400.00
Arkansas Industrial Development Foundation	$11,500.00
Arkansas Junior Deputy Sheriffs' Association	$100.00
Arkansas Junior Deputy Sheriffs' Association (Negro)	$100.00
Arkansas Lighthouse for the Blind	$25.00

Arkansas Opportunity Fund	$24,291.00
Arkansas Science Fair Association	$50.00
Arkansas State Council on Economic Education	$250.00
Arkansas State Publicity and Parks Commission	$132,602.49
Arkansas State Publicity and Parks Commission, World Fair Expenses	$5,215.61
Arkansas State Teachers College	$10,000.00
Arthritis and Rheumatic Foundation	$250.00
Associated Industries of Arkansas	$500.00
Auxiliary of University Hospital	$32.50
Big Brothers of America	$100.00
Bigelow School	$25.00
Boy Land of Arkansas	$5,000.00
Boy Scouts of America	$11,062.50
Boy Scouts of America	$11,559.38
Boys' Clubs of America	$25.00
Chartered Flights for Charities	$12,270.06
Christian Record for the Blind	$25.00
Cloverdale Benefit Concert	$5.00
Colonial Williamsburg, Inc.	$102.30
Conway County Fair Association	$50.00
Conway County Mental Health Association	$25.00
Conway County Road Improvement	$8,824.00
Conway County Special Fund	$2,228.97
Conway County Tuberculosis Association	$50.00
Council of California Growers	$598.30
Council of Jewish Women	$10.00
Desert Hospital Building Commission	$5,000.00
Disabled American Veterans	$20.00
Ducks Unlimited	$25.00
First Methodist Church	$50.00
Flight Safety Foundation	$1,000.00
Graduate Institute of the Southwest	$598.00
Hockaday School Building Fund	$51,625.00
Hospitalized Veterans Association	$100.00
International Institute on Education	$438.48
Jack Kriendler Memorial Fund	$200.00
Joint Center for Urban Studies	$281.25
Kiwanis Activities, Benefit	$75.00
Little Rock Boys' Club	$100.00
Little Rock Police Department	$25.00
Lonoke County Tuberculosis Association	$5.00
Loomis School	$238,650.00
Loomis School, Alumni Fund	$1,000.00
Loomis School, miscellaneous	$81.33
Loomis School, Psychiatry Fund	$2,000.00
Loomis School, Special Fund	$1,000.00

Middle East Institute	$5,000.00
Miss Hospitality Scholarship	$100.00
National Association for Mental Health	$3,601.16
National Conference of Christians and Jews	$100.00
National Conference on Rural Youth	$2,519.14
National Council of Churches of Christ in the USA	$5,100.00
National Fund for Medical Education	$500.00
National Urban League	$22,398.90
National Wildlife Federation	$5.00
New York City USO Commission	$2,000.00
New York University Medical Center	$83,362.50
North Hills Exceptional Children's School	$50.00
North Little Rock Firemen's Charity Benefit	$10.00
Ouachita Baptist College	$750.00
Ouachita Girl Scout Council	$25.00
Plummerville Boys' Baseball Team	$25.00
Pulaski County Tuberculosis Association	$500.00
Rockwin Fund	$50,934.37
Seventh Day Adventists	$10.00
Shepherd of the Hills Home	$30.00
Shrine Circus Benefit Fund	$24.00
Soil Conservation Society of America	$50.00
Soldiers', Sailors', and Airmen's Club, NY	$100.00
Trinity School Scholarship and Development Fund	$100.00
Unitarian Service Committee	$5,000.00
United Fund	$10,559.38
United Negro College Fund	$500.00
University of Arkansas, Fayetteville	$60.00
University of Arkansas, Endowment and Trust Fund	$250.00
Urban League of Greater Little Rock	$3,214.85
Valeria Home	$500.00
Vanderbilt University	$342.20
Yale Club of New York City	$5.00
Yale University Alumni Fund	$1,000.00
Yale University, Class of 1937	$5,000.00
Yale University, Scholarship and Library Fund	$12.00
Yale University, Yale in China Association	$1,000.00
YMCA	$500.00
TOTAL	**$1,236,083.17**

1964

A.M.E. Church	$5.00

American Legion	$40.00
American Red Cross	$50.00
American Red Cross	$100.00
Arkansas, State of	$48,666.98
Arkansas A&M	$1,000.00
Arkansas Arts Center	$52,069.41
Arkansas Association for Mental Health	$2,215.65
Arkansas Association for Mental Health	$6,341.99
Arkansas Association for the Crippled	$100.00
Arkansas Association of University Women	$96.00
Arkansas Children's Hospital	$25.00
Arkansas Council on Human Relations	$2,707.50
Arkansas Foundation of Associated Colleges	$500.00
Arkansas Foundation of Associated Colleges	$19,882.50
Arkansas Heart Association	$50.00
Arkansas Inventors Congress	$120.00
Arkansas Junior Deputy Sheriffs' Association	$200.00
Arkansas Lighthouse for the Blind	$25.00
Arkansas Opportunity Fund	$26,241.40
Arkansas Science Fair Association	$50.00
Arkansas State Council of Economic Education	$1,000.00
Arkansas State Publicity and Parks Commission	$1,218.65
Arkansas State Publicity and Parks Commission	$72,656.25
Arthritis Foundation, Arkansas Branch	$250.00
Association for the Preservation of Virginia Antiques	$10.00
Big Brothers of America	$100.00
Boy Land of Arkansas	$4,569.50
Boy Scouts of America	$25.00
Boy Scouts of America	$100.00
Boy Scouts of America	$100.00
Boy Scouts of America	$100.00
Boys' Clubs of America	$25.00
Carlisle Playground Association	$100.00
Christian Record Braille Foundation	$50.00
Conway County Fair Association	$50.00
Conway County Tuberculosis Association	$50.00
Disabled American Veterans	$20.00
Ducks Unlimited	$50.00
Easter Seal Sheltered Workshop	$10.00
Father Flanagan's Boys' Home	$10.00
Finch College	$500.00
Fine Arts Club	$210.00

Flight Safety Foundation	$902.50	Soldiers', Sailors', and Airmen's Club, NY	$100.00
Hampton Institute	$200.00	Southern Historical Association	$100.00
Hospitalized Veterans Service	$100.00	Spellman College	$550.00
Institute of International Education	$398.56	St. Anthony's Hospital	$100.00
Jack Kriendler Memorial Fund	$100.00	St. Nicholas School	$510.00
Kiwanis Activities	$112.50	Travel Expenses in Connection with Charities	$5,088.44
Lakewood Methodist Church	$10,000.00		
Little Rock Boys' Club	$50.00	Travel Expenses in Connection with Charities	$32,136.08
Little Rock Boys' Club Auxiliary	$100.00		
Little Rock Chamber of Commerce	$300.00	U.S. Committee for United Nations	$50.00
Little Rock Fire Department	$25.00	U.S. Olympic Commission	$100.00
Little Rock School District	$2,500.00	United Fund of Pulaski County	$9,955.63
Little Rock Sertoma Club	$10.00	United Negro College Fund	$500.00
Little Rock University	$16,673.13	University of Arkansas, Endowment and Trust	$250.00
Loomis Alumni Fund	$1,000.00		
Loomis Institute	$3,800.00	University of Arkansas Medical Center	$9,941.25
Mental Health Association of St. Louis	$1,500.00	University of Colorado	$200.00
Morrilton School District	$64.47	Urban League of Little Rock	$4,140.00
Morrilton School District	$4,717.90	USO of New York City	$2,707.50
National Association for Mental Health	$4.00	Walnut Ridge High School	$500.00
National Conference of Christians and Jews	$300.00	Watson Chapel High School	$500.00
		Winrock Farms, contribution names not itemized	$10.00
National Foundation for Medical Education	$500.00	Women's City Club	$30.00
National Urban League	$19,882.50	WSCS of Henderson Methodist Church	$594.45
Navy League of the U.S., Pemberton House Fund	$500.00	Yale Club of Arkansas	$30.00
North Little Rock Firemen's Benefit	$10.00	Yale Club of New York City	$12.00
Opera Association of New Mexico	$4,956.88	Yale University, Alumni Fund	$1,000.00
Ouachita Girl Scouts Council	$25.00	Yale University, Class of 1935	$9,927.50
Partnership Contributions, Winrock Development Company	$3,507.00	Yale in China Association	$1,000.00
Philander Smith College	$24,784.38	**TOTAL**	**$716,835.39**
Pilgrim's Rest A.M.E. Church	$10.00		
Protestant Council of the City of New York	$400.00	**1965**	
Pulaski County Mental Health Association	$26.94	American Hospital in Beirut	$2,500.00
		American Red Cross	$100.00
Pulaski County Tuberculosis Association	$500.00	Arkansas Arts Center	$280,846.25
Radio Free Europe	$100.00	Arkansas Association for Mental Health	$1,054.18
Recording for the Blind	$50.00	Arkansas Children's Hospital	$25.00
Rehearsal Club	$1,000.00	Arkansas College	$50,375.00
Rockwin Fund	$100,781.25	Arkansas Council on Human Relations	$2,782.50
Rural Youth Organization	$1,484.82		
Sacred Heart School	$24,784.38	Arkansas Foundation of Associated Colleges	$25,187.50
Salvation Army	$20.00	Arkansas Junior Chamber of Commerce	$3,442.50
Sarah Clark Little League Baseball Team	$25.00		
Sealantic Fund.	$168,829.50	Arkansas Lighthouse for the Blind	$25.00
Seventh Day Adventist	$10.00	Arkansas Lighthouse for the Blind	$1,192.50
Shepherd of the Hills Home	$30.00	Arkansas Opportunity Fund	$27,030.00
Shrine Circus	$36.00	Arkansas State Council on Economic Education	$1,000.00

Arkansas State Publicity and Parks Commission	$4,218.90
Arkansas State Publicity and Parks Commission	$34,632.50
Arkansas State Teacher's Band	$150.00
Boy Land of Arkansas	$4,931.55
Boy Scouts of America	$25.00
Charitable Contributions, not itemized or named	$2,029.73
Conway County Fair Association	$50.00
Conway County Mounted Patrol	$50.00
Conway County Tuberculosis Association	$50.00
Crowley's Ridge Girl Scouts	$500.00
Cumberland Fund, Alcoholic Hospital	$500.00
Farm and Ranch Youth Center Club	$9,906.25
Fine Arts of El Dorado	$5,151.25
Flight Safety Foundation	$1,192.50
Graduate Institute of the Southwest	$50,375.00
Harlem Hospital	$618.60
Hendrix College	$50,375.00
Hockaday School	$2,823.63
Institute of International Education	$329.03
Jack Kriendler Memorial Fund	$200.00
Jewish Hospital of St. Louis	$1,000.00
Kiwanis Club Activities	$112.50
Langston University	$500.00
Leslie Municipal Hospital	$800.00
Little Rock Boys' Club	$500.00
Little Rock University	$17,392.50
Little Rock YMCA	$250.00
Loomis Institute	$2,100.00
Middle East Institute	$2,437.50
Morrilton Board of Education	$14,820.00
Museum of Science and Natural History	$500.00
National Association for Mental Health	$35,423.58
National Beauty Conference	$288.15
National Conference of Christians and Jews	$250.00
National Conference on State Parks	$1,000.00
National Foundation for Medical Education	$500.00
National Urban League	$20,272.50
Ouachita Baptist College	$50,375.00
Ouachita Girl Scout Council	$25.00
Pine Bluff High School Choir	$500.00
Protestant Council of the City of New York	$400.00
Rehearsal Club	$500.00
Rockwin Fund	$45,333.75
Sealantic Fund	$60,817.50

Seventh Day Adventist	$10.00
Shawnee Boys' Ranch	$500.00
Shepherd of the Hills Home	$30.00
St. Andrews Presbyterian Church	$395.00
Texas A & M University	$950.00
Travel Expense in Connection with Charities	$117,921.18
United Fund of Pulaski County	$23,172.50
University of Arkansas, Fayetteville	$2,040.00
University of Arkansas Medical Center	$800.00
University of Virginia	$1,027.00
Urban League of Little Rock	$4,276.25
USO of New York City	$1,987.50
Vanderbilt University	$207.80
Winthrop Rockefeller Trust Fund	$4,573.75
WSCS of Henderson Methodist Church	$500.00
Yale University	$1,192.50
Yale in China Association	$1,000.00
TOTAL	**$980,350.83**

1966

A.M.E. Church	$5.00
American Red Cross	$100.00
Arkansas Arts Center	$201,850.69
Arkansas Association for Mental Health	$2,376.06
Arkansas Basin Association	$150.00
Arkansas Children's Hospital	$25.00
Arkansas Council on Human Relations	$6,000.00
Arkansas Enterprises for the Blind	$1,012.00
Arkansas Foundation of Associated Colleges	$25,300.00
Arkansas Lighthouse for the Blind	$25.00
Arkansas Opportunity Fund	$27,300.00
Arkansas State Council of Economic Education	$1,100.00
Arkansas State Publicity and Parks Commission	$22,137.50
Boy Land of Arkansas	$12,667.50
Boy Scouts of America	$25.00
Boy Scouts of America	$25.00
Boy Scouts of America	$100.00
Boy Scouts of America	$2,000.00
Brown, Robert K. (Bishop)	$500.00
Charitable Expenses (Travel)	$79,208.10
College of the Ozarks	$50,800.00
Contributions through Partnerships	$100.00
Conway County Fair Association	$50.00
Conway County Tuberculosis Association	$50.00

Election Research Council	$15,886.25
Flight Safety Foundation	$1,012.00
Harding College	$50,800.00
Henderson Methodist Church	$600.00
Hockaday School	$1,000.00
John Brown University	$50,800.00
Levi Memorial Hospital	$5,000.00
Little Rock University	$16,867.50
Loomis Institute	$4,400.00
National Association for Mental Health	$97,200.18
National Conference of Christians and Jews	$250.00
National Foundation for Medical Education	$500.00
National Urban League	$20,111.25
Oklahoma Herford Breeders Association	$9.50
Ouachita Girl Scout Council	$25.00
Ozarks, Inc.	$2,747.50
Rehearsal Club of New York	$500.00
Rockefeller, Jeannette, contributions	$6,884.37
Rockwin Fund	$116,299.58
Rural Youth Organization	$7,557.57
Salvation Army Building Fund	$5,102.50
Sealantic Fund	$60,009.38
Seventy-seventh Infantry Division Association	$1,000.00
Shepherd of the Hills Home	$30.00
Southern Baptist College	$50,800.00
St. Vincent Infirmary	$1,000.00
Texas A&M University	$1,625.00
Travel Expenses in Connection with Charities	$4,553.10
United Fund of Pulaski County	$15,894.38
University of Arkansas, Fayetteville	$250.00
University of Arkansas Medical Center	$3,450.00
University of California	$5,060.00
USO of New York City	$2,011.13
Valley Education and Research Fund	$12,620.30
Washburn University of Topeka	$500.00
Winrock Farms, contribution names not itemized	$125.65
Winthrop Rockefeller Trust Fund	$2,460.00
Yale in China Association	$1,000.00
Yale University Alumni Fund	$1,012.00
TOTAL	**$999,860.99**

1967

Adona School	$100.00
A.M.E. Church	$25.00
American Cancer Society	$25.00
American Legion	$354.35
American Red Cross	$50.00
American Red Cross	$250.00
Arizona College	$4,253.16
Arkansas, State of	$388,759.85
Arkansas Arts Center	$250.00
Arkansas Arts Center	$255,627.56
Arkansas Association for Mental Health	$5,988.18
Arkansas Basin Association	$150.00
Arkansas Foundation of Associated Colleges	$25,169.38
Arkansas Industrial Development Foundation	$2,146.22
Arkansas Industrial Development Foundation	$6,186.88
Arkansas Jaycees	$1,800.00
Arkansas Opportunity Fund	$22,443.75
Arkansas State Council on Economic Education	$1,500.00
Arkansas State Publicity and Parks Commission	$500.00
Arkansas Technical College Band	$250.00
Boy Scouts of America	$25.00
Boy Scouts of America	$10,260.00
California Institute of the Arts	$500.00
Carlisle Booster Club	$40.00
Charitable Contributions, not itemized or named	$2,528.51
Contributions through Partnerships	$175.00
Cystic Fibrosis	$8,609.12
Girl Scouts of America	$25.00
Governmental Efficiency Study Commission	$7,925.60
Hockaday School	$1,000.00
J. C. Brand (State Park)	$1,400.00
Jewish Relief Fund	$500.00
Johns Hopkins University	$800.00
League of Women Voters	$100.00
Lonoke Fire Department	$50.00
Loomis Institute	$2,600.00
Louisiana State University	$250.00
Metropolitan Museum of Art	$2,000.00
Museum of Science and Natural History	$500.00
National Association of Mental Health	$691.60
National Conference of Christians and Jews	$35.00
National Conference of Christians and Jews	$350.00
National Fund for Medical Education	$500.00
National Jewish Hospital	$250.00
North Little Rock Women's Softball Team	$500.00
Pocantico Hills Church	$19,625.00

Protestant Council of New York City	$600.00
Razorback Fund	$3,786.25
Rehearsal Club	$500.00
Rockefeller, Jeannette, contributions	$8,426.96
Rockwin Fund	$131,726.25
Salvation Army Building Fund	$5,407.83
Second Baptist Church	$4,165.13
St. Andrews Presbyterian Church	$250.00
State College of Arkansas	$8,681.88
Territorial Capital	$1,310.50
Trammel S. Crow Fund	$10,600.00
Travel Expenses in Connection with Charities	$82,750.32
U.S. Olympics	$338.03
United Fund of Pulaski County	$680.00
University of Arkansas, Fayetteville	$350.00
University of Arkansas, Fayetteville	$1,250.00
Urban League	$2,550.00
Veterans of America Conference	$339.97
Warren High School Band	$500.00
Winrock Farms, contribution names not itemized	$116.52
Winthrop Rockefeller Trust Fund	$2,092.00
Yale in China Association	$1,000.00
Yale University	$1,000.00
YMCA	$290.00
TOTAL	**$1,045,780.80**

1968

Agriculture, USA	$427.50
Amalgamated Choraliers	$100.00
American Cancer Society	$100.00
American Musical and Dramatic Academy	$3,000.00
Arkansas, State of	$253,622.99
Arkansas AM&N Cappella Choir	$100.00
Arkansas Arts Center	$234,311.70
Arkansas Association for Mental Health	$546.28
Arkansas Barrel Racing Association	$350.00
Arkansas Basin Association	$150.00
Arkansas Basin Association	$540.00
Arkansas Council on Human Relations	$5,608.13
Arkansas for Revised Constitution	$5,000.00
Arkansas Industrial Development Foundation	$12,298.25
Arkansas Jaycees	$1,359.06
Arkansas Opportunity Fund	$27,790.00
Arkansas Orchestra Society	$500.00
Arkansas Poultry Federation	$100.00

Arkansas Society of Sons of American Revolution	$100.00
Arkansas State Council on Economic Education	$1,500.00
Arkansas State Elks	$525.00
Arkansas State Publicity and Parks Commission	$1,500.00
Auburn University	$1,645.08
Boy Scouts of America	$100.00
Boy Scouts of America	$100.00
Boy Scouts of America	$200.00
California Mental Health Association	$6,933.87
Camp Mitchell	$4,575.00
Carlisle Community Building Fund	$100.00
Carlisle School	$1,000.00
Charitable Contributions, not itemized or named	$989.98
Charity Fund	$100.00
Citizens for Good Government	$2,000.00
Contributions through Partnerships	$168.00
Conway County Hospital	$50,351.25
Cystic Fibrosis	$2,370.45
District of Columbia Mental Health Association	$770.00
Economic Opportunity Agency Athletic Department	$100.00
Election Research Council	$1,157.50
Flight Safety Foundation	$2,070.63
Governor's Youth Council	$1,500.00
Hall High School	$296.20
Headstart Program	$1,707.40
Heart Fund	$100.00
Helena Central High School Band	$500.00
Henderson Methodist Church	$1,350.00
Hockaday School	$1,000.00
Jack Kriendler Memorial Fund	$200.00
Joint Committee on Mental Health of Children	$1,284.51
Kiwanis Activities	$150.00
Little Rock Men's Baseball League	$200.00
Little Rock Vocational School	$1,280.00
Loomis Institute	$100,465.00
Mayor's Commission on Youth	$300.00
Meeting Street School for Retarded	$100.00
Metropolitan New York Committee, 1968 Olympics	$100.00
Moral Rearmament, Inc.	$250.00
Morrilton High School Library Fund	$100.00
Morrilton Vocational School	$5,987.00
National Association for Mental Health	$10,028.72
National Conference of Christians and Jews	$600.00

National Fund for Medical Education	$500.00
National Institute of Child Health	$559.82
National Jewish Hospital at Denver	$250.00
National Urban League	$20,341.88
New York University Medical Center	$400.00
Northern Virginia Cooperative School for Handicapped Children	$200.00
One-Eyed Jacks Softball Team	$500.00
People to People	$250.00
President's Committee on Mental Retardation	$4,498.02
Rehearsal Club	$500.00
Rockefeller, Jeannette, contributions	$14,173.00
Rockwin Fund	$156,419.39
Sealantic Fund	$60,390.00
Second Baptist Church, Hope	$150.00
St. Vincent's, returned portion from 1966 contribution	$(1,000.00)
State College of Arkansas	$16,470.00
State Department of Education	$500.00
Trammel S. Crow Fund	$120,000.00
Travel Expenses in Connection with Charities	$53,000.45
Tucker Prison Chapel Fund	$5,000.00
United Fund	$2,000.00
United Fund of Pulaski County	$22,052.00
Universal Seltoma Club for Speech and Hearing Defects	$100.00
University of Arkansas	$1,000.00
University of Arkansas Creative Writing Program	$2,081.25
University of Arkansas Endowment and Trust	$250.00
University of Arkansas Special Art Project	$3,766.50
University of Texas College of Business Administration Foundation	$500.00
Urban League	$10,729.91
USO of New York City	$4,254.38
Vanderbilt University	$260.00
Wiltwyck School for Boys'	$240.00
Winrock Farms, contribution names not itemized	$210.00
Winthrop Rockefeller Trust Fund	$4,517.50
Yale in China Association	$1,000.00
Yale University Alumni Fund	$1,000.00
YMCA	$916.00
Young Life Forward Fund for Arkansas	$250.00
Youth Home, Inc.	$457.80
TOTAL	**$1,260,447.40**

1969

305th Infantry Division Association	$17.00
American Musical and Dramatic Academy	$3,000.00
American Red Cross	$682.00
Arkansas, State of	$325,556.00
Arkansas 4-H Club Foundation	$250.00
Arkansas Acre at Valley Forge	$100.00
Arkansas Arts Center	$270,241.00
Arkansas Association for Mental Health	$140.00
Arkansas Association for Retarded Children	$650.00
Arkansas Athletic Association	$25.00
Arkansas Council on Human Relations	$2,517.00
Arkansas Foundation of Associated Colleges	$50,156.00
Arkansas Industrial Development Foundation	$6,338.00
Arkansas Opportunity Fund	$31,498.00
Arkansas Orchestra Society	$500.00
Arkansas Razorback Fund	$12,213.00
Arkansas Rehabilitation Service	$972.00
Arkansas Service Organization	$13,700.00
Arkansas Society of Sons of American Revolution	$100.00
Arkansas State Council on Economic Education	$1,500.00
Arkansas State Publicity and Parks Commission	$1,600.00
Arkansas Teachers Association	$250.00
Arkansas Tuberculosis and Respiratory Disease Association	$50.00
Bendameer Grotto Fun-Tac-U-Lar	$10.00
Camden Fairview Band	$500.00
Catholic High School Equipment Fund	$5.00
Charitable Contributions, not itemized or named	$80.00
Charitable expenses for various organizations	$2,443.00
Citywide Religious Pictures	$25.00
Community Concert Association	$50.00
Contributions through Partnerships	$182.00
District of Columbia Mental Health Association	$2,500.00
Douglas F. Burton Memorial Scholarship Fund	$100.00
Ducks Unlimited	$50.00
Education Commission of the State	$25.00
Education Commission of the State	$433.00
Election Research Council	$12,373.00
Fayetteville High School Band	$1,000.00

Finch College	$25,603.00
Flight Safety Foundation	$1,000.00
Franklin County Library Building Fund	$25.00
Governor's Youth Council	$10,515.00
Greater Little Rock Council of Garden Clubs	$20.00
Henderson Student Scholarship Fund	$50.00
Inspiration Point Fine Arts Academy	$100.00
Institute of International Education	$1,275.00
Institute of Rehabilitative Medicine	$200.00
Jack Kriendler Memorial Fund	$200.00
Joint Committee on Mental Health of Children	$289.00
Kiwanis Activities	$120.00
Little Rock Hadassah	$200.00
Little Rock Men's Baseball League	$100.00
Little Rock Schools Athletic Department	$50.00
Loomis Institute	$101,062.00
Loomis, Chaffee Annual Fund	$2,000.00
M. M. Eberts Post #1 American Legion	$37.00
Maharry College	$91.00
March of Dimes	$100.00
Marion Coffee Shop Breakfast Club	$50.00
Martin Luther King Jr. Memorial Hospital	$2,448.00
McClellan Band Boosters	$150.00
McClellan High School Lionettes	$100.00
Mental Health Association Staff Council	$4,997.00
Mental Retardation Center, UCLA	$864.00
Museum of Science and Natural History	$500.00
National Association for Mental Health	$3,642.00
National Association for Retarded Children	$1,050.00
National Conference of Christians and Jews	$350.00
National Council for Children and Youth	$100.00
National Fund for Medical Education	$500.00
National Institute of Childhood Disease	$1,627.00
National Jewish Hospital	$250.00
National Medical Association Foundation	$3,155.00
National Urban League	$20,160.00
Office of Economic Opportunity, Tackle Football League	$50.00
One-Eyed Jacks Softball Team	$500.00
Operation Headstart	$5,586.00
Optimist Club of Greater Little Rock	$50.00
People to People	$250.00

Pine Bluff Community Concert Association	$16.00
Portal's House Benefit	$10,122.00
Presbyterian Pan American School	$100.00
President's Committee on Mental Retardation	$3,319.00
Pulaski County Tuberculosis Association	$500.00
Rehearsal Club	$500.00
Rockefeller, Jeannette, contributions	$8,995.00
Rockwin Fund	$218,690.00
Sealantic Fund	$60,637.00
Second Baptist Church	$100.00
Seventy-seventh Infantry Division Association	$20.00
Shrine Circus Fund	$25.00
South End Boys' Club Building Fund	$2,500.00
South Walton County Fire Department	$500.00
Souvenir Program of Arkansas Association of Colored Women's Clubs	$60.00
St. Joseph's Orphanage	$52.00
State College of Arkansas	$25,144.00
State Festival of Arkansas	$80.00
Symposium on Mental Retardation	$3,693.00
Travel Expenses in Connection with Charities	$34,702.00
Trinity United Methodist Church	$25.00
Tucker Prison Chapel Fund	$5,000.00
United Fund	$2,000.00
United Fund of Pulaski County	$21,240.00
University of Arkansas Endowment and Trust Fund	$425.00
Up with People	$170.00
Urban League	$25,317.00
USO of New York City	$5,250.00
Vanderbilt University	$126,417.00
Winrock Farms, contribution names not itemized	$220.00
Winthrop Rockefeller Fund	$1,500.00
Winthrop Trust Association	$200.00
Yale Club of New York City	$17.00
Yale in China Association	$1,000.00
Yale University	$1,000.00
YMCA	$290.00
TOTAL	**$1,491,073.00**

1970

American Red Cross	$550.00
Arcadia National Park	$357.00
Arkadelphia Little League	$545.00
Arkansas, State of	$437,672.00

Arkansas Arts Center	$138,931.00
Arkansas Association for Mental Health	$497.00
Arkansas Audubon Society	$10.00
Arkansas Barrel Racing Association	$350.00
Arkansas Council on Human Relations	$2,850.00
Arkansas Foundation of Associated Colleges	$25,303.00
Arkansas High School Rodeo Association	$50.00
Arkansas Industrial Development Foundation	$7,575.00
Arkansas Junior Miss Pageant	$15.00
Arkansas Opportunity Fund	$33,238.00
Arkansas Orchestra Society	$500.00
Arkansas Service Organization	$900.00
Arkansas Society of Sons of American Revolution	$100.00
Arkansas State Council on Economic Education	$1,500.00
Arkansas State Publicity and Parks Commission	$1,500.00
Arkansas State University Indian Club	$10.00
Arkansas Travelers	$35.00
Arkansas Wildlife Federation	$500.00
Arkansas Youth Council	$15.00
Athletic and Teenage Club	$2,000.00
Bendameer Grotto Fun-Tac-U-Lar	$15.00
Boy Scouts of America	$550.00
Catholic High School	$1,000.00
Community Concert Association	$16.00
Concern for Prisoners of War, Arkansas Chapter	$100.00
Conference on Controlled Environment and Food Technology	$5,447.00
Contributions through Partnerships	$75.00
Ducks Unlimited	$10.00
Election Research Council	$30,000.00
Everett Dirksen Library Fund	$61.00
Exchange Club of Jonesboro	$100.00
Festival of American Folklore	$350.00
Flight Safety Foundation	$1,000.00
Forest City Band Booster Club	$200.00
Gordon Gale Post #99 American Legion	$40.00
Governor's Youth Council	$11,500.00
Greater Little Rock Council of Garden Clubs	$22.00
Hot Springs Jaycettes	$1,200.00
Infantry Museum	$576.00
Jack Kriendler Memorial Fund	$200.00
Jackson Theological Seminary	$500.00
John Brown University	$200.00
Kiwanis Activities	$150.00
Little Rock Hadassah	$200.00
Little Rock Jaycees	$100.00
Loomis Institute	$206,325.00
M. M. Eberts Post #1 American Legion	$40.00
Marion Coffee Shop Breakfast Club	$50.00
Museum of Science and Natural History	$500.00
National Conference of Christians and Jews	$350.00
National Fund for Medical Education	$500.00
National Jewish Hospital	$250.00
National Tennis Education Foundation	$100.00
National Urban League	$51,518.00
Opportunities Industrialization Center	$100.00
Optimist Club of Greater Little Rock	$50.00
Ouachita Girl Scouts	$70.00
People to People	$250.00
Pine Bluff Boys' Club	$250.00
Pine Bluff Community Concert Association	$50.00
President's Committee on Mental Retardation	$5,069.00
President's Task Force	$477.00
Pulaski County Youth Service	$700.00
Quigley Stadium Athletic Department	$50.00
Rehearsal Club	$500.00
Rockefeller (Abby Aldrich) Scholarship Fund	$3,325.00
Rockefeller (Winthrop) Trust Fund	$3,956.00
Rockefeller, Jeannette, contributions	$56,146.00
Rockwin Fund	$160,569.00
Seventy-seventh Infantry Division Association	$5.00
Shrine Circus Fund	$25.00
Southwestern at Memphis	$250.00
St. Joseph's Orphanage	$50.00
Stadium Commission, War Memorial, Little Rock, AR	$1,000.00
Third Marine Division Association	$135.00
Travel Expenses in Connection with Charities	$26,166.00
Union Congregational Church of Seal Harbor	$7,119.00
Union County Center for the Handicapped	$20.00
United Fund	$2,000.00
United Fund of Pulaski County	$29,707.00
University of Arkansas Endowment and Trust Fund	$450.00

University of Michigan School of Public Health	$5,000.00
Urban League	$5,561.00
USO of New York City	$2,529.00
Vanderbilt University	$123,987.00
Winrock Farms, contribution names not itemized	$1,254.00
Yale Club of New York City	$25.00
Yale in China Association	$1,000.00
Yale University	$1,000.00
TOTAL	**$1,407,093.00**

1971

A. Wade Martin Foundation	$250.00
Abby Aldrich Rockefeller Scholarship Fund	$3,572.00
American Legion	$42.00
Arkansas, State of	$22,758.00
Arkansas Arts Center	$113,369.00
Arkansas Association for the Crippled	$50.00
Arkansas Audubon Society	$10.00
Arkansas Colony for Crippled Children	$25.00
Arkansas Council on Human Relations	$2,668.00
Arkansas Foundation of Associated Colleges	$25,200.00
Arkansas Guild Foundation	$50.00
Arkansas Human Resources Council	$40.00
Arkansas Jaycees	$1,500.00
Arkansas Junior Miss Pageant	$15.00
Arkansas Opportunity Fund	$34,732.00
Arkansas Orchestra Society	$500.00
Arkansas Society of Sons of American Revolution	$100.00
Arkansas State Council on Economic Education	$1,500.00
Arkansas State Hospital	$440.00
Arkansas State University Indian Club	$10.00
Arkansas Travel Council	$2,500.00
Arkansas Youth Forum	$3,605.00
Auburn University	$1,950.00
Big Brothers of Pulaski County	$25.00
Boy Scouts of America	$100.00
Catholic High School	$500.00
College of the Ozarks	$8,843.00
Community Concert Association	$16.00
Conway County Hospital	$25.00
Conway County, Arkansas	$204,098.00
Department of State Parks	$1,500.00
DePaww University	$200.00
Douglas Burton Memorial Fund	$100.00
Ducks Unlimited	$20.00

Eisenhower Medical Center and Eisenhower College	$1,000.00
Election Laws Institute	$6,125.00
Everett Dirksen Library Fund	$550.00
Firefighters Charity Ball	$25.00
Flight Safety Foundation	$1,000.00
Geyer Springs Community Association	$250.00
Governor's Youth Council	$2,900.00
Greater Little Rock Optimist Club	$100.00
Infantry Museum	$6,553.00
Jack Kriendler Memorial Fund	$200.00
Kiwanis Club	$150.00
Knickerbocker Hospital	$250.00
L. McGillicuddy Scholarship Fund	$200.00
Little Rock Hadassah	$200.00
Little Rock Jaycees	$2,100.00
Loomis Institute	$100,375.00
McClellan Band Boosters	$1,000.00
Middle Tennessee University	$1,775.00
Mississippi State University	$1,800.00
Museum of Science and Natural History	$500.00
National 4-H Club Foundation	$500.00
National Conference of Christians and Jews	$450.00
National Fund for Medical Education	$500.00
National Jewish Hospital	$250.00
New York University Medical Center	$10,281.00
Old Eureka Unitarian Church	$775.00
Opportunities Industrialization Center	$25.00
People to People	$250.00
Philander Smith College	$25,300.00
Quigley Stadium Athletic Department	$50.00
Rehearsal Club	$500.00
Rockwin Fund	$207,912.00
Shorter College	$10,547.00
Shrine Circus Fund	$24.00
Southwest University	$5,159.00
Travel Expenses in Connection with Charities	$2,008.00
Union Memorial Hospital	$100.00
United Fund of Pulaski County	$18,360.00
United Negro College Fund	$5,365.00
University of Arkansas, Fayetteville	$2,155.00
Urban League	$1,557.00
USO of New York City	$2,631.00
Vanderbilt University Chancellor's Council	$10,308.00
VFW	$2.00
Winrock Farms, contribution names not itemized	$2,288.00
Winthrop Rockefeller Fund	$3,956.00

Women's Auxiliary of Desert Hospital	$50.00
Yale Club of New York City	$25.00
Yale in China Association	$1,000.00
Yale University	$1,000.00
YMCA Running Track Fund	$200.00
TOTAL	**$870,894.00**

1972

4-H Club Foundation	$50.00
Abby Aldrich Rockefeller Scholarship Fund	$3,125.00
Alcoholism Council of Greater Los Angeles	$500.00
American Cancer Society	$20.00
American Legion	$2.00
Arkansas, State of	$28,973.00
Arkansas Arts Center	$123,250.00
Arkansas Arts Center Foundation	$100,000.00
Arkansas Audubon Society	$10.00
Arkansas Boys' State	$40.00
Arkansas Council on Human Relations	$2,500.00
Arkansas Foundation of Associated Colleges	$30,000.00
Arkansas Jaycees	$1,500.00
Arkansas Junior Miss Pageant	$15.00
Arkansas Opportunity Fund	$45,763.00
Arkansas Orchestra Society	$500.00
Arkansas Parks, Recreation and Tourism	$500.00
Arkansas Service Organization	$100.00
Arkansas State Council on Economic Education	$1,700.00
Arkansas State Hospital	$513.00
Arkansas State University	$10.00
Arkansas Travel Council	$1,000.00
Arkansas Travelers	$100.00
Auburn University	$20.00
Boy Scouts of America	$20.00
Boy Scouts of America	$25,000.00
Boys' State	$40.00
Carlisle High School	$40.00
Catholic High School	$500.00
Charitable Expenses (Travel)	$22,495.00
College of the Ozarks	$21,328.00
Commandant's House, Department of the Navy	$100.00
Community Concert Association	$16.00
Conway County, Arkansas	$14,025.00
Conway County Hospital Auxiliary	$25.00
Cummins Prison Chapel Fund	$10,164.00
Desert Hospital Auxiliary	$50.00
Disabled American Veterans	$400.00

Ducks Unlimited	$200.00
Election Laws Institute (TEL, Inc.)	$51,653.00
Flight Safety Foundation	$7,250.00
Future Farmers of America	$50.00
Game and Fish Commission National Convention	$100.00
Geyer Springs Community Association	$250.00
Heart Fund	$10.00
Hendrix College Scholarship Fund	$10,500.00
Hockaday School Scholarship Fund	$15,000.00
Jack Kriendler Memorial Fund	$200.00
Kiwanis Activities of Little Rock	$150.00
Lillian McGillicuddy Scholarship Fund	$384.00
Little Rock Central High School	$250.00
Little Rock Jaycees	$100.00
Little Rock Optimist Clubs	$100.00
Little Rock Schools Athletic Department	$50.00
Lonoke County Exceptional School	$50.00
Loomis Institute	$261,200.00
Loomis, Chaffee Fund	$2,000.00
March of Dimes	$50.00
Museum of Science and Natural History	$550.00
National Conference of Christians and Jews	$450.00
National Fund for Medical Education	$500.00
National Infantry Museum (Infantry Museum Association, Inc.)	$30,745.00
National Jewish Hospital	$250.00
National Urban League	$20,000.00
Old Euseba Baptist Church	$25.00
Osborne Association	$10,140.00
Ouachita Baptist University	$1,000.00
People to People International	$250.00
Phi Lambda Chi	$100.00
Philander Smith College "Take Care of Philander" Benefit	$1,000.00
Rehearsal Club	$500.00
Resources, Inc.	$10,461.00
Reynolds PTA	$25.00
Rockwin Fund	$178,389.00
Rural Resources Institute	$25,113.00
Southern Christian Home	$25.00
St. Vincent Infirmary	$10,370.00
Third Marine Division Association	$135.00
United Fund	$4,050.00
United Fund of Pulaski County	$18,148.00
United Negro College Fund	$45.00
University of Arkansas, Fayetteville	$21,353.00
University of Arkansas Endowment and Trust	$450.00

University of Tennessee	$20.00	Arkansas Audubon Society	$10.00
University of the South	$150.00	Arkansas Orchestra Society	$100.00
Urban League of Little Rock	$33.00	Catholic High School	$500.00
Urban League of Little Rock	$1,650.00	Election Laws Institute	$3,000.00
USO of New York City	$2,500.00	National Infantry Museum	$300.00
Vanderbilt University	$4,500.00	People to People International	$250.00
Vanderbilt University	$927,000.00	Resources, Inc.	$16,350.00
VFW	$2.00	Rockwin Fund	$46,863.00
Winthrop Rockefeller Distinguished Lecture Series	$51.00	Rural Resources Institute	$15,000.00
		Scimitar Shrine Temple	$25.00
Winthrop Rockefeller Fund	$2,300.00	State College of Arkansas	$200.00
Yale Club of New York City	$25.00	Travel Expenses in Connection with Charities	$4,335.00
Yale in China Association	$1,000.00		
Yale University Alumni Fund	$1,000.00	Winrock Farms, contribution names not itemized	$75.00
YMCA	$1,320.00		
TOTAL	**$2,059,566.00**	YMCA	$560.00
		TOTAL	**$127,568.00**

1973

Arkansas Arts Center	$40,000.00	**Grand Total 1934–1975**	**$19,680,668.83**

APPENDIX B

Winthrop Rockefeller Charitable Trust, 1974–2001

Year	Organization	Amount
1974	American Cattlemen's Association	$25,000.00
1985	American Farmland Trust	$150,000.00
1984	American Heart Association (San Francisco)	$500.00
1990	Arkansas Aerospace Education Center	$3,026,609.00
1975	Arkansas Arts Center	$210,890.00
1976	Arkansas Arts Center Foundation	$3,832,514.80
1990	Arkansas Center for Health Improvement	$1,820,000.00
2001	Arkansas Community Foundation	$11,500,000.00
2001	Arkansas Governors Mansion Association	$100,000.00
1987	Arkansas State Council on Economic Education	$12,500.00
1992	Central Arkansas Library System, Perry County Public Library	$250,000.00
1979	Center for Community Change	$160,000.00
1996	Central Arkansas Library System	$50,000.00
1984	Citizens' Participation Project	$100,000.00
1984	Close Up Foundation	$25,000.00
1974	College of the Ozarks	$11,193.68
1977	Colonial Williamsburg Foundation	$9,500,000.00
1988	Hendrix College	$1,000,000.00
1974	Infantry Museum Association, Inc.	$100,000.00
1975	Loomis Institute	$698,500.00
1982	Museum of Automobiles	$384,694.50
2000	National Audubon Society	$450,000.00
1976	National Rural Center	$1,950,000.00
2001	Nature Conservancy	$239,580.00
1981	Rockefeller University	$111,733.33
1973	Rockwin	$605,193.00
1975	Rural Housing Alliance	$15,000.00
1976	Society of New York Hospital	$100,000.00
1981	Arkansas, State of	$50.00
1976	Arkansas Department of Parks and Tourism	$475,900.00
1991	TCU Ranch Management	$1,050,000.00
1974	United Fund of Pulaski County	$20,000.00
1980	University of Arkansas Foundation	$505,000.00
1975	Vanderbilt University	$500,000.00

1987	Winrock International	$86,524,885.44
1975	Winthrop Rockefeller Foundation	$39,098,432.24
1983	Worldwatch Institute	$645,000.00
1979	Yale University	$300,000.00
1979	YMCA Metropolitan Little Rock	$200,000.00
Pending	Lonoke County Task Force on Child Abuse	$250,000.00
Pending	Philander Smith College	$2,000,000.00
TOTAL GRANTS		**$165,748,175.99**

APPENDIX C

Winthrop Rockefeller Foundation Grants, 1975–1999

1975

Arkansas Community Foundation	$9,000.00
College of the Ozarks	$30,000.00
Department of Finance and Administration	$9,450.00
Election Laws Institute	$8,575.00
Episcopal Diocese of Arkansas (Rockwin)	$2,000.00
Governor's Economic Development Study Commission	$100,000.00.00
Group Homes (Rockwin)	$5,000.00
Independent Community Consultants	$5,342.00
Institute of International Education (Rockwin)	$2,500.00
Legal Aid Bureau of Pulaski County	$10,000.00
National Commerce Corporation (Rockwin)	$9,000.00
National Community Education Association	$62,306.00
National Merit Scholarship Corporation	$50,447.00
Pulaski County Council on Aging	$6,000.00
Scott Area Action Council (Rockwin)	$6,000.00
University of Arkansas, Little Rock	$26,784.00
Winrock International Livestock Research and Training Center	$100,000.00
Winthrop (Rockwin), City of,	$10,000.00
Winthrop Rockefeller Scholarships	$3,890.00
Youth Bridge (Rockwin)	$3,000.00
TOTAL	**$459,294.00**

1976

Arkansas Community Foundation	$50,000.00
Arkansas State University, Beebe	$25,000.00
Charter House Tenants	$6,100.00
College of the Ozarks and Arkansas College	$30,000.00
Department of Local Services	$50,000.00
Independent Community Consultants	$597.75
Little Rock Chamber of Commerce Foundation	$5,000.00
NAACP, Legal Defense Fund	$50,000.00
National Community Education Association	$93,000.00
National Merit Scholarship Corporation	$51,509.00
National Wildlife Federation	$15,000.00
Neighborhood Housing Services	$10,000.00
Pulaski County Council on Aging	$20,000.00
Rural Development Discretionary Fund	$15,000.00
Save the Children, Community Development Fund	$20,000.00
University of Arkansas for Medical Sciences	$30,259.00
University of Arkansas, Little Rock	$19,105.00
University of Arkansas, Little Rock	$37,165.00
Winthrop Rockefeller Scholarships	$3,859.50
TOTAL	**$531,595.25**

1977

Arkansas Advocates for Children and Families	$34,000.00
Arkansas College	$10,000.00
Arkansas Community Foundation	$50,000.00
Arkansas Issues	$45,000.00
Arkansas Library Commission	$22,000.00
College of the Ozarks	$6,000.00
Community Council of Central Arkansas	$58,150.00
Department of Local Services	$15,649.00
Election Laws Institute	$5,335.00
Independent Community Consultants	$2,437.00
Independent Community Consultants	$4,000.00

Independent Community Consultants	$850.00
Independent Community Consultants	$9,110.00
Little Rock, City of,	$500.00
Little Rock Public Schools	$3,300.00
National Merit Scholarship Corporation	$43,387.00
Rural Community Education Project	$100,000.00
University of Arkansas for Medical Sciences	$30,765.00
University of Arkansas	$48,369.00
Winthrop Rockefeller Scholarships	$3,905.00
Youth Home	$14,450.00
TOTAL	**$507,207.00**

1978

Arkansas Community Foundation	$50,000.00
Arkansas Issues	$31,000.00
Arkansas College	$10,000.00
Arkansas College	$54,400.00
Department of Local Services	$20,000.00
Department of Natural and Cultural Heritage	$10,000.00
Arkansas Consumer Research	$360.00
Arkansas Consumer Research	$1,000.00
Arkansas Repertory Theater	$21,380.00
Arkansas State University	$35,800.00
ARVAC (Rural Industries)	$43,939.00
CARTI, Central Arkansas Radiation Therapy Institute	$42,050.00
Heifer Project International	$40,000.00
Human Service Providers Association of Arkansas	$68,443.00
Independent Community Consultants	$402.00
Institute of Cultural Affairs	$1,000.00
Little Rock Panel of American Women	$3,604.00
Little Rock Public Schools	$16,800.00
Little Rock Public Schools	$900.00
Little Rock Public Schools	$1,000.00
National Merit Scholarship Corporation	$47,533.00
Neighborhood Housing Services	$15,000.00
Ozark Action	$3,750.00
Save the Children	$90,000.00
Southern Arkansas University	$1,000.00
University of Arkansas	$10,000.00
University of Arkansas, Little Rock	$3,030.00
University of Arkansas, Little Rock	$17,660.00
Urban League of Greater Little Rock, GYST House	$950.00
Urban League of Greater Little Rock, GYST House	$46,090.00

Wilderness Society	$900.00
Winthrop Rockefeller Scholarships	$3,905.00
Youth Program Development	$7,596.00
TOTAL	**$699,492.00**

1979

Arkansas Advocates for Children and Families	$17,500.00
Arkansas Business Development Corporation	$4,900.00
Arkansas Business Development Corporation	$31,477.00
Arkansas College	$925.00
Arkansas Community Education Development Association	$5,000.00
Arkansas Community Foundation	$120,000.00
Arkansas Consumer Research	$1,000.00
Arkansas Consumer Research	$29,726.00
Arkansas Consumer Research	$1,000.00
Arkansas Family Day-Care Providersfor Quality Child Care	$11,000.00
Arkansas Issues	$88,000.00
Arkansas Opera Theatre	$2,746.00
Arkansas State University	$43,542.00
ARVAC (Rural Industries)	$41,505.00
CARTI, Central Arkansas Radiation Therapy Institute	$20,000.00
Criminal Justice Institute	$48,000.00
Department of Correction	$5,000.00
Department of Education	$106,400.00
Department of Health	$5,000.00
Department of Health	$20,000.00
Department of Natural and Cultural Heritage	$50,000.00
Health Center of Pulaski County	$19,513.00
Human Service Providers Association of Arkansas	$66,027.00
Human Service Providers Association of Arkansas	$20,543.00
Independent Community Consultants	$5,700.00
Little Rock Public Schools	$1,620.00
Museum of Science and Natural History	$830.00
NAACP, Legal Defense Fund	$50,000.00
National Endowment for the Humanities	$12,000.00
National Endowment for the Humanities	$20,000.00
National Merit Scholarship Corporation	$27,705.00
Neighborhood Housing Services	$5,000.00
PEDCO	$100,000.00
Saving the Children (Arkansas Delta Project)	$90,000.00

Special Learning Center of Fort Smith	$20,000.00
Total Health Services	$15,000.00
University of Arkansas, Little Rock	$6,950.00
University of Arkansas for Medical Sciences	$14,000.00
University of Arkansas for Medical Sciences	$24,760.00
1979 Mini-grants (6)	$3,908.00
TOTAL	**$1,156,277.00**

1980

Arkansas Business Development Corporation	$38,947.00
Arkansas Coalition Against Domestic Violence	$17,131.00
Arkansas Community Education Development Association	$25,000.00
Arkansas Issues	$30,000.00
Arkansas Land and Farm Development Association	$35,500.00
Baptist Medical Center (Central Baptist)	$3,000.00
Camp Aldersgate	$45,737.00
Central Arkansas Area Agency on Aging	$1,500.00
Central Arkansas YWCA	$12,700.00
Criminal Justice Institute	$56,930.00
Department of Correction	$55,000.00
Department of Energy	$64,000.00
Department of Natural and Cultural Heritage	$50,000.00
Heifer Project International	$25,000.00
Human Service Providers Association of Arkansas	$21,128.00
Meadowcreek Project	$42,000.00
National Merit Scholarship Corporation	$18,005.00
National Wildlife Federation	$18,733.00
New Earth Health Center	$31,283.00
Ozark Legal Services	$12,200.00
Ozark Legal Services	$41,724.00
PEDCO	$100,000.00
Pulaski County Council on Aging	$24,809.00
Save the Children	$90,000.00
Union Medical Center	$54,625.00
United Methodist Church, Board of Global Ministries	$5,400.00
University of Arkansas	$62,290.00
University of Arkansas	$185,042.00
University of Arkansas for Medical Sciences	$53,820.00
Winrock International Livestock Research and Training Center	$40,559.00
Winrock International Livestock Research and Training Center	$15,000.00

Women's Education and Development Institute	$2,500.00
1980 Discretionary Grants (19)	$20,653.00
TOTAL	**$1,300,216.00**

1981

Arkansas Civil Liberties Foundation	$21,500.00
Arkansas Community Education Development Association	$25,000.00
Arkansas Community Foundation	$40,000.00
Arkansas Community Foundation	$75,000.00
Arkansas Delta Housing Development Corporation	$21,500.00
Arkansas Issues	$86,000.00
Boy Scouts of America, South Central Region	$44,171.00
Camp Aldersgate	$83,971.00
Center for Education and Communication	$32,010.00
Central Arkansas Area Agency on Aging	$19,845.00
Central Arkansas Legal Services	$33,691.00
Central Arkansas Library System	$15,421.00
Displaced Homemakers Network	$36,200.00
Fayetteville Open Channel	$5,615.00
Friends of KLRE-FM	$22,500.00
Heifer Project International	$25,000.00
Independent Community Consultants	$5,000.00
Independent Community Consultants	$30,868.00
Little Rock Public Schools	$3,546.00
Little Rock Public Schools	$45,122.00
Meadowcreek Project	$59,000.00
Morris-Booker Memorial College	$28,567.00
National Homecaring Council	$12,500.00
National Merit Scholarship Corporation	$8,645.00
Nature Conservancy	$250,000.00
Ozark Legal Services	$14,552.00
Southeast Arkansas Educational Cooperative	$25,000.00
Southwest Arkansas Educational Cooperative	$25,000.00
State Council on Economic Education	$15,000.00
Union Medical Center	$25,108.00
United Methodist Church	$14,100.00
United Way of Pulaski County	$12,542.00
University of Arkansas	$86,000.00
University of Arkansas	$65,239.00
University of Arkansas, Little Rock	$30,400.00
Violet Hill School District #1	$27,561.00
Winrock International Livestock Research and Training Center	$4,500.00

Winrock International Livestock Research and Training Center	$53,000.00
1981 Discretionary Grants (30)	$27,078.00
TOTAL	**$1,455,752.00**

1982

Arkansas Advocates for Children and Families	$33,983.00
Arkansas Coalition for the Handicapped	$20,000.00
Arkansas Community Education Development Association	$10,000.00
Arkansas Community Education Development Association	$25,000.00
Arkansas Community Foundation	$10,000.00
Arkansas Community Foundation	$41,138.00
Arkansas Family Planning Council	$53,500.00
Arkansas Interfaith Hunger Task Force	$5,000.00
Arkansas Interfaith Hunger Task Force	$25,000.00
Arkansas Land and Farm Development Corporation	$66,200.00
Arkansas League for Nursing	$5,000.00
Camp Mitchell, Camp and Conference Center	$26,300.00
Central Arkansas Legal Services	$35,345.00
Dartmouth College	$5,800.00
Ecocenter	$7,556.00
Fayetteville Open Channel	$5,000.00
Friends of KLRE-FM	$14,500.00
Heifer Project International	$25,000.00
Human Service Providers Association of Arkansas	$21,050.00
Little Rock Public Schools	$47,077.00
Meadowcreek Project	$57,000.00
Morris-Booker Memorial College	$37,704.00
National Homecaring Council	$17,500.00
Pathfinder Schools	$4,196.00
Presbyterian Urban Council	$50,000.00
Save the Children, Arkansas Delta Project	$31,887.00
Southeast Arkansas Educational Cooperative	$25,000.00
Southern Coalition for Educational Equity	$31,000.00
Southwest Arkansas Educational Cooperative	$25,000.00
United Methodist Church	$45,000.00
United Way of Pulaski County	$24,854.00
University of Arkansas	$22,000.00
University of Arkansas	$70,028.00
University of Arkansas, Little Rock	$65,144.00
University of Arkansas, Little Rock	$25,366.00
University of Arkansas, Little Rock	$15,200.00
University of Arkansas for Medical Sciences	$88,108.00
Wilton, City of,	$15,000.00
1982 Discretionary Grants (17)	$16,212.00
TOTAL	**$1,148,648.00**

1983

Archaeological Conservancy	$1,000.00
Arkansas Advocates for Children and Families	$32,942.00
Arkansas Advocates for Children and Families	$6,100.00
Arkansas Bureau of Legislative Research	$788.00
Arkansas Coalition for the Handicapped	$20,445.00
Arkansas Community Education Development Association	$600.00
Arkansas Community Foundation	$20,000.00
Arkansas Community Foundation	$6,928.00
Arkansas Delta Housing Development Corporation	$59,382.00
Arkansas Department of Education	$15,370.00
Arkansas Department of Higher Education	$24,943.00
Arkansas Endowment for the Humanities/Humanities Council	$1,000.00
Arkansas Family Planning Council	$86,135.00
Arkansas Interfaith Hunger Task Force	$30,000.00
Arkansas Issues	$71,952.00
Arkansas Justice Foundation	$1,000.00
Arkansas Land and Farm Development Corporation	$98,000.00
Central Arkansas Area Agency on Aging	$1,000.00
Central Arkansas Legal Services	$34,398.00
College Station Community Development Fund	$15,000.00
Criminal Justice Ministries	$52,000.00
Economic Development Agency	$1,000.00
Economic Opportunity Agency	$1,950.00
Heifer Project International	$4,000.00
Historic Preservation Alliance of Arkansas	$125,555.00
Human Service Providers Association of Arkansas	$1,000.00
Human Service Providers Association of Arkansas	$1,000.00
Independent Community Consultants	$900.00
Kiwanis Activities of Little Rock	$28,204.00
Life Options Program	$5,129.00
Literacy Council of Pulaski County	$500.00

Little Rock Public Schools	$25,266.00
Manpower Demonstration Research Corporation	$50,000.00
Mississippi Action for Community Education	$1,000.00
Morris-Booker Memorial College	$40,968.00
Nature Conservancy	$350,000.00
Ouachita Baptist University	$11,650.00
Ozark Guidance Center	$1,000.00
Peace Links Worldwide	$55,000.00
Quapaw Quarter Association	$1,000.00
Southeast Arkansas Educational Cooperative	$25,000.00
Southern Arkansas University	$1,000.00
Southern Arkansas University	$7,500.00
Southwest Arkansas Educational Cooperative	$25,000.00
Stepping Stone	$800.00
United Methodist Church	$43,600.00
United Way of Pulaski County	$22,187.00
University of Arkansas for Medical Sciences	$99,961.00
University of Arkansas Foundation	$1,000.00
University of Arkansas	$10,000.00
University of Arkansas	$2,000.00
University of Arkansas	$950.00
University of Arkansas, Little Rock	$1,000.00
University of Arkansas, Little Rock	$160,238.00
University of Arkansas, Little Rock	$22,392.00
University of Arkansas, Little Rock	$28,992.00
University of Arkansas, Little Rock	$4,575.00
University of Arkansas, Little Rock	$41,620.00
University of Arkansas, Little Rock	$57,423.00
University of Arkansas, Little Rock	$67,209.00
University of Arkansas, Little Rock	$68,800.00
University of Arkansas, Little Rock	$7,050.00
University of Arkansas, Little Rock	$939.00
University of Central Arkansas	$1,000.00
University of Central Arkansas	$1,000.00
University of Central Arkansas	$1,000.00
University of Central Arkansas	$1,000.00
Wilowe Institute	$1,000.00
Wilowe Institute	$53,980.00
Youth Bridge	$1,000.00
TOTAL	**$2,043,321.00**

1984

American Indian Center of Arkansas	$1,000.00
Arkansas Advocates for Children and Families	$17,337.00
Arkansas Arts Council	$1,000.00
Arkansas Association of Conservation Districts	$1,000.00

Arkansas Coalition for the Handicapped	$20,000.00
Arkansas Council for International Visitors	$1,000.00
Arkansas Delta Housing Development Corporation	$40,000.00
Arkansas Department of Higher Education	$12,450.00
Arkansas Department of Higher Education	$800.00
Arkansas Department of Parks and Tourism	$450.00
Arkansas Educational Television Network	$1,000.00
Arkansas Endowment for the Humanities/Humanities Council	$1,000.00
Arkansas Endowment for the Humanities/Humanities Council	$1,000.00
Arkansas Endowment for the Humanities/Humanities Council	$1,000.00
Arkansas Endowment for the Humanities/Humanities Council	$1,000.00
Arkansas Family Planning Council	$94,749.00
Arkansas Foodbank Network	$1,000.00
Arkansas Historical Association	$25,000.00
Arkansas Interfaith Hunger Task Force	$1,000.00
Arkansas Interfaith Hunger Task Force	$24,900.00
Arkansas Interfaith Hunger Task Force	$30,000.00
Arkansas Issues	$105,160.00
Arkansas Land and Farm Development Corporation	$1,000.00
Birdsong, City of,	$925.00
Boys', Girls', Adults' Community Development Center	$8,700.00
Camden, City of,	$1,000.00
Carroll County Learning Center	$500.00
College Station YMCA	$7,000.00
Cornucopia Project	$37,028.00
Delta Foundation	$73,500.00
Economic Development Agency of Lonoke	$20,000.00
Economic Opportunity Agency of Washington County	$1,000.00
Economic Opportunity Agency of Washington County	$2,450.00
First House Training/Economic Development Center	$1,000.00
Friends of the Zoo	$1,000.00
Interfaith Community Center	$1,000.00
Jefferson City Recreation Association	$1,000.00
LaGrange, City of,	$540.00
League of Women Voters Education Fund	$1,000.00

Literacy Council of Polk County	$1,000.00	Arkansas Coalition for the Handicapped	$20,750.00
Manpower Demonstration Corporation	$60,000.00	Arkansas Community Foundation	$20,000.00
Meadowcreek Project	$54,000.00	Arkansas Delta Housing Development Corporation	$20,000.00
Nature Conservancy	$250,000.00	Arkansas Department of Education	$15,000.00
Nonprofit Resources	$6,000.00	Arkansas Department of Education	$20,176.00
Parent Center	$37,260.00	Arkansas Educational Television Network	$196,488.00
Peace Links Worldwide	$55,000.00		
Philander Smith College	$76,550.00	Arkansas Endowment for the Humanities/Humanities Council	$3,000.00
Planned Parenthood Federation	$1,000.00	Arkansas Family Planning Council	$16,500.00
Police Chaplaincy Program	$1,000.00	Arkansas Federated Children	$4,627.00
Pulaski Heights Presbyterian Church	$24,838.00	Arkansas Human Development Corporation	$30,000.00
Radio Station KABF	$750.00	Arkansas Hunger Project	$8,437.00
Service Corps of Retired Executives	$1,000.00	Arkansas Land and Farm Development Corporation	$80,670.00
Service Corps of Retired Executives	$2,000.00		
Southern Arkansas University	$39,851.00	Augusta Public Schools	$10,000.00
Southern Coalition for Educational Equity	$29,000.00	Bay Public Schools	$10,000.00
		Benton Public Schools	$10,000.00
St. Luke African Methodist Church	$6,400.00	Board of Global Ministries	$22,900.00
Texarkana School District	$8,500.00	Boys', Girls', Adults' Community Development Center	$21,000.00
United Methodist Church	$25,000.00		
United Way of Pulaski County	$16,060.00	Cabot Public Schools	$2,000.00
University of Arkansas for Medical Sciences	$93,236.00	College Station Community Development Program	$20,500.00
University of Arkansas Foundation	$10,000.00	College Station YMCA	$4,000.00
University of Arkansas Foundation	$2,000.00	Crowley's Ridge Educational Service Cooperative	$2,000.00
University of Arkansas	$10,000.00		
University of Arkansas, Little Rock	$15,000.00	Danville Public Schools	$1,800.00
University of Arkansas, Little Rock	$17,700.00	Danville Public Schools	$10,000.00
University of Arkansas, Little Rock	$19,822.00	Dardanelle Public Schools	$10,000.00
University of Arkansas, Little Rock	$59,465.00	Dardanelle Public Schools	$2,000.00
University of Arkansas, Little Rock	$60,200.00	Dawson Education Service Cooperative	$10,000.00
University of Arkansas, Little Rock	$64,693.00	Dermott Concerned Citizens	$8,000.00
University of Arkansas, Water Resources Research Center	$1,000.00	Fayetteville Public Schools	$10,000.00
Urban League of Arkansas	$1,000.00	Focus	$17,550.00
Voter Education Project	$20,000.00	Gould Community Service Corporation	$10,000.00
Watershed II	$1,000.00		
Wilowe Institute	$37,000.00	Historic Preservation Alliance, Main Street Arkansas	$68,375.00
TOTAL	**$1,647,814.00**	Hot Springs School District	$2,000.00

1985

Americans for Civic Participation, Project Vote	$38,000.00	League of Women Voters Education Fund	$5,000.00
Arkansas ABLE	$17,525.00	Little Rock Panel	$32,152.00
Arkansas ABLE	$22,112.00	Little Rock Public Schools	$1,530.00
Arkansas Advocates for Children and Families	$4,910.00	Little Rock Public Schools	$1,784.00
		Little Rock Public Schools	$1,989.00
Arkansas Association of LeadAR Alumni	$5,000.00	Manpower Demonstration Research Corporation	$40,000.00
Arkansas Coalition Against Violence to Women and Children	$19,965.00	Meadowcreek Project	$46,000.00
		Nature Conservancy	$300,000.00

Nonprofit Resources	$14,910.00
Nonprofit Resources	$4,959.00
North Crossett Elementary School	$2,000.00
North Little Rock Public Schools	$2,000.00
Ozarks Unlimited Resources	$2,000.00
Parent Center	$34,355.00
Peace Links Worldwide	$49,500.00
Philander Smith College	$50,800.00
Pulaski County Special School District	$10,000.00
Pulaski Heights Presbyterian Church	$21,065.00
Pulaski Heights Presbyterian Church, Home Grown Markets	$30,750.00
Russellville School District	$9,996.00
Sheridan Public Schools	$63,105.00
Southern Arkansas University	$41,400.00
Sparkman Public Schools	$2,000.00
United Methodist Church	$20,000.00
University of Arkansas, Little Rock	$12,900.00
University of Arkansas, Little Rock	$123,445.00
University of Arkansas, Little Rock	$43,000.00
University of Arkansas, Monticello	$10,000.00
Voter Education Project	$20,000.00
Walnut Ridge School District	$1,434.00
West Fork Public Schools	$1,950.00
Western Arkansas Education Cooperative	$7,800.00
Wilowe Institute	$16,500.00
Winrock International	$8,875.00
1985 Discretionary Grants (29)	$28,300.00
TOTAL	**$1,856,784.00**

1986

Advocates for Battered Women	$1,000.00
AFACT	$459.00
American Association of Retired Persons	$180.00
American Indian Center of Arkansas	$1,000.00
Americans for Civic Participation, Project Vote	$65,320.00
Archaeological Conservancy	$1,000.00
Arkansas (handbook for deputy registrars)	$1,000.00
Arkansas Advocates for Children and Families	$1,000.00
Arkansas Advocates for Children and Families	$35,530.00
Arkansas Broadcasting Foundation	$28,075.00
Arkansas Community Foundation	$108,371.00
Arkansas Community Foundation	$24,984.00
Arkansas Community Foundation	$500.00
Arkansas Conference of Churches and Synagogues	$41,500.00

Arkansas Cultural Enterprises	$1,000.00
Arkansas Department of Education	$11,107.00
Arkansas Department of Education	$14,085.00
Arkansas Endowment for the Humanities/Humanities Council	$1,000.00
Arkansas Enterprise Group	$1,000,000.00
Arkansas Human Development Corporation	$1,000.00
Arkansas Institute for Social Justice	$20,000.00
Arkansas Land and Farm Development Corporation	$42,260.00
Arkansas Tech University	$8,000.00
ARVAC (Rural Industries)	$10,000.00
Augusta Public Schools	$10,000.00
Bay Public Schools	$10,000.00
Benton Public Schools	$10,000.00
Boys', Girls', Adults' Community Development Center	$1,000.00
Boys', Girls', Adults' Community Development Center	$18,000.00
Bryant Public Schools	$850.00
College Station Community Development Fund	$20,500.00
College Station YMCA	$2,000.00
Community Resource Group	$23,800.00
Council on Foundations	$500.00
Danville Public Schools	$10,000.00
Dardanelle Public Schools	$10,000.00
Dawson Education Service Cooperative	$10,000.00
Deer Consolidated Schools	$10,000.00
Delta Foundation	$1,000.00
Delta Improvement Corporation	$47,057.00
Economic Opportunity Agency of Washington County	$1,000.00
Environmental Policy Institute	$10,000.00
Fayetteville Public Schools	$10,000.00
Heckatoo Heritage Foundation	$1,000.00
Heifer Project International	$19,050.00
Hendrix College	$2,710.00
Historic Preservation Alliance of Arkansas	$57,125.00
Hugh O'Brian Youth Foundation	$500.00
Institute for Industrial and Commercial Ministries	$1,000.00
Jonesboro Public Schools	$2,000.00
League of Women Voters Education Fund	$4,000.00
Literacy Council of Jefferson County	$26,138.00
Literacy Council of Pulaski County	$1,000.00
Little Rock Panel	$11,800.00
Little Rock Panel	$20,000.00
Little Rock Public Schools	$10,000.00

Meadowcreek Project	$32,850.00
Meadowcreek Project	$50,000.00
National Council of Negro Women	$500.00
Nonprofit Resources	$2,666.00
Nonprofit Resources	$23,539.00
Old State House	$1,000.00
Ozark Institute	$1,000.00
Ozark Institute	$38,496.00
Parent Center	$34,276.00
Partnership for the Future	$15,000.00
Peace Links Worldwide	$44,550.00
Perryville Public Schools	$30,000.00
Philander Smith College	$33,590.00
Phillips County Community College	$1,000.00
Presbytery of Arkansas	$55,714.00
Pulaski Activity Center	$10,000.00
Pulaski County Paratransit System	$1,000.00
Pulaski County Special School District	$10,000.00
Regenerative Agriculture Project	$62,930.00
Russellville School District	$4,979.00
SEARK Concert of the Arts	$1,000.00
Sheridan Public Schools	$110,855.00
Southeast Arkansas Arts and Science Center	$1,000.00
Southern Arkansas University	$40,993.00
Southern Development Bancorporation	$2,850,000.00
Springdale School District	$10,000.00
Springdale School District	$2,000.00
Texarkana, City of,	$1,000.00
Trumann Public Schools	$1,000.00
University of Arkansas	$900.00
University of Arkansas, Little Rock	$1,000.00
University of Arkansas, Little Rock	$1,000.00
University of Arkansas, Little Rock	$146,856.00
University of Arkansas, Little Rock	$15,000.00
University of Arkansas, Little Rock	$40,298.00
University of Arkansas, Little Rock	$44,362.00
University of Arkansas, Little Rock	$51,600.00
University of Arkansas, Little Rock	$900.00
University of Arkansas, Little Rock	$950.00
University of Central Arkansas	$1,000.00
Urban League of Arkansas	$22,144.00
Urban League of Greater Little Rock	$1,000.00
Van Buren Public Schools	$500.00
Western Arkansas Education Service Cooperative	$10,000.00
Wilowe Institute	$41,500.00
Winrock International	$30,000.00
Wolf-Kelly Community Development Council	$10,000.00

Women's Project	$20,000.00
TOTAL	**$5,690,349.00**

1987

Agenda for Tax Reform in Arkansas	$3,444.00
Amity Public Schools	$10,000.00
Arkansas Advocates for Children and Families	$1,000.00
Arkansas Advocates for Children and Families	$24,728.00
Arkansas Advocates for Children and Families	$41,954.00
Arkansas Broadcasting Foundation	$6,379.00
Arkansas Chapter, National Association of Minority Contractors	$6,000.00
Arkansas Children's Hospital	$1,000.00
Arkansas Community Foundation	$1,000.00
Arkansas Community Foundation	$36,747.00
Arkansas Community Foundation	$50,000.00
Arkansas Department of Education	$11,284.00
Arkansas Educational Television Network Foundation	$60,000.00
Arkansas Endowment for the Humanities/Humanities Council	$1,000.00
Arkansas Endowment for the Humanities/Humanities Council	$10,000.00
Arkansas Family Planning Council	$1,000.00
Arkansas Human Development Corporation	$15,000.00
Arkansas Human Development Corporation	$26,000.00
Arkansas Institute for Social Justice	$10,000.00
Arkansas Land and Farm Development Corporation	$35,816.00
Arkansas Museum of Science and History	$500.00
Arkansas Wildlife Federation	$5,551.00
Arts Live	$1,000.00
Ashdown School District	$1,080.00
Bay Public Schools	$10,000.00
Benton Public Schools	$1,200.00
Benton Public Schools	$10,000.00
Blytheville School District	$2,000.00
Boy Scouts of America, National Council	$1,000.00
Boys', Girls', Adults' Community Development Center	$15,000.00
Bryant Public Schools	$520.00
Cabot Public Schools	$1,500.00
Cats Climb	$10,000.00
College Station Community Development Fund	$20,000.00
Conway Public Schools	$1,200.00
Conway Public Schools	$2,000.00

Council on Foundations	$500.00	National Association of State Boards of Education	$7,910.00
Crossett Public Schools	$1,000.00	National Federation of Parents for Drug-Free Youth	$1,000.00
Dardanelle Public Schools	$800.00	Nonprofit Resources	$20,000.00
Deer Consolidated Schools	$10,000.00	Nonprofit Resources	$35,272.00
Delta Improvement Corporation	$1,000.00	North Little Rock Public Schools	$1,500.00
Delta Improvement Corporation	$32,276.00	North Little Rock Public Schools	$1,610.00
Department of Arkansas Heritage	$40,236.00	Ouachita Girl Scout Council	$1,000.00
DeQueen Mena Education Service Cooperative	$2,000.00	Ozark Regional Land Trust	$8,345.00
Division of Vocational Education	$35,000.00	Partnership for the Future	$1,000.00
Domestic and Foreign Missionary Society	$1,000.00	Peace Links Worldwide	$40,095.00
Drew Central School District	$2,000.00	Perryville Public Schools	$30,000.00
Economic Development in Arkansas: Obstacles and Opportunities	$17,721.00	Pine Bluff Public Schools	$1,000.00
Educational Reform Study	$148,495.00	Presbytery of Arkansas	$55,700.00
El Dorado Public Schools	$1,500.00	Pulaski Activity Center	$13,446.00
Eureka Springs School District	$1,000.00	Pulaski County Special School District	$1,200.00
Family Service Agency of Central Arkansas	$24,070.00	Pulaski County Special School District	$500.00
Fayetteville Public Schools	$1,000.00	Pulaski County Special School District	$673.00
Fayetteville Public Schools	$600.00	Rodale Institute	$29,750.00
Federation of Small Towns	$10,000.00	Rogers Junior Auxiliary	$1,000.00
Fort Smith Public Schools	$1,500.00	Rural Special School District	$2,000.00
Friends of KLRE-FM	$20,000.00	Russellville School District	$603.00
Fulbright, J. William (documentary biography)	$5,885.00	Sheridan Public Schools	$165,549.00
Grady School District	$400.00	South Conway County School District	$1,000.00
Health Care: The Crisis in Arkansas	$16,495.00	Southern Arkansas University	$35,326.00
Heifer Project International	$20,000.00	Southern Development Bancorporation	$250,000.00
Henderson State University	$14,450.00	Springdale School District	$10,000.00
Jasper School District	$1,290.00	Stuttgart Public Schools	$1,100.00
JOBS, Inc.	$29,100.00	University of Arkansas for Medical Sciences	$18,350.00
Jonesboro Public Schools	$1,000.00	University of Arkansas Foundation	$25,000.00
League of Women Voters Education Fund	$5,700.00	University of Arkansas	$1,000.00
Lee County School District	$44,975.00	University of Arkansas	$1,000.00
Lincoln Consolidated Schools	$2,000.00	University of Arkansas	$19,085.00
Literacy Council of Jefferson County	$26,138.00	University of Arkansas	$2,500.00
Literacy Council of Jefferson County	$600.00	University of Arkansas, Little Rock	$1,000.00
Little Rock Public Schools	$1,000.00	University of Arkansas, Little Rock	$1,000.00
Little Rock Public Schools	$1,500.00	University of Arkansas, Little Rock	$15,000.00
Little Rock Public Schools	$2,000.00	University of Arkansas, Little Rock	$40,678.00
Little Rock Public Schools	$2,000.00	University of Arkansas, Little Rock	$43,039.00
Little Rock Public Schools	$5,000.00	University of Arkansas, Little Rock	$58,400.00
Lonoke Public Schools	$1,356.00	Urban League of Arkansas	$13,024.00
Mid-America Museum	$1,000.00	Urban League of Greater Little Rock	$20,000.00
Mid-South Astronomical Research Society	$1,000.00	Warren School District	$835.00
Mount Saint Mary Academy	$1,500.00	Watson, City of,	$1,000.00
NAACP	$1,000.00	Wilowe Institute	$22,000.00
Nashville School District	$500.00	Winrock International	$50,000.00

Women's Project	$1,000.00
Yellville Summit School District	$1,500.00
TOTAL	**$2,024,480.00**

1988

American Planning Association	$1,350.00
Amity Public Schools	$1,000.00
Arkansas (domestic violence)	$550.00
Arkansas ABLE	$23,150.00
Arkansas Advocates for Children and Families	$26,578.00
Arkansas Advocates for Children and Families	$7,500.00
Arkansas Coalition Against Violence to Women and Children	$17,995.00
Arkansas Coalition for the Handicapped	$38,270.00
Arkansas Community Foundation	$10,000.00
Arkansas Community Foundation	$14,800.00
Arkansas Community Foundation	$35,100.00
Arkansas Community Foundation	$50,000.00
Arkansas Enterprise Group	$1,000,000.00
Arkansas Enterprise Group	$250,000.00
Arkansas Human Development Corporation	$26,000.00
Arkansas Institute for Social Justice	$46,820.00
Arkansas Institute for Social Justice	$5,000.00
Arkansas Land and Farm Development Corporation	$29,000.00
Arkansas Repertory Theater	$500.00
Arkansas Repertory Theater	$900,000.00
Arkansas Revenue Report	$11,064.00
Arkansas Rice Depot	$1,000.00
Arkansas School for the Deaf	$1,500.00
Arkansas School Reform Study	$102,884.00
Arkansas Seniors Organized for Progress	$15,000.00
Arkansas Soil and Water Conservation Commission	$18,000.00
Arkansas State University	$1,000.00
Arkansas Tech University	$300.00
Arkansas Wildlife Federation	$500.00
Ashley County Adult Education	$2,000.00
Beebe Public Schools	$1,330.00
Blevins, City of,	$7,500.00
Boys', Girls', Adults' Community Development Center	$2,000.00
Boys', Girls', Adults' Community Development Center	$30,000.00
Bradford Special School District	$1,000.00
Camden School District	$16,130.00
CARTI Foundation	$2,000.00
Central Arkansas Legal Services	$1,640.00
Council on Foundations	$500.00

Criminal Justice Ministry of Arkansas	$1,000.00
Crossett Public Schools	$1,000.00
Crossett Public Schools	$7,622.00
Danville Public Schools	$10,000.00
Dardanelle Public Schools	$1,000.00
Dardanelle Public Schools	$1,000.00
Dardanelle Public Schools	$30,000.00
Dawson Educational Cooperative	$10,000.00
Deer Consolidated Schools	$10,000.00
Delta Community Development Corporation	$10,000.00
Delta Improvement Corporation	$24,034.00
Earle School District	$1,500.00
East Arkansas Community College	$2,000.00
Economic Opportunity Agency of Washington County	$1,000.00
Edukashun: The High Cost of Failure	$41,880.00
Edutainment, Video Distribution	$8,236.00
El Dorado Public Schools	$1,000.00
El Dorado Public Schools	$1,000.00
ElderCare of Eastern Arkansas	$10,000.00
Eureka Springs School District	$1,500.00
Fayetteville Public Schools	$1,000.00
Fayetteville Public Schools	$1,000.00
Fayetteville Public Schools	$10,000.00
Fayetteville Public Schools	$762.00
Forrest City Public Schools	$1,500.00
Fort Smith Public Schools	$1,000.00
Fort Smith Symphony	$2,000.00
Friends of KLRE-FM	$15,000.00
Gould Public Schools	$1,000.00
Gould Public Schools	$1,000.00
Grassroots Leadership	$20,089.00
Green Forest School District	$2,000.00
Harrison School District	$1,000.00
Helena-West Helena School District	$29,976.00
Henderson State University	$15,173.00
Hendrix College	$42,200.00
Historic Preservation Alliance of Arkansas	$37,000.00
Holly Grove Educational Club	$7,500.00
Hospice of the Ozarks	$1,000.00
Huntsville School District	$2,000.00
Institute for Educational Leadership	$10,000.00
JOBS	$2,000.00
JOBS	$29,100.00
Jonesboro Public Schools	$2,000.00
Kensett Special School District	$1,200.00
Kirby Public Schools	$1,250.00
Kiwanis Activities of Little Rock	$30,000.00

Lake View School District	$1,000.00
Lee County Conservation District	$1,000.00
Lee County School District	$38,000.00
Literacy Council of Pulaski County	$1,000.00
Literacy Council of Pulaski County	$1,635.00
Little Rock Panel of American Women	$2,000.00
Little Rock Panel	$30,000.00
Little Rock Public Schools	$1,000.00
Little Rock Public Schools	$1,000.00
Little Rock Public Schools	$1,000.00
Little Rock Public Schools	$1,200.00
Little Rock Public Schools	$1,961.00
Little Rock Public Schools	$2,000.00
Little Rock Public Schools	$500.00
Little Rock Public Schools	$55,000.00
Little Rock Public Schools	$600.00
Lonoke Public Schools	$1,000.00
Lonoke Public Schools	$1,000.00
Lonoke Public Schools	$30,000.00
Malvern Public Schools	$900.00
Meadowcreek Project	$2,000.00
Meadowcreek Project	$50,000.00
Mena Public Schools	$1,000.00
Mid-South Astronomical Research Society	$2,000.00
Mount Holly School District	$1,995.00
Murfreesboro Public Schools	$1,000.00
NAACP, Fair Share	$1,500.00
Nonprofit Resources	$25,000.00
North Little Rock Public Schools	$1,000.00
Okolona Love Council	$7,500.00
Our Lady of Holy Souls	$1,000.00
Ozark Institute	$2,000.00
Ozark Regional Land Trust	$44,993.00
Ozark Regional Land Trust	$992.00
Pea Ridge School District	$1,000.00
Pea Ridge School District	$940.00
Peace Links Worldwide	$35,982.00
Perryville Public Schools	$30,000.00
Philander Smith College	$1,000.00
Planned Parenthood of Arkansas	$29,250.00
Pulaski Activity Center	$10,000.00
Pulaski County Special School District	$550.00
Pulaski County Special School District	$905.00
Rape Crisis	$1,000.00
Rogers Public Schools	$1,000.00
Rogers Public Schools	$1,500.00
Russellville School District	$500.00
Save the Children Federation	$49,500.00

Searcy Public Schools	$816.00
Second Crisis in Little Rock	$9,776.00
Shepherd's Center of Southwest Little Rock	$1,000.00
Sheridan Public Schools	$155,000.00
South Arkansas Symphony	$2,000.00
Southern Education Foundation	$10,000.00
Springdale School District	$10,000.00
Texarkana School District	$775.00
Tri-County Community Center	$1,000.00
Tuckerman Public Schools	$1,000.00
University of Arkansas for Medical Sciences	$80,000.00
University of Arkansas Foundation	$25,000.00
University of Arkansas System	$64,000.00
University of Arkansas	$1,000.00
University of Arkansas	$10,600.00
University of Arkansas	$19,085.00
University of Arkansas	$2,000.00
University of Arkansas	$60,000.00
University of Arkansas, Little Rock	$1,000.00
University of Arkansas, Little Rock	$1,500.00
University of Arkansas, Little Rock	$14,400.00
University of Arkansas, Little Rock	$37,500.00
University of Arkansas, Little Rock	$40,000.00
University of Arkansas, Little Rock	$500.00
University of Arkansas, Little Rock	$800.00
University of Arkansas, Monticello	$2,000.00
Urban Family Outreach	$1,000.00
Valley Springs School District	$1,500.00
Vietnam Women's Memorial Project	$2,000.00
Washington County Juvenile Court	$12,500.00
Water for Arkansas's Future	$22,800.00
Watershed Human and Community Development Agency	$2,000.00
Western Arkansas Cooperative	$35,000.00
Wilowe Institute	$10,000.00
Wilowe Institute	$500.00
Witts Springs School District	$1,275.00
Women's Project	$40,043.00
Wrightsville, City of,	$7,500.00
Yellville Summit School District	$1,000.00
TOTAL	**$4,305,256.00**

1989

AFS International/Intercultural Programs	$750.00
American Center for International Leadership	$500.00
Arkansas ABLE	$9,704.00
Arkansas Advocates for Children and Families	$45,000.00
Arkansas AIDS Foundation	$2,000.00

Arkansas Arts Center	$1,000.00
Arkansas Citizen Participation	$49,630.00
Arkansas Coalition Against Violence to Women and Children	$9,185.00
Arkansas Coalition for the Handicapped	$30,770.00
Arkansas Community Foundation	$16,000.00
Arkansas Community Foundation	$2,000.00
Arkansas Community Foundation	$35,100.00
Arkansas Community Foundation	$50,000.00
Arkansas Department of Higher Education	$41,200.00
Arkansas Development Finance Authority	$1,000.00
Arkansas Enterprise Group	$250,000.00
Arkansas Institute for Social Justice	$36,000.00
Arkansas Institute for Social Justice	$734.00
Arkansas Museum of Science and History	$500.00
Arkansas Revenue Report	$4,481.00
Arkansas School Reform Study	$12,956.00
Arkansas Volunteer Lawyers for the Elderly	$500.00
Arkansas–Soviet Union Exchange	$10,000.00
Bald Knob School District	$28,630.00
Batesville School District	$1,000.00
Batesville School District	$515.00
Bentonville Public Schools	$950.00
Bismarck Public Schools	$900.00
Black Community Developers Program	$5,000.00
Blevins Public Schools	$1,700.00
Boys', Girls', Adults' Community Development Center	$2,000.00
Boys', Girls', Adults' Community Development Center	$27,000.00
Brookland Public Schools	$1,000.00
Cabot Public Schools	$1,000.00
Camden Housing Authority	$700.00
Camden School District	$11,570.00
CARTI Foundation	$3,000.00
Cedarville Public Schools	$1,000.00
Cedarville Public Schools	$514.00
Community Organization for Poverty Elimination (COPE)	$2,000.00
Conway Public Schools	$725.00
Council on Foundations	$500.00
County Line Public Schools	$25,320.00
Crossett Public Schools	$4,750.00
Dardanelle Public Schools	$30,000.00
Dawson Educational Cooperative	$10,000.00
Decatur Public Schools	$1,000.00
Delta Community Development Corporation	$68,500.00
Delta Improvement Corporation	$19,862.00
Dollarway School District	$1,000.00
Dollarway School District	$900.00
Domestic and Foreign Missionary Society	$2,000.00
Earle School District	$1,500.00
Edukashun: The High Cost of Failure	$21,483.00
Edutainment, Video Distribution	$13,880.00
Fayetteville Public Schools	$1,000.00
Fayetteville Public Schools	$280.00
Fayetteville Public Schools	$950.00
Forrest City Public Schools	$26,500.00
Forrest City Public Schools	$650.00
Fort Smith Public Schools	$1,000.00
Fort Smith Public Schools	$1,291.00
Fort Smith Public Schools	$2,000.00
Greenbrier Public Schools	$990.00
Harding University	$1,000.00
Helena, Main Street Helena	$2,000.00
Helena-West Helena School District	$30,015.00
Henderson State University	$15,932.00
Henderson State University	$2,000.00
Henderson State University	$51,240.00
Hendrix College	$41,950.00
Hot Springs School District	$1,000.00
Housing: The Low- to Moderate-Income Piece of the Puzzle	$12,000.00
Izard County Consolidated School District	$1,000.00
Junior Deputy Sheriffs of Pulaski County	$2,000.00
Kiwanis Activities of Little Rock	$2,000.00
Kiwanis Activities of Little Rock	$30,000.00
Learning Club of Southwest Arkansas	$10,000.00
Lee County Library	$2,000.00
Lee County	$2,000.00
Literacy Council of Pulaski County	$20,573.00
Little Rock Public Schools	$1,000.00
Little Rock Public Schools	$1,000.00
Little Rock Public Schools	$1,000.00
Little Rock Public Schools	$1,250.00
Little Rock Public Schools	$1,500.00
Little Rock Public Schools	$1,500.00
Little Rock Public Schools	$1,941.00
Little Rock Public Schools	$25,000.00
Little Rock Public Schools	$784.00
Lonoke County Task Force on Child Abuse and Neglect	$1,000.00
Lonoke Public Schools	$30,000.00
Marion School District	$500.00

Marion School District	$750.00
Meadowcreek Project	$50,000.00
Monticello School District	$1,000.00
Mountain Home School District	$1,000.00
Nashville School District	$1,500.00
National Conference of Christians and Jews	$1,695.00
National Conference of Christians and Jews	$2,000.00
Nettleton Public Schools	$1,000.00
Newton County Resource Council	$31,100.00
Nonprofit Resources	$15,000.00
Nonprofit Resources	$41,655.00
Norfork School District	$500.00
Northeast Arkansas School District	$1,000.00
Our Lady of Good Counsel School	$1,000.00
Ozark Regional Land Trust	$44,000.00
Pea Ridge School District	$800.00
Peace Links Worldwide	$1,000.00
Perryville Public Schools	$26,500.00
Pine Bluff Public Schools	$30,000.00
Pine Bluff Youth Services Center	$500.00
Plainview-Rover School District	$1,000.00
Plainview-Rover School District	$1,000.00
Planned Parenthood of Arkansas	$37,650.00
Pulaski County Special School District	$1,200.00
Pulaski County Special School District	$2,000.00
Pulaski County Special School District	$900.00
Pulaski County Special School District	$917.00
Rape Crisis	$1,500.00
Recycling and Integrated Solid Waste Management	$26,403.00
Reorganized Church of Jesus Christ of Latter Day Saints	$1,000.00
Rogers Public Schools	$1,000.00
Russellville School District	$35,746.00
Russellville School District	$500.00
Sandflat-Glendale Neighborhood Development Corporation	$10,000.00
Save the Children Federation	$50,000.00
Searcy County Airport Commission	$10,000.00
Second Crisis in Little Rock	$14,053.00
Serenity House	$2,000.00
Sheridan Public Schools	$1,000.00
Shirley Community Service and Development Corporation	$9,770.00
Siloam Springs Public Schools	$1,000.00
Soil and Water Conservation Commission	$13,450.00
Solutions	$2,000.00

Solutions	$46,303.00
Southeast Arkansas Economic Development District	$1,500.00
Southern Education Foundation	$17,500.00
Southern Growth Policy Board	$71,440.00
St. Francis County	$1,200.00
Talent Equal Access to Media (TEAM)	$2,000.00
Texarkana Regional Arts and Humanities Council	$25,000.00
Texarkana School District	$1,500.00
Tri-County Community Center	$10,000.00
University of Arkansas for Medical Sciences	$80,000.00
University of Arkansas Foundation	$15,000.00
University of Arkansas System	$28,333.00
University of Arkansas	$18,050.00
University of Arkansas	$60,000.00
University of Arkansas, Little Rock	$1,500.00
University of Arkansas, Little Rock	$32,500.00
University of Arkansas, Little Rock	$40,000.00
University of Arkansas, Little Rock	$500.00
University of Arkansas, Pine Bluff	$15,000.00
University of Arkansas, Pine Bluff	$5,000.00
University of Central Arkansas Foundation	$10,200.00
University of Central Arkansas	$1,000.00
University of North Carolina, Chapel Hill	$11,920.00
Viola Public Schools	$1,000.00
Washington County Juvenile Court	$4,000.00
Watershed Human and community Development Agency	$5,000.00
Watson Chapel School District	$1,670.00
Weiner Public Schools	$1,735.00
Western Arkansas Education Cooperative	$19,329.00
Women's Project	$37,419.00
TOTAL	**$2,268,443.00**

1990

Amendment 59—Education and Economic Development	$29,109.00
Arkadelphia Public Schools	$1,325.00
Arkansas (meeting of Technical Education Enhancement Commission)	$1,200.00
Arkansas (video to train poll workers)	$500.00
Arkansas Association of LeadAR Alumni	$10,000.00
Arkansas Aviation Historical Society	$500,000.00
Arkansas Aviation Historical Society	$54,000.00
Arkansas Children's Hospital	$2,000.00

Arkansas Coalition Against Violence to Women and Children	$22,170.00
Arkansas College	$41,300.00
Arkansas Community Foundation	$10,000.00
Arkansas Community Foundation	$13,000.00
Arkansas Community Foundation	$50,000.00
Arkansas Delta Law Foundation Corporation	$1,500.00
Arkansas Delta Law Foundation Corporation	$10,000.00
Arkansas Department of Education	$1,645.00
Arkansas Department of Education	$53,703.00
Arkansas Department of Health	$1,000.00
Arkansas Department of Higher Education	$37,100.00
Arkansas Disability Coalition	$10,000.00
Arkansas Enterprise Group	$250,000.00
Arkansas Institute for Social Justice	$28,000.00
Arkansas Land and Farm Development Corporation	$39,650.00
Arkansas Literacy Councils	$1,320.00
Arkansas Public Policy Panel	$2,000.00
Arkansas Rice Depot	$1,000.00
Arkansas State University	$2,000.00
Arkansas Tech University	$1,300.00
Arkansas Territorial Restoration Foundation	$1,500.00
Artisan Source	$10,000.00
Atkins Public Schools	$500.00
Augusta Public Schools	$846.00
Bald Knob School District	$24,000.00
Boys', Girls', Adults' Community Development Center	$10,000.00
Boys', Girls', Adults' Community Development Center	$24,000.00
Bryant Public Schools	$330.00
Cabot Public Schools	$982.00
Calico Rock Public Schools	$1,000.00
Camden School District	$11,570.00
Camden School District	$917.00
Center to Prevent Handgun Violence	$7,300.00
Centers for Youth and Families	$10,000.00
Close Up Foundation	$1,000.00
Commission for Arkansas's Future	$5,000.00
Council of Better Business Bureaus Foundation	$1,000.00
Council on Foundations	$500.00
County Line Public Schools	$26,950.00
Crossett Public Schools	$2,720.00
Dardanelle Public Schools	$30,000.00
Delta Community Development Corporation	$58,500.00
Dermott Community Action	$10,000.00
Dollarway School District	$592.00
Dollarway School District	$766.00
Dollarway School District	$966.00
Dream and the Mission	$27,057.00
Drew Central School District	$435.00
Dumas, City of,	$2,000.00
Edutainment, Video Distribution	$4,896.00
El Dorado Public Schools	$1,685.00
Emerson School District	$760.00
Emma Elease Webb Community Center	$10,000.00
Emmet Public Schools	$1,200.00
Fayetteville Public Schools	$2,000.00
Fayetteville Public Schools	$884.00
Financing Ozarks Rural Growth and Economy	$10,000.00
For Our Children and Us	$1,125.00
Forrest City Public Schools	$23,750.00
Fort Smith Public Schools	$1,000.00
Fort Smith Public Schools	$1,500.00
Fort Smith Public Schools	$2,000.00
Fort Smith Public Schools	$2,000.00
Fouke School District	$2,000.00
Future Builders	$10,000.00
Future Builders	$40,000.00
Grady School District	$780.00
Greene County Technical School District	$834.00
Hamburg School District	$1,500.00
Hector School District	$1,000.00
Helena-West Helena School District	$1,500.00
Helena-West Helena School District	$29,716.00
Henderson State University	$1,000.00
Henderson State University	$1,500.00
Henderson State University	$35,868.00
Hendrix College	$45,825.00
Housing: The Low- to Moderate-Income Piece of the Puzzle	$3,438.00
Increasing Philanthropy in Arkansas	$21,270.00
Jonesboro Public Schools	$1,000.00
Jonesboro Public Schools	$1,900.00
Junior Achievement	$2,000.00
Kirby Public Schools	$1,558.00
Kiwanis Activities of Little Rock	$30,000.00
Lakeside School District	$880.00
Learning Club of Southwest Arkansas	$10,000.00
Lee County School District	$28,125.00
Literacy Council of Pulaski County	$18,073.00
Little Rock Police Department	$2,000.00
Little Rock Port Authority	$2,000.00

Little Rock Public Schools	$1,936.00
Little Rock Public Schools	$2,000.00
Little Rock Public Schools	$42,500.00
Little Rock Public Schools	$500.00
Little Rock, City of,	$1,000.00
Little Rock, City of,	$700.00
Lonoke Public Schools	$30,000.00
Lonoke/Prairie County Regional Library System	$1,200.00
Marion School District	$1,000.00
Meadowcreek Project	$1,000.00
Meadowcreek Project	$50,000.00
Metroplan	$2,000.00
Metropolitan Education Services Center	$500.00
Minimum Performance Test and Teaching and Learning	$720.00
NAACP	$24,636.00
National Conference of Christians and Jews	$21,500.00
National Conference of Christians and Jews	$700.00
National Society of Fund Raising Executives	$500.00
Nettleton Public Schools	$808.00
Newark School District	$1,000.00
Newton County Resource Council	$30,550.00
Nonprofit Resources	$39,660.00
Norfork School District	$1,535.00
Northeast Arkansas School District	$1,350.00
Oak Ridge Associated Universities	$2,000.00
Ozark Recycling Enterprise	$45,000.00
Ozark Regional Land Trust	$44,900.00
Perryville Public Schools	$27,000.00
Philander Smith College	$217,000.00
Pine Bluff Public Schools	$1,361.00
Pine Bluff Public Schools	$30,000.00
Pine Bluff Public Schools	$900.00
Project Raft	$2,000.00
Pulaski County Special School District	$1,900.00
Pulaski County Special School District	$26,878.00
Reading is Fundamental	$10,000.00
Recycling and Integrated Solid Waste Management	$18,598.00
Russellville School District	$700.00
Searcy County Airport Commission	$50,000.00
Service Corps of Retired Executives	$1,000.00
Sheridan Public Schools	$2,000.00
Shirley Community Service and Development Corporation	$24,920.00
Siloam Springs Public Schools	$325.00
Southeast Arkansas Arts and Science Center	$2,000.00
Southeast Arkansas Educational Cooperative	$2,000.00
Southern Arkansas University	$39,985.00
Southern Education Foundation	$7,500.00
Southwest Arkansas Community Development Corporation	$5,000.00
Springdale School District	$1,500.00
Texarkana Regional Arts and Humanities Council	$25,000.00
Tri-County Community Center	$10,000.00
Union County Libraries	$1,500.00
University of Arkansas for Medical Sciences	$500.00
University of Arkansas for Medical Sciences	$80,000.00
University of Arkansas Foundation	$125,280.00
University of Arkansas Foundation	$15,000.00
University of Arkansas System	$28,333.00
University of Arkansas	$60,000.00
University of Arkansas, Little Rock	$1,300.00
University of Arkansas, Little Rock	$12,000.00
University of Arkansas, Little Rock	$2,000.00
University of Arkansas, Little Rock	$53,025.00
University of Arkansas, Little Rock	$600.00
University of Arkansas, Little Rock	$935.00
University of Arkansas, Monticello	$15,254.00
University of Arkansas, Pine Bluff	$2,000.00
University of Central Arkansas	$2,000.00
University of Central Arkansas	$3,770.00
Watershed Human and Community Development Agency	$1,400.00
Westark Community College	$1,000.00
Western Arkansas Education Cooperative	$19,361.00
Wilbur D. Mills Education Service Cooperative	$2,000.00
Wilowe Institute	$2,000.00
Women's Project	$1,500.00
Women's Project	$37,419.00
YMCA	$2,000.00
TOTAL	**$3,128,759.00**

1991

ACORN Housing Corporation	$30,000.00
Alpena Public Schools	$924.00
Alread Community Resource and Development Council	$10,000.00
Alread Community Resource and Development Council	$5,000.00
Altheimer-Sherrill Public Schools	$1,500.00
Amendment 59 Follow-up	$5,996.00
Arkadelphia Public Schools	$1,000.00

Arkadelphia Public Schools	$1,245.00
Arkansans for Drug-Free Youth, Union County	$2,000.00
Arkansas (training program for school administrators)	$1,000.00
Arkansas (video for the hearing and visual impaired)	$1,000.00
Arkansas 4-H Foundation	$2,000.00
Arkansas ABLE	$38,253.00
Arkansas Advocates for Children and Families	$47,821.00
Arkansas Association of LeadAR Alumni	$3,000.00
Arkansas Baptist State Convention	$2,000.00
Arkansas City Public Schools	$1,000.00
Arkansas Coalition Against Violence to Women and Children	$49,830.00
Arkansas College	$39,800.00
Arkansas Community Foundation	$1,000.00
Arkansas Community Foundation	$1,500.00
Arkansas Community Foundation	$2,000.00
Arkansas Council for International Visitors	$500.00
Arkansas Delta Housing Development Corporation	$2,000.00
Arkansas Delta Housing Development Corporation	$30,000.00
Arkansas Department of Human Services	$1,000.00
Arkansas Department of Human Services	$1,500.00
Arkansas Disability Coalition	$3,000.00
Arkansas Disability Coalition	$34,975.00
Arkansas Education Renewal Consortium	$70,000.00
Arkansas Historical Association	$1,900.00
Arkansas Human Development Corporation	$35,000.00
Arkansas Land and Farm Development Corporation	$35,000.00
Arkansas Public Policy Panel	$40,121.00
Arkansas School for the Deaf	$456.00
Arkansas Scottish Rite Foundation	$1,250.00
Arkansas Seniors Organized for Progress	$3,000.00
Arkansas Seniors Organized for Progress	$730.00
Arkansas State University, Beebe	$400.00
Artisan Source	$2,000.00
Artisan Source	$35,000.00
Arts Live	$9,150.00
Atkins Public Schools	$993.00
Bald Knob School District	$23,500.00
Benton Public Schools	$2,000.00

Berryville Public Schools	$2,000.00
Berryville Public Schools	$800.00
Boy Scouts of America, National Council	$2,000.00
Boys', Girls', Adults' Community Development Center	$23,544.00
Boys', Girls', Adults' Community Development Center	$3,000.00
Bryant Public Schools	$1,000.00
Cats Climb	$1,500.00
Cedarville Public Schools	$1,000.00
Centers for Youth and Families	$8,000.00
Commission for Arkansas's Future	$1,500.00
Conway Public Schools	$1,000.00
Conway Public Schools	$1,000.00
Council on Foundations	$500.00
County Line Public Schools	$1,500.00
County Line Public Schools	$25,190.00
Dardanelle Public Schools	$1,200.00
Dardanelle Public Schools	$825.00
Delight Public Schools	$2,000.00
Delta Community Development Corporation	$10,000.00
Delta Community Development Corporation	$30,075.00
Delta Community Development Corporation	$48,500.00
Delta Research, Education and Development Foundation	$10,000.00
Delta Research, Education and Development Foundation	$7,000.00
DeQueen School District	$1,657.00
Dermott Community Action	$3,000.00
DeVall's Bluff School District	$1,500.00
Dollarway School District	$1,769.00
Dollarway School District	$520.00
Edutainment, Video Distribution	$5,103.00
Emerson School District	$1,600.00
Fairview Public Schools	$1,490.00
Faulkner County Literacy Council	$1,530.00
Fayetteville Public Schools	$1,000.00
Fayetteville Public Schools	$900.00
Financing Ozarks Rural Growth and Economy	$3,000.00
Forrest City Public Schools	$445.00
Fort Smith Public Schools	$900.00
Friends of the Museum	$2,000.00
Future Builders	$10,000.00
Future Builders	$40,000.00
Gentry Public Schools	$920.00
Gillett Public Schools	$900.00
Greene County Technical School District	$990.00

Greenwood Public Schools	$500.00	Newton County Resource Council	$25,550.00
Gurdon Public Schools	$1,170.00	Newton County Resource Council	$3,000.00
Harmony Grove Public Schools	$1,000.00	Newton County Resource Council	$30,000.00
Harmony Grove Public Schools	$684.00	Nonprofit Resources	$10,715.00
Henderson State University	$20,496.00	Nonprofit Resources	$51,140.00
Hot Springs Community Band	$1,000.00	North Little Rock Public Schools	$650.00
Housing: The Low- to Moderate-Income Piece of the Puzzle	$3,234.00	Northside Redevelopment Corporation	$10,000.00
Increasing Philanthropy in Arkansas	$12,215.00	Ola Public Schools	$700.00
Jackson County	$10,000.00	Ouachita Public Schools	$1,700.00
Jasper School District	$422.00	Pangburn Public Schools	$1,100.00
Jonesboro Public Schools	$1,000.00	Perryville Public Schools	$20,500.00
Kirby Public Schools	$430.00	Philander Smith College	$2,000.00
Lakeside School District	$500.00	Philander Smith College	$72,334.00
Lavaca Public Schools	$1,600.00	Pine Bluff Public Schools	$1,100.00
Learning Club of Southwest Arkansas	$10,000.00	Pine Bluff Public Schools	$30,000.00
Legal Services of Arkansas	$1,500.00	Pine Bluff Public Schools	$500.00
Lewisville Public Schools	$996.00	Pine Bluff Public Schools	$600.00
Literacy Council of Ouachita-Calhoun Counties	$1,110.00	Pine Bluff Public Schools	$700.00
Literacy Council of Pulaski County	$15,573.00	Plainview-Rover School District	$800.00
Little River County Leadership Council	$10,000.00	Pulaski County Quorum Court	$10,000.00
Little River County Leadership Council	$5,000.00	Pulaski County Special School District	$1,000.00
Little Rock Chamber of Commerce Foundation	$1,500.00	Pulaski County Special School District	$23,554.00
Little Rock Public Schools	$1,000.00	Pulaski County Special School District	$966.00
Little Rock Public Schools	$1,000.00	Quapaw Quarter Association	$1,000.00
Little Rock Public Schools	$1,200.00	Rape Crisis	$1,500.00
Little Rock Public Schools	$1,590.00	Rogers Public Schools	$1,248.00
Little Rock Public Schools	$2,000.00	Rural Advancement Foundation International, USA	$2,000.00
Little Rock Public Schools	$42,500.00	Save the Children Federation	$30,000.00
Little Rock Public Schools	$710.00	Searcy County Airport Commission	$50,000.00
Lonoke Public Schools	$1,000.00	Second Genesis Ministries	$10,000.00
Marion School District	$1,000.00	Shepherd's Ranch	$2,000.00
Meadowcreek Project	$1,500.00	Sheridan Public Schools	$600.00
Minimum Performance Test and Teaching and Learning	$77,630.00	Shirley Community Service and Development Corporation	$23,220.00
Murfreesboro Community Foundation	$6,200.00	Siloam Springs Public Schools	$1,500.00
National Conference of Christians and Jews	$16,000.00	Southeast Arkansas Community Action Corporation	$10,000.00
National Conference of Christians and Jews	$2,000.00	Southern Arkansas University	$29,942.00
National Dunbar Alumni Association of Little Rock	$1,500.00	Southern Ventures	$250,000.00
NCTR Associated Universities	$22,547.00	Southwest Arkansas Community Development Corporation	$10,000.00
Nemo Vista Public Schools	$1,975.00	Southwest Arkansas Community Development Corporation	$6,800.00
Nettleton Public Schools	$1,000.00	Springdale School District	$1,325.00
Nettleton Public Schools	$1,200.00	Springdale School District	$500.00
Newton County Resource Council	$2,000.00	Stuttgart Public Schools	$975.00
		Teach for America	$60,000.00
		Texarkana Regional Arts and Humanities Council	$25,000.00

Tri-County Community Center	$3,000.00
Universal Housing Development Corporation	$30,000.00
University of Arkansas for Medical Sciences	$1,600.00
University of Arkansas Foundation	$100,000.00
University of Arkansas Foundation	$15,000.00
University of Arkansas Foundation	$2,000.00
University of Arkansas System	$28,334.00
University of Arkansas, Little Rock	$2,000.00
University of Arkansas, Little Rock	$30,000.00
University of Arkansas, Little Rock	$49,550.00
University of Arkansas, Little Rock	$680.00
University of Arkansas, Pine Bluff	$1,000.00
University of Arkansas, Pine Bluff	$18,000.00
University of Central Arkansas	$1,000.00
Urban League of Greater Little Rock	$30,000.00
Vilonia Public Schools	$1,000.00
Vilonia Public Schools	$1,500.00
Watson Chapel School District	$1,468.00
Watson Chapel School District	$900.00
Western Arkansas Education Service Cooperative	$17,126.00
Western Yell County Schools	$700.00
Wilowe Institute	$1,500.00
Wilowe Institute	$22,100.00
WR Foundation, "The Dream and the Mission," film	$940.00
WR Foundation, Networking Conference	$7,314.00
TOTAL	**$2,312,115.00**

1992

ACORN Housing Corporation	$30,000.00
Acorn School District	$1,500.00
Alpena Public Schools	$1,590.00
Alread Community Resource and Development Council	$3,000.00
Amendment 59, Education and Economic Development Study	$17,777.00
American Forum	$33,317.00
American Lung Association of Arkansas	$1,000.00
Arch Ford Education Service Cooperative	$15,750.00
Arkadelphia Public Schools	$1,000.00
Arkadelphia Public Schools	$1,000.00
Arkadelphia Public Schools	$1,050.00
Arkadelphia Public Schools	$1,150.00
Arkansas (Martin Luther King Jr., National Youth Assembly)	$750.00
Arkansas Advocates for Children and Families	$35,270.00

Arkansas Association of Conservation Districts	$700.00
Arkansas Association of Conservation Districts	$725.00
Arkansas Aviation Historical Society	$1,000.00
Arkansas Chapter National Association of Black Social Workers	$1,000.00
Arkansas College	$39,800.00
Arkansas College	$5,000.00
Arkansas Community Foundation	$1,120.00
Arkansas Delta Foundation	$50,000.00
Arkansas Delta Foundation	$6,000.00
Arkansas Delta Housing Development Corporation	$30,000.00
Arkansas Department of Education	$1,000.00
Arkansas Department of Education	$450.00
Arkansas Department of Health	$6,000.00
Arkansas Department of Higher Education	$35,000.00
Arkansas Department of Human Services	$800.00
Arkansas Disability Coalition	$31,793.00
Arkansas Education Renewal Consortium	$70,000.00
Arkansas Endowment for the Humanities/Humanities Council	$77,394.00
Arkansas Extension Homemakers Council, Tri-County	$1,500.00
Arkansas Geological Commission	$1,800.00
Arkansas Human Development Corporation	$30,000.00
Arkansas Land and Farm Development Corporation	$30,000.00
Arkansas Land and Farm Development Corporation	$44,500.00
Arkansas Regional Minority Purchasing Council	$50,000.00
Arkansas River Education Service Cooperative	$2,000.00
Arkansas River Education Service Cooperative	$49,500.00
Arkansas Rural Development Commission	$1,000.00
Arkansas Sheriffs' Boys' Ranch	$2,000.00
Arkansas State University	$1,000.00
Arkansas State University	$4,916.00
Arkansas State University	$6,000.00
Arkansas Tech University	$6,000.00
Arkansas Territorial Restoration Foundation	$27,267.00
Arkansas, Bavaria Youth Exchange	$500.00
Artisan Source	$35,000.00
Association for Supervision and Curriculum Development	$79,539.00
Augusta Public Schools	$1,006.00

Bald Knob School District	$855.00
Bentonville Public Schools	$1,000.00
Bismarck Public Schools	$1,200.00
Black Community Developers	$2,000.00
Cabot Public Schools	$1,500.00
Cedarville Public Schools	$1,000.00
Centers for Youth and Families	$1,125.00
Centers for Youth and Families	$7,000.00
Central Arkansas Library System	$250.00
Christian Ministerial Alliance	$2,000.00
Community Alternative Prevention Program	$10,000.00
Community Development Corporation Handbook	$13,000.00
Conway Public Schools	$786.00
Corning Public Schools	$1,000.00
Council on Foundations	$500.00
Cradle Care Food Program	$6,500.00
Crowley's Ridge Development Council	$10,000.00
Deer Consolidated Schools	$1,893.00
Delta Community Development Corporation	$22,575.00
Delta Community Development Corporation	$3,000.00
Delta Research, Education and Development Foundation	$3,000.00
Delta Research, Education and Development Foundation	$55,735.00
Dermott, City of,	$1,075.00
Dermott, City of,	$54,994.00
Drew Central School District	$1,742.00
Dumas Public Schools	$900.00
East Poinsett County School District	$354.00
East-Central Arkansas Economic Development Corporation	$15,000.00
Economic Opportunity Agency of Washington County	$16,200.00
Economic Opportunity Agency of Washington County	$37,789.00
Edutainment, Video Distribution	$2,500.00
El Dorado Public Schools	$1,450.00
ElderCare of Eastern Arkansas	$10,000.00
ElderCare of Eastern Arkansas	$893.00
Emma Elease Webb Community Center	$10,000.00
Fairview Public Schools	$1,400.00
Fairview Public Schools	$2,000.00
Fayetteville Public Schools	$1,500.00
Fayetteville Public Schools	$2,000.00
Fayetteville Public Schools	$891.00
Fort Smith Public Schools	$1,000.00
Fort Smith Public Schools	$2,000.00
Frances A. Allen School for Exceptional Children	$700.00
Friends of the Mid-America Museum	$2,000.00
Future Builders	$3,000.00
Future Builders	$40,000.00
Gould Public Schools	$1,000.00
Governor's Commission on Adult Literacy	$66,120.00
Great Rivers Education Service Cooperative	$49,750.00
Greater Little Rock Community Development Corporation	$7,500.00
Green Forest School District	$740.00
Greenbrier Public Schools	$1,500.00
Greenwood Public Schools	$1,200.00
Grubbs Special School District	$215.00
GYST House	$1,500.00
Heber Springs School District	$500.00
Henderson State University	$1,000.00
Henderson State University	$6,000.00
Home Visit Booklet	$463.00
Huntsville School District	$2,000.00
Independent College Fund of Arkansas	$1,000.00
International Association of Missions	$1,000.00
John Brown University	$5,977.00
Jonesboro Public Schools	$1,000.00
Jonesboro Public Schools	$1,375.00
Kirby Public Schools	$287.00
Kirby Public Schools	$560.00
Lake Hamilton School District	$900.00
Lakeside School District	$1,000.00
Lincoln Consolidated Schools	$1,200.00
Little River County Leadership Council	$3,000.00
Little Rock Chamber Foundation	$2,000.00
Little Rock City Beautiful Commission	$1,300.00
Little Rock Public Schools	$1,000.00
Little Rock Public Schools	$1,088.00
Little Rock Public Schools	$800.00
Local Initiatives Support Corporation	$25,000.00
Lonoke Public Schools	$1,000.00
Love Center	$500.00
Marion School District	$400.00
Minimum Performance Test and Teaching and Learning	$15,421.00
Monticello School District	$1,000.00
National Association for Education and Motivation of Young People	$1,250.00
National Coalition Against the Death Penalty	$2,000.00

National Conference of Christians and Jews	$3,100.00
National Conference of Christians and Jews	$6,000.00
National Faculty	$36,000.00
NCTR Associated Universities	$10,450.00
Nettleton Public Schools	$1,400.00
Nevada School District	$1,000.00
Nevada School District	$970.00
Newton County Resource Council	$30,000.00
Nonprofit Resources	$97,454.00
North Little Rock Public Schools	$1,000.00
North Little Rock Public Schools	$1,850.00
Northeast Arkansas School District	$580.00
Northeast Arkansas School District	$900.00
Northside Redevelopment Corporation	$3,000.00
Northwest Arkansas Rape Crisis Center	$1,000.00
Oasis Resources	$50,000.00
Ola Public Schools	$2,000.00
Operation Lifesaver	$1,000.00
Ouachita Girl Scout Council	$20,000.00
Ozan-Inghram/Iron Mountain Neighborhood Development Corporation	$10,000.00
Ozark Alternative Training and Promotion Association	$10,000.00
Paris Public Schools	$1,000.00
Perry County Extension Homemakers Council	$10,000.00
Pine Bluff Downtown Development	$5,000.00
Planned Parenthood of Greater Arkansas	$1,000.00
Pulaski County Child and Family Services	$250.00
Pulaski County Circuit Chancery Court	$10,000.00
Pulaski County Junior Deputy Program	$1,000.00
Pulaski County Special School District	$1,000.00
Pulaski County Special School District	$1,995.00
Pulaski County Special School District	$750.00
RAIN Arkansas	$15,000.00
Rison Public Schools	$800.00
Rural Advancement Foundation International, USA	$2,000.00
Safe Agricultural Insecticides and Related Products	$10,000.00
Sanctuary	$10,000.00
Sandflat-Glendale Neighborhood Development Corporation	$10,000.00
Searcy County Airport Commission	$50,000.00
Second Genesis Ministries	$3,000.00
Shirley Community Service and Development Corporation	$20,770.00
Siloam Springs Public Schools	$874.00
Sloan-Hendrix School District	$700.00
Smithsonian Institution	$1,000.00
Social, Economic and Educational Development Corporation	$10,000.00
Southeast Arkansas Community Development Corporation	$69,040.00
Southeast Arkansas Education Service Cooperative	$49,750.00
Southeastern Archeological Conference	$600.00
Southern Center for International Studies	$2,000.00
Southwest Arkansas Community Development Corporation	$3,000.00
Southwest Arkansas Community Development Corporation	$71,100.00
Spa Area Independent Living Services	$10,000.00
Springdale School District	$265.00
St. Michael's School	$1,000.00
Star City Public Schools	$1,000.00
Star City Public Schools	$2,000.00
Stuttgart Public Schools	$1,031.00
Teach for America	$50,000.00
Texarkana School District	$1,000.00
Texarkana School District	$1,000.00
Texarkana School District	$1,000.00
Texarkana School District	$1,500.00
United Way of Fort Smith	$1,000.00
Universal Housing Development Corporation	$30,000.00
University of Arkansas for Medical Sciences	$1,000.00
University of Arkansas Foundation	$1,000.00
University of Arkansas Foundation	$105,300.00
University of Arkansas Foundation	$73,811.00
University of Arkansas	$1,563.00
University of Arkansas	$5,527.00
University of Arkansas	$6,000.00
University of Arkansas, Little Rock	$1,000.00
University of Arkansas, Little Rock	$1,980.00
University of Arkansas, Little Rock	$12,525.00
University of Arkansas, Little Rock	$2,000.00
University of Arkansas, Little Rock	$30,000.00
University of Arkansas, Little Rock	$6,000.00
University of Arkansas, Little Rock	$700.00
University of Arkansas, Monticello	$2,000.00
University of Arkansas, Monticello	$6,000.00

University of Arkansas, Pine Bluff	$1,000.00	Arkansas Chapter of the National Association of Minority Contractors	$2,000.00
University of Arkansas, Pine Bluff	$1,500.00	Arkansas College	$30,000.00
University of Arkansas, Pine Bluff	$6,000.00	Arkansas College	$42,750.00
University of Arkansas, Pine Bluff	$80,050.00	Arkansas Community Foundation	$1,500.00
University of Central Arkansas	$1,000.00	Arkansas Community Foundation	$1,500.00
University of Central Arkansas	$6,000.00	Arkansas Community Foundation	$2,000.00
Urban League of Greater Little Rock	$30,000.00	Arkansas Delta Housing Development Corporation	$30,000.00
Valley Springs School District	$1,300.00	Arkansas Department of Education	$36,000.00
Watson Chapel School District	$766.00	Arkansas Disability Coalition	$31,006.00
Watson Chapel School District	$812.00	Arkansas Economic Corporation	$55,000.00
We Care of Pulaski County	$1,000.00	Arkansas Education Renewal Consortium	$68,500.00
Weiner Public Schools	$1,500.00	Arkansas Educational Television Network Foundation	$20,000.00
Westside Consolidated School District	$465.00	Arkansas Endowment for the Humanities/Humanities Council	$43,070.00
Westside School District	$2,000.00	Arkansas Human Development Corporation	$25,000.00
White County Central School District	$1,400.00	Arkansas Land and Farm Development Corporation	$26,000.00
Wilowe Institute	$22,500.00	Arkansas Land and Farm Development Corporation	$44,500.00
Wilowe Institute	$400.00	Arkansas Partners in Education	$46,325.00
Winthrop Rockefeller Foundation, At-Risk Program	$5,094.00	Arkansas Repertory Theater	$140,420.00
Winthrop Rockefeller Foundation, Housing Initiative	$4,391.00	Arkansas Rice Depot	$2,000.00
Winthrop Rockefeller Foundation, Networking Conference	$6,680.00	Arkansas River Education Service Cooperative	$40,000.00
Women's Project	$1,000.00	Arkansas River Education Service Cooperative	$47,000.00
YMCA of Metropolitan Little Rock	$1,000.00	Arkansas River Valley Art Center Foundation	$5,000.00
Youth Advocate and Resources Network	$5,000.00	Arkansas School for the Blind	$7,500.00
TOTAL	**$2,627,710.00**	Arkansas Seniors Organized for Progress	$15,000.00

1993

ACORN Housing Corporation	$30,000.00	Arkansas State University	$6,000.00
Alread Community Resource and Development Council	$250.00	Arkansas State University	$75,459.00
Alread Community Resource and Development Council	$3,740.00	Arkansas State University	$750.00
AMDPA Foundation	$2,000.00	Arkansas Tech University	$6,000.00
American Forum	$35,000.00	Arkansas Territorial Restoration Foundation	$20,850.00
American Planning Association	$1,250.00	Arkansas Wildlife Federation	$8,030.00
Arch Ford Education Service Cooperative	$12,100.00	Artisan Source	$35,000.00
Arkadelphia Public Schools	$1,200.00	Arts Live	$45,000.00
Arkansas Advocates for Children and Families	$1,500.00	Arts Live	$5,000.00
		ARVAC (Rural Industries)	$98,662.00
Arkansas Advocates for Children and Families	$950.00	Ashley County Board of Education	$2,000.00
Arkansas AIDS Foundation	$2,000.00	Association for Supervision and Curriculum Development	$86,000.00
Arkansas Association of Community Development	$75,000.00	Association of Black Engineers in Arkansas	$12,160.00
Arkansas Association of LeadAR Alumni	$50,000.00	Bentonville Public Schools	$7,500.00
Arkansas Baptist State Convention	$10,000.00		

Berryville Public Schools	$1,800.00
Berryville Public Schools	$2,000.00
Biggers-Reyno School District	$1,447.00
Bismarck Public Schools	$1,126.00
Blytheville-Gosnell Area Food Pantry	$5,000.00
Blytheville-Gosnell Area Food Pantry	$50,000.00
Boston Mountain Education Cooperative	$1,463.00
Bryant Public Schools	$1,665.00
Cabot Public Schools	$1,150.00
Caddo Hills School District	$1,959.00
Camden School District	$7,500.00
Carthage High School	$7,500.00
Carthage, Community Local Action Center	$10,000.00
Central Arkansas Legal Services	$860.00
Child Development	$1,200.00
Child Welfare League of America	$1,920.00
Christian Methodist Episcopal Church	$2,000.00
Clear Spring School	$5,000.00
Cleburne County Cares	$5,000.00
Community Development Corporation Handbook	$16,000.00
Community School of Cleburne County	$1,570.00
Community Solutions in Progress	$1,000.00
Conway Public Schools	$1,000.00
Conway Public Schools	$7,500.00
Corning Public Schools	$770.00
Crawford County Art Association	$5,000.00
Crittenden County Clients Council (West Memphis)	$10,000.00
Cross County School District	$2,000.00
Dallas County Good Samaritans Center	$10,000.00
Dardanelle Public Schools	$2,000.00
Dardanelle Public Schools	$7,500.00
Delta Community Development Corporation	$100,000.00
Delta Community Development Corporation	$16,075.00
Delta Community Development Corporation	$2,000.00
Delta Community Development Corporation	$207,068.00
Delta Research, Education and Development Foundation	$60,000.00
Department of Arkansas Heritage	$1,500.00
Department of Human Services	$1,500.00
Dermott, City of,	$44,012.00
Dumas Public Schools	$1,477.00
Dumas Public Schools	$1,750.00
East Arkansas Legal Services	$56,201.00
East Arkansas Regional Mental Health Center	$1,500.00
East-Central Arkansas Economic Development Corporation	$56,000.00
Economic Opportunity Agency of Washington County	$16,200.00
Economic Opportunity Agency of Washington County	$21,289.00
Economic Opportunity Agency of Washington County	$473.00
Edutainment, Video Distribution	$2,500.00
El Dorado Public Schools	$7,500.00
Emerson School District	$823.00
Evangelical Lutheran Good Samaritan Society	$1,000.00
Financing Ozarks Rural Growth and Economy	$50,000.00
Floyd Brown-Fargo Agricultural School Museum	$2,000.00
Fort Smith Literacy Council	$2,211.00
Fort Smith Public Schools	$1,948.00
Friends of the Rogers Historical Museum	$5,000.00
Friendship School for Exceptional Children	$2,000.00
Future Builders	$67,000.00
Gaines House	$1,750.00
Garland County Community College	$1,700.00
Girl Scouts of America, Conifer Council	$1,500.00
Good Neighbor-Love Center	$5,000.00
Good News Ministries	$5,000.00
Gould Community Service Corporation	$10,000.00
Gravette School District	$1,824.00
Great Rivers Education Service Cooperative	$40,600.00
Greater Little Rock Community Development Corporation	$10,000.00
Greenbrier Public Schools	$7,500.00
Guardianship	$20,000.00
Gurdon Public Schools	$1,000.00
Gurdon Public Schools	$1,377.00
Gurdon Public Schools	$1,419.00
Harding University	$15,000.00
Heifer Project International	$2,000.00
Helena Community Renewal Corporation	$20,053.00
Helena-West Helena School District	$1,230.00
Hempstead County Arts Council	$5,000.00
Henderson State University	$60,000.00
Home Visit Booklet	$945.00

Hospice Home Care	$1,500.00
Hot Springs Development Foundation	$1,500.00
Immanuel Rescue Mission	$1,800.00
IMPAC Learning Systems	$60,000.00
International Life Services	$2,500.00
Jennette, City of,	$10,000.00
Jennette, City of,	$900.00
John Brown University	$30,000.00
Johnson County Helping Hands	$10,000.00
Jonesboro Church Health Center	$2,000.00
Junction City School District	$1,490.00
Junction City School District	$1,826.00
Kirby Public Schools	$7,500.00
Kirby Public Schools	$825.00
Lakeside School District	$1,000.00
Lakeside School District	$1,000.00
Lakeside School District	$1,900.00
League of Women Voters Education Fund	$12,025.00
Literacy Council of Ouachita-Calhoun Counties	$500.00
Little River County Leadership Council	$1,036.00
Little Rock Chamber Foundation	$6,000.00
Little Rock Public Schools	$1,500.00
Little Rock Public Schools	$1,575.00
Little Rock Public Schools	$1,760.00
Little Rock Public Schools	$1,800.00
Little Rock Public Schools	$1,980.00
Little Rock Public Schools	$7,500.00
Little Rock Public Schools	$950.00
Local Initiatives Support Corporation	$25,000.00
Magazine School District	$1,200.00
Magazine School District	$10,000.00
Mallalieu Black Community Developers	$55,000.00
Mammoth Spring School District	$1,500.00
March of Dimes Birth Defects Foundation	$5,000.00
Montessori Cooperative School	$1,340.00
Mother to Mother Ministry of Northwest Arkansas	$1,951.00
NAACP	$510.00
National Conference of Christians and Jews	$49,010.00
National Faculty	$36,000.00
NCTR Associated Universities	$20,000.00
Nettleton Public Schools	$1,000.00
Nettleton Public Schools	$1,180.00
Nettleton Public Schools	$1,857.00
Nettleton Public Schools	$1,880.00
Nettleton Public Schools	$7,500.00
Nevada School District	$1,390.00
Nevada School District	$1,472.00
Newark School District	$1,000.00
Newton County Resource Council	$30,000.00
Newton County Resource Council	$5,000.00
Newton County Resource Council	$50,000.00
Nonprofit Resources	$91,160.00
North Garland County Youth Center	$10,000.00
North Little Rock Public Schools	$7,500.00
North Little Rock Public Schools	$7,500.00
North Little Rock, City of,	$2,000.00
Northeast Arkansas School District	$1,500.00
Northeast Arkansas School District	$1,991.00
Northwest Arkansas Rape Crisis Center	$10,000.00
Northwest Arkansas Rape Crisis Center	$335.00
Oasis Renewal Center	$1,000.00
Oasis Resources	$10,000.00
Ouachita County	$15,000.00
Ouachita Girl Scout Council	$16,000.00
Ozan-Inghram/Iron Mountain Neighborhood Development Corporation	$10,000.00
Ozan-Inghram/Iron Mountain Neighborhood Development Corporation	$27,500.00
Ozark Foothills Resource Conservation and Development Council	$25,000.00
Ozark Heritage and Arts Center	$2,000.00
Ozark Recycling Enterprise	$1,000.00
Ozark Small Farm Viability Project	$2,000.00
Palestine-Wheatley School District	$1,800.00
Pankey Community Improvement	$10,000.00
Parent Involvement Manual	$4,170.00
Parent Teach Association, Arkansas Congress	$22,106.00
Paris Public Schools	$10,000.00
Paris School District	$1,915.00
Parkin School District	$400.00
Pine Bluff Public Schools	$500.00
Prairie Grove School District	$1,350.00
Project for Arkansas Compensation Education	$2,000.00
Public Servant: Positive Role Model	$7,000.00
Pulaski County Special School District	$1,987.00
Pulaski County	$1,340.00
Pulaski County	$2,000.00
RAIN Arkansas	$15,000.00

Retired Senior Volunteer Program of Central Arkansas	$5,000.00
Rogers Little Theater	$5,000.00
Rural Profile (1993 revision of 1990 publication)	$10,000.00
Russellville School District	$22,400.00
Samaritan Center	$1,500.00
Sanctuary	$10,000.00
Sandflat-Glendale Neighborhood Development Corporation	$1,085.00
Sandflat-Glendale Neighborhood Development Corporation	$27,500.00
Saratoga School District	$1,554.00
SCAN Volunteer Service	$5,000.00
Searcy County Airport Commission	$29,500.00
Searcy Public Schools	$2,000.00
Setting Captives Free Ministries	$1,000.00
Sheridan Public Schools	$1,112.00
Sheridan Public Schools	$1,924.00
Shirley Community Service and Development Corporation	$56,910.00
Shorter College	$84,000.00
Siloam Springs Public Schools	$1,500.00
Siloam Springs Public Schools	$23,860.00
South Arkansas Community Action Authority	$2,000.00
Southeast Arkansas Community Development Corporation	$64,246.00
Southern Center for International Studies	$44,352.00
Southside School District	$1,950.00
Southside School District	$900.00
Southwest Arkansas Community Development Corporation	$5,000.00
Southwest Arkansas Community Development Corporation	$63,990.00
Springdale School District	$1,002.00
Springdale School District	$1,500.00
Springdale School District	$7,500.00
Stork's Nest Charity Fund	$1,600.00
Stuttgart Public Schools	$1,685.00
Sulphur Rock School District	$1,000.00
Support for Education Progress	$2,989.00
Teach for America	$40,000.00
Texarkana School District	$2,000.00
Texarkana, City of,	$27,500.00
Twin Groves, City of,	$10,000.00
Undoing Racism and Organizing	$6,367.00
Universal Housing Development Corporation	$30,000.00
University of Arkansas for Medical Sciences	$1,000.00
University of Arkansas Foundation	$1,480.00
University of Arkansas Foundation	$180,600.00

University of Arkansas Foundation	$58,505.00
University of Arkansas Foundation	$75,736.00
University of Arkansas	$60,000.00
University of Arkansas, Little Rock	$1,000.00
University of Arkansas, Little Rock	$1,500.00
University of Arkansas, Little Rock	$1,600.00
University of Arkansas, Little Rock	$2,000.00
University of Arkansas, Little Rock	$30,000.00
University of Arkansas, Little Rock	$43,800.00
University of Arkansas, Little Rock	$60,200.00
University of Arkansas, Monticello	$6,000.00
University of Arkansas, Pine Bluff	$60,000.00
University of Central Arkansas	$2,000.00
University of Central Arkansas	$60,000.00
University of the Ozarks	$1,000.00
Urban League of Greater Little Rock	$30,000.00
Vilonia Public Schools	$1,000.00
Volunteers of America	$30,000.00
Waldron School District	$2,000.00
Watson Chapel School District	$1,500.00
Weiner Public Schools	$1,990.00
Weiner Public Schools	$7,500.00
Westside Consolidated School District	$1,065.00
Westside Consolidated School District	$1,095.00
Westside Consolidated School District	$521.00
White County Central School District	$1,950.00
White River Area Agency on Aging	$3,000.00
William O. Darby Ranger Memorial Foundation	$4,736.00
Wilmar, City of,	$10,000.00
Winrock International	$15,000.00
Winthrop Rockefeller Foundation Housing Initiative	$3,608.00
Winthrop Rockefeller Foundation Presidential Transition	$13,816.00
Winthrop Rockefeller Foundation, Networking Conference	$4,876.00
Women's Project	$1,000.00
Wynne School District	$1,535.00
YMCA of Metropolitan Little Rock	$61,260.00
Youth Advocate and Resources Network	$1,500.00
YWCA	$1,800.00
TOTAL	**$4,768,137.00**

1994

A Better Chance	$37,650.00
Acorn School District	$750.00
All Our Children, West Memphis	$10,000.00

American Forum	$35,000.00
Amity Public Schools	$1,647.00
Amity Public Schools	$1,842.00
Argenta Community Development Corporation	$10,000.00
Arkadelphia Public Schools	$1,750.00
Arkansas ABLE	$2,000.00
Arkansas Advocates for Children and Families	$19,443.00
Arkansas Advocates for Children and Families	$200.00
Arkansas Arts Center Foundation	$2,000.00
Arkansas Association of LeadAR Alumni	$36,800.00
Arkansas Cattlemen's Foundation	$50,000.00
Arkansas Community Foundation	$1,500.00
Arkansas Community Foundation	$10,000.00
Arkansas Community Foundation	$150,000.00
Arkansas Council for the Social Studies	$2,000.00
Arkansas Delta Housing Development Corporation	$2,000.00
Arkansas Delta Housing Development Corporation	$43,000.00
Arkansas Department of Correction	$1,200.00
Arkansas Disability Coalition	$30,975.00
Arkansas Economic Corporation	$98,880.00
Arkansas Education Renewal Consortium	$65,250.00
Arkansas Endowment for the Humanities/Humanities Council	$104,117.00
Arkansas Endowment for the Humanities/Humanities Council	$40,663.00
Arkansas Epilepsy Society	$1,500.00
Arkansas Friends for Better Schools	$57,882.00
Arkansas Handicapped Athletic Association	$1,000.00
Arkansas Land and Farm Development Corporation	$1,000.00
Arkansas Land and Farm Development Corporation	$44,500.00
Arkansas Low-Income Housing Coalition	$57,194.00
Arkansas Public Policy Panel	$69,816.00
Arkansas Repertory Theater	$140,419.00
Arkansas River Education Service Cooperative	$40,000.00
Arkansas School for Mathematics and Sciences	$2,000.00
Arkansas School for the Blind	$7,500.00
Arkansas State Police	$1,500.00
Arkansas State University	$30,000.00
Arkansas State University	$67,591.00
Arkansas Tech University	$30,000.00

Arkansas Territorial Restoration Foundation	$17,250.00
Arts Live	$30,000.00
ARVAC (Rural Industries)	$88,599.00
Association for Supervision and Curriculum Development	$49,525.00
Association of Black Engineers in Arkansas	$13,940.00
Augusta Public Schools	$968.00
Bald Knob School District	$1,500.00
Batesville School District	$1,000.00
Bentonville Public Schools	$7,500.00
Black Community Developers	$2,000.00
Blytheville Community Samaritan Ministries	$2,000.00
Boy Scouts of America	$100,000.00
Boys', Girls', Adults' Community Development Center	$53,335.00
Boys', Girls', Adults' Community Development Center, Highlander Research and Education Center	$2,000.00
Break the Mold Process Observers	$11,511.00
Bryant Public Schools	$1,324.00
Buffalo Island Central School District	$963.00
Cabot Public Schools	$900.00
Camden School District	$57,036.00
Camden School District	$7,500.00
Carthage High School	$7,500.00
Centers for Youth and Families	$48,192.00
Central Arkansas Legal Services	$1,150.00
Chapter 1 Study	$39,808.00
Christian Church Disciples of Christ (General Assembly)	$1,000.00
Citizen Participation in Arkansas, An Update	$70,000.00
Clinton School District	$313.00
Colt Community Development Corporation	$1,200.00
Colt Community Development Corporation	$10,000.00
Community Development Corporation Handbook and Network Development	$1,000.00
Community Planning Empowerment Zone	$49,223.00
Conference of Southwest Foundations	$1,000.00
Conway Public Schools	$1,104.00
Conway Public Schools	$1,500.00
Conway Public Schools	$1,842.00
Conway Public Schools	$2,000.00
Conway Public Schools	$7,500.00
Corning Public Schools	$1,475.00
Corning Public Schools	$1,738.00

Corporate Connections Update	$6,500.00	Greenbrier Public Schools	$7,500.00
Cross County School District	$1,883.00	Greenwood Public Schools	$1,250.00
Crowley's Ridge Educational		Harding University	$15,500.00
Cooperative	$20,000.00	Harmony Grove Public Schools	$2,000.00
Crowley's Ridge Regional Library	$3,500.00	Harrisburg School District	$713.00
Cushman School District	$1,000.00	Helena Community Renewal	
Dardanelle Public Schools	$7,500.00	Corporation	$50,000.00
Dawson Education Service		Henderson State University	$60,000.00
Cooperative	$20,000.00	Home Visit Booklet	$6,659.00
Deer Consolidated Schools	$2,000.00	Hope School District	$1,379.00
Delta Community Development		Hot Springs, City of,	$500.00
Corporation	$182,623.00	Jacksonville Care Channel	$10,000.00
Delta Research, Education and		Jennette, City of,	$1,677.00
Development Foundation	$49,995.00	Jessieville School District	$1,260.00
Dermott, City of,	$39,313.00	John Brown University	$30,000.00
DeVall's Bluff School District	$1,500.00	Kids Voting USA	$2,000.00
Drew Central School District	$1,728.00	Kirby Public Schools	$1,078.00
East Arkansas Legal Services	$44,300.00	Kirby Public Schools	$7,500.00
East Central Arkansas Economic		Lakeside School District	$1,000.00
Development Corporation	$40,000.00	Lakeside School District	$1,200.00
East End School District	$1,871.00	Lakeside School District	$1,995.00
Economic Opportunity Agency		Lakeside School District	$2,000.00
of Washington County	$16,200.00	Lakeside School District	$990.00
Economic Opportunity Agency		Laubach Literacy International	$5,000.00
of Washington County	$25,000.00	Lavaca School District	$1,500.00
Economic Opportunity Agency		League of Women Voters Education	
of Washington County	$52,100.00	Fund	$2,000.00
El Dorado Public Schools	$7,500.00	Literacy League of Craighead County	$1,000.00
Elizabeth McGill Drop-In Center	$60,000.00	Little River County Leadership	
Elkins School District	$1,575.00	Council	$24,000.00
Extension Homemakers Council,		Little Rock Chamber Foundation	$500.00
Little River County	$10,000.00	Little Rock Public Schools	$1,500.00
Fayetteville Public Schools	$1,100.00	Little Rock Public Schools	$1,662.00
Fayetteville Public Schools	$1,441.00	Little Rock Public Schools	$2,000.00
Financial Management Workshops	$25,000.00	Little Rock Public Schools	$2,000.00
Financing Ozarks Rural Growth		Little Rock Public Schools	$2,000.00
and Economy	$50,000.00	Little Rock Public Schools	$250.00
Forrest City Community Voices	$10,000.00	Little Rock Public Schools	$7,500.00
Fort Smith Public Schools	$1,000.00	Little Rock, City of,	$1,500.00
Fort Smith Public Schools	$1,949.00	Little Rock, City of,	$2,000.00
Fort Smith Public Schools	$2,000.00	Local Initiatives Support	
Foundation for the Mid-South	$50,000.00	Corporation	$50,000.00
Foundation for Women's Resources	$1,000.00	Lockesburg School District	$1,584.00
Frances A. Allen School for		Love Center	$1,500.00
Exceptional Children	$2,000.00	Lyon College	$26,333.00
Future Builders	$63,668.00	Lyon College	$30,000.00
Gentry Public Schools	$1,000.00	Madison, City of,	$10,000.00
Gentry Public Schools	$1,520.00	Madison, City of,	$2,000.00
Gladney Fund, Arkansas Auxiliary	$10,000.00	Magnolia School District	$1,800.00
Global Learning Center	$10,000.00	Mallalieu Black Community	
Global Learning Center	$2,000.00	Developers	$55,000.00
Governor's Commission on Adult		Martin Luther King Jr.	
Literacy	$27,800.00	Commission	$50,000.00
Greater Friendship	$10,000.00		

Martin Luther King Jr. Commission	$6,548.00
McGehee School District	$1,800.00
Mid-South Astronomical Research Society	$2,000.00
Monticello School District	$2,000.00
Mountain Home School District	$1,200.00
Mountain Home School District	$2,000.00
Mountain View School District	$1,000.00
Murfreesboro Community Fund	$2,000.00
Nashville School District	$1,992.00
National Conference of Christians and Jews	$49,010.00
Nebboa Community Services	$1,000.00
Nettleton Public Schools	$1,000.00
Nettleton Public Schools	$1,500.00
Nettleton Public Schools	$673.00
Nettleton Public Schools	$7,500.00
New Horizons Church and Its Ministries	$24,000.00
New Reality	$1,000.00
Newton County Housing Council	$30,000.00
Newton County Resource Council	$50,000.00
Nonprofit Resources	$82,897.00
North Little Rock Housing Authority	$500.00
North Little Rock Public Schools	$7,500.00
North Little Rock Public Schools	$7,500.00
Northeast Arkansas School District	$1,450.00
Northwest Arkansas Education Service Cooperative	$2,000.00
Oasis Resources	$50,000.00
Office of Human Concern	$1,500.00
Office of Rural Advocacy	$1,000.00
Olive Garden Development Corporation	$10,000.00
Ouachita County	$57,180.00
Ouachita Girl Scout Council	$12,000.00
Ozan-Inghram/Iron Mountain Neighborhood Development Corporation	$27,500.00
Ozark Foothills Resource Conservation and Development Council	$10,000.00
Ozark Heritage and Arts Center	$1,930.00
Ozark Small Farm Viability Project	$2,000.00
Parent Involvement Manual	$3,459.00
Parent Teach Association, Arkansas Congress	$42,908.00
Paris School District	$1,585.00
Parkers Chapel School District	$1,000.00
People are Concerned	$1,500.00
Person to Person Citizen Advocacy	$7,000.00
Philander Smith College	$1,975.00
Philander Smith College	$2,000.00
Pine Bluff Public Schools	$30,505.00

Pope County 4-H Association	$10,000.00
Prescott School District	$1,998.00
Pulaski County Special School District	$30,175.00
Pulaski Metropolitan Initiative Neighborhood Development Corporation	$50,000.00
RAIN Arkansas	$1,500.00
RAIN Arkansas	$15,000.00
Reading Recovery Video	$5,269.00
Russellville School District	$10,551.00
Sandflat-Glendale Neighborhood Development Corporation	$27,500.00
SCAN Volunteer Services	$80,940.00
Searcy County Airport Commission	$24,500.00
Second Genesis Ministries	$30,695.00
Service Corps of Retired Executives (SCORE)	$1,500.00
Shepherd's Center of Little Rock	$2,000.00
Shepherd's Ranch	$2,000.00
Shirley Community Service and Development Corporation	$50,910.00
Shirley School District	$2,000.00
Siloam Springs Public Schools	$17,160.00
Social, Economic, and Education Development, Monticello	$10,000.00
South Arkansas Community Action Authority	$1,800.00
South Conway County School District	$2,000.00
South Mississippi County School District	$2,000.00
South Mississippi County School District	$2,000.00
South-Central Education Service Cooperative	$20,000.00
Southeast Arkansas Community Development Corporation	$62,532.00
Southern Development Bancorporation	$250,000.00
Southwest Arkansas Community Development Corporation	$56,880.00
Springdale School District	$2,000.00
Springdale School District	$7,500.00
Stuttgart Public Schools	$1,685.00
Teach for America	$36,129.00
Texarkana, City of,	$27,500.00
U.S. Catholic Conference, Trinity Junior High	$2,000.00
Undoing Racism and Organizing	$4,536.00
United Way of Pulaski County	$855.00
Universal Housing Development Corporation	$31,623.00
University of Arkansas for Medical Sciences	$1,500.00

University of Arkansas for Medical Sciences	$2,000.00
University of Arkansas for Medical Sciences	$8,000.00
University of Arkansas Foundation	$1,850.00
University of Arkansas Foundation	$113,200.00
University of Arkansas Foundation	$2,000.00
University of Arkansas Foundation	$52,100.00
University of Arkansas Foundation	$65,285.00
University of Arkansas, Little Rock	$1,000.00
University of Arkansas, Little Rock	$1,000.00
University of Arkansas, Little Rock	$1,004.00
University of Arkansas, Little Rock	$2,000.00
University of Arkansas, Little Rock	$2,000.00
University of Arkansas, Little Rock	$30,000.00
University of Arkansas, Little Rock	$60,200.00
University of Arkansas, Pine Bluff	$2,000.00
University of Arkansas, Pine Bluff	$60,000.00
University of Arkansas, Pine Bluff	$85,088.00
Van Buren Public Schools	$1,000.00
Ventures in Education	$33,000.00
Volunteers of America	$30,000.00
Warren School District	$9,923.00
Watershed Human and Community Development Agency	$1,500.00
Weiner Public Schools	$1,500.00
Weiner Public Schools	$7,500.00
West Memphis School District	$1,235.00
Western Arkansas Education Service Cooperative	$20,000.00
Westside Consolidated School District	$1,000.00
Westside School District	$1,000.00
White Hall School District	$2,000.00
White River Planning and Development District	$7,100.00
Winslow School District	$835.00
Winthrop Rockefeller Foundation, At-Risk Program Documentation	$5,369.00
Winthrop Rockefeller Foundation, Housing Initiative	$2,001.00
Winthrop Rockefeller Foundation, Networking Conference	$13,871.00
Witts Spring School District	$1,032.00
Woodruff County Economic Development Council	$15,000.00
Yellville Summit School District	$1,000.00
YMCA of Metropolitan Little Rock	$45,937.00
Youth Programs and Services Inventory	$22,506.00
TOTAL	**$5,515,747.00**

1995

A Better Chance	$56,950.00
Acorn School District	$1,000.00
African American Men of Distinction	$2,000.00
American Lung Association of Arkansas	$400.00
Arch Ford Education Service Cooperative	$10,000.00
Arkadelphia Public Schools	$1,905.00
Arkadelphia Public Schools	$2,000.00
Arkansans for Drug-Free Youth, Union County	$18,000.00
Arkansas (Photo Identification Program)	$1,000.00
Arkansas (Prosecutor's Pre-charging Diversion Program)	$2,000.00
Arkansas ABLE	$49,750.00
Arkansas Advocates for Children and Families	$15,000.00
Arkansas Advocates for Children and Families	$84,402.00
Arkansas Association of Community Development Corporations	$75,000.00
Arkansas Association of LeadAR Alumni	$29,050.00
Arkansas Aviation Historical Society	$2,000.00
Arkansas Chapter of the National Association of Black Social Workers	$1,000.00
Arkansas Community Foundation	$150,000.00
Arkansas Crisis Intervention Center	$1,500.00
Arkansas Delta Housing Development Corporation	$32,000.00
Arkansas Department of Human Services	$1,000.00
Arkansas Development Finance uthority	$125,000.00
Arkansas Disability Coalition	$30,950.00
Arkansas Economic Corporation	$113,500.00
Arkansas Extension Homemakers Council	$10,000.00
Arkansas Friends for Better Schools	$58,237.00
Arkansas Gay and Lesbian Task Force	$25,100.00
Arkansas Human Development Corporation	$1,500.00
Arkansas Land and Farm Development Corporation	$44,500.00
Arkansas Low-Income Housing Coalition	$68,394.00
Arkansas Office of the Attorney General	$1,200.00
Arkansas Public Policy Center	$2,328.00
Arkansas Public Policy Panel	$64,289.00

Arkansas Repertory Theater	$140,420.00
Arkansas River Education Service Cooperative	$1,388.00
Arkansas River Education Service Cooperative	$10,000.00
Arkansas River Valley Regional Library System	$2,000.00
Arkansas River Valley Resource Conservation and Development	$16,800.00
Arkansas Rural Development Commission	$135,000.00
Arkansas Seniors Organized for Progress	$50,000.00
Arkansas Single Parent Scholarship Fund	$12,980.00
Arkansas State University	$30,000.00
Arkansas State University	$37,355.00
Arkansas Tech University	$30,000.00
Armoel School District	$2,000.00
Artisan Source	$2,000.00
Arts Live	$2,000.00
Arts Live	$20,000.00
ARVAC (Rural Industries)	$41,317.00
Association for Children for Enforcement of Support	$10,000.00
Association for Supervision and Curriculum Development	$59,914.00
Association for Supervision and Curriculum Development	$86,700.00
Association of Black Engineers in Arkansas	$9,850.00
Atkins Public Schools	$2,000.00
Augusta Public Schools	$1,772.00
Autism Society of America	$1,986.00
Batesville School District	$1,000.00
Benton Public Schools	$1,250.00
Bentonville Public Schools	$9,500.00
Berryville Public Schools	$1,500.00
Block Grant Planning	$4,375.00
Boy Scouts of America	$75,000.00
Boys' and Girls' Club of Bentonville	$1,500.00
Boys', Girls', Adults' Community Development Center	$40,000.00
Break the Mold Process Observers	$2,747.00
Cabot Public Schools	$1,600.00
Cabot Public Schools	$1,750.00
Camden School District	$29,539.00
Camden School District	$9,500.00
Carthage High School	$9,500.00
Cassatot Technical College	$72,755.00
Centers for Youth and Families	$61,259.00
Chapter 1 Study	$92,876.00
Cleburne County Cares	$6,115.00

College Station Community Development Corporation	$1,700.00
Community Local Action Center	$77,519.00
Community Resource Group	$48,000.00
Conway Public Schools	$1,000.00
Conway Public Schools	$9,500.00
Corning Public Schools	$1,992.00
Corporation Connections Update	$1,000.00
Cotter School District	$1,414.00
Crowley's Ridge Education Cooperative	$10,000.00
Dardanelle Public Schools	$9,500.00
Daughters of Charity Services of Arkansas	$2,000.00
Dawson Education Service Cooperative	$10,000.00
Deer Consolidated Schools	$1,600.00
Delta Community Development Corporation	$130,627.00
Delta Community Development Corporation	$710.00
Delta Research, Education and Development Foundation	$39,995.00
DeQueen-Mena Educational Cooperative	$10,000.00
Dodson Street Family Life Center	$10,000.00
Dumas Public Schools	$1,500.00
East Arkansas Legal Services	$30,166.00
East End School District	$1,000.00
East End School District	$1,845.00
East-Central Arkansas Economic Development Corporation	$2,000.00
East-Central Arkansas Economic Development Corporation	$234.00
Economic Opportunity Agency of Washington County	$49,100.00
El Dorado Public Schools	$9,500.00
Elizabeth McGill Drop-In Center	$60,000.00
Family Community Development Corporation	$33,323.00
Fayetteville Public Schools	$1,000.00
Fayetteville Public Schools	$1,500.00
Fayetteville Public Schools	$1,692.00
Financial Management Workshops	$10,000.00
Fort Smith Public Schools	$1,500.00
Fort Smith Public Schools	$2,000.00
Fort Smith Public Schools	$7,500.00
Fort Smith Symphony Association	$14,150.00
Frances A. Allen School for Exceptional Children	$1,000.00
Future Builders	$44,399.00
Future Builders	$62,153.00
Girl Scouts of America, Conifer Council	$20,359.00

Girl Scouts of America, Crowley's Ridge Girl Scout Council	$1,990.00
Gladney Fund, Arkansas Auxiliary	$10,000.00
Global Learning Center	$2,000.00
Global Learning Center	$25,000.00
Governor's Commission on Adult Literacy	$27,800.00
Gravette School District	$1,991.00
Greenbrier Public Schools	$9,500.00
Greene County Technical School District	$992.00
Group Living	$10,000.00
Guardianship	$28,000.00
Hazen School District	$1,685.00
Heifer Project International	$2,000.00
Heifer Project International	$26,750.00
Helena Community Renewal Corporation	$45,000.00
Henderson State University	$60,000.00
House of Lydia	$10,000.00
Housing Authority of Camden	$1,500.00
Huntsville School District	$1,500.00
Huntsville School District	$2,000.00
In Affordable Housing	$45,000.00
International Business Education	$2,000.00
International Life Services	$1,000.00
J & J Christian Riding School	$2,000.00
Jessieville School District	$2,000.00
Jessieville School District	$2,000.00
John Brown University	$30,000.00
Kirby Public Schools	$9,500.00
Lakeside School District	$1,400.00
Lakeside School District	$1,412.00
Lakeside School District	$1,500.00
Lamar School District	$1,953.00
League of Women Voters Education Fund	$10,000.00
League of Women Voters Education Fund	$29,450.00
Lee County School District	$1,500.00
Leslie School District	$1,495.00
Little Rock Public Schools	$1,000.00
Little Rock Public Schools	$1,500.00
Little Rock Public Schools	$1,500.00
Little Rock Public Schools	$500.00
Little Rock Public Schools	$9,500.00
Little Rock, City of,	$800.00
Lonoke Public Schools	$1,000.00
Lyon College	$13,750.00
Lyon College	$2,000.00
Lyon College	$30,000.00
Magnolia School District	$1,998.00
Mallalieu Black Community Developers	$55,000.00
Martin Luther King Jr. Commission	$54,037.00
Micro-Loan Funds	$6,675.00
Monticello School District	$1,731.00
My House	$13,640.00
National Dunbar Alumni Association of Little Rock	$1,000.00
National Trust for Historic Preservation	$2,000.00
National Urban League	$45,000.00
Native American Coalition of Arkansas	$47,150.00
Nettleton Public Schools	$1,000.00
Nettleton Public Schools	$1,775.00
Nettleton Public Schools	$9,500.00
Nevada School District	$1,960.00
New Horizons Church and its Ministries	$58,000.00
Newton County Housing Council	$30,000.00
Newton County Library	$1,148.00
Newton County Resource Council	$50,000.00
Nonprofit Resources	$49,260.00
Nonprofit Resources	$58,600.00
North Garland County Youth Center	$57,000.00
North Little Rock Housing Authority	$500.00
North Little Rock Public Schools	$9,500.00
North-central Arkansas Education Service Center	$10,000.00
Northeast Arkansas Educational Cooperative	$2,000.00
Northside Development Corporation	$1,500.00
Northwest Arkansas Community College	$800.00
Northwest Arkansas Education Service Cooperative	$10,000.00
Northwest Arkansas Education Service Cooperative	$890.00
Old State House Museum Associates	$1,000.00
Operation Lifesaver	$1,500.00
Ouachita County Youth Aid	$75,000.00
Ouachita Public Schools	$2,000.00
Ozan-Inghram/Iron Mountain Neighborhood Development Corporation	$27,500.00
Ozark Legal Services	$2,000.00
Ozark Recycling Enterprise	$1,500.00
Parent-Teacher Association, Arkansas Congress	$25,615.00
Pine Bluff Public Schools	$1,985.00
Pine Bluff Public Schools	$17,930.00
Pottsville School District	$1,700.00

Prescott School District	$1,388.00
Prescott School District	$1,983.00
Pulaski County Juvenile Services	$59,563.00
Pulaski County Special School District	$1,000.00
Pulaski County Special School District	$1,137.00
Pulaski County Special School District	$18,150.00
Pulaski County Special School District	$2,000.00
Pulaski Metropolitan Initiative Neighborhood Development Corporation	$50,000.00
Pulaski Metropolitan Initiative Neighborhood Development	$49,280.00
Quapaw Quarter Association	$43,140.00
Russellville School District	$1,369.00
Russellville School District	$12,079.00
Russellville School District	$2,000.00
Sandflat-Glendale Neighborhood Development Corporation	$27,500.00
SCAN Volunteer Services	$53,489.00
Scotland School District	$1,550.00
Second Genesis Ministries	$22,425.00
Sevier County	$1,500.00
Shepherd's Ranch	$40,000.00
Shirley Community Service and Development Corporation	$43,140.00
South Conway County School District	$1,750.00
South Mississippi County School District	$1,500.00
South-Central Arkansas Service Cooperative	$10,000.00
Southern Regional Council	$7,500.00
Springdale School District	$1,740.00
Star City Public Schools	$1,000.00
Texarkana Arkansas School District	$2,000.00
Texarkana, City of,	$27,500.00
Trumann Public Schools	$1,500.00
U.S. Catholic Conference	$1,000.00
U.S. Catholic Conference	$1,500.00
Undoing Racism and Organizing	$20,000.00
United Way of Union County	$10,000.00
Universal Housing Development Corporation	$33,870.00
University of Arkansas for Medical Sciences	$75,000.00
University of Arkansas for Medical Sciences	$89,200.00
University of Arkansas Foundation	$1,500.00
University of Arkansas Foundation	$1,920.00
University of Arkansas Foundation	$115,250.00

University of Arkansas Foundation	$28,400.00
University of Arkansas Foundation	$37,845.00
University of Arkansas Foundation	$87,325.00
University of Arkansas	$60,000.00
University of Arkansas, Little Rock	$30,000.00
University of Arkansas, Little Rock	$30,000.00
University of Arkansas, Little Rock	$60,200.00
University of Arkansas, Pine Bluff	$1,000.00
University of Arkansas, Pine Bluff	$10,000.00
University of Arkansas, Pine Bluff	$2,000.00
University of Arkansas, Pine Bluff	$60,000.00
University of Arkansas, Pine Bluff	$80,000.00
University of Central Arkansas	$1,000.00
University of Central Arkansas	$60,000.00
Valley Springs School District	$1,650.00
Ventures in Education	$34,000.00
Volunteers of America	$30,000.00
Watershed Human and Community Development Agency	$2,000.00
Watson Chapel School District	$1,500.00
Weiner Public Schools	$1,025.00
Weiner Public Schools	$9,500.00
West Memphis School District	$800.00
Western Arkansas Education Service Cooperative	$10,000.00
Westside Consolidated School District	$585.00
Wildwood Center for the Performing Arts	$2,000.00
Winthrop Rockefeller Foundation At-Risk Program Documentation	$7,207.00
Winthrop Rockefeller Foundation, Networking Conference	$10,106.00
Woodruff County Economic Development Council	$15,000.00
YMCA of Metropolitan Little Rock	$31,436.00
Youth Home	$18,383.00
Youth Programs and Services Inventory	$9,400.00
TOTAL	**$5,710,328.00**

1996

A Better Chance	$73,200.00
ACORN Housing Corporation	$1,400.00
Advocates and Relatives for Kids	$8,250.00
Aid in Community Development	$10,000.00
Aldersgate	$1,375.00
Arch Ford Education Service Cooperative	$10,000.00
Arkadelphia Public Schools	$1,100.00
Arkansans for Drug-Free Youth, Union County	$17,500.00
Arkansas ABLE	$35,332.00

Arkansas Advocates for Children and Families	$2,000.00
Arkansas Advocates for Children and Families	$36,664.00
Arkansas Association of Community Development Corporations	$75,000.00
Arkansas Baptist College	$40,000.00
Arkansas Broadcasting Foundation	$50,930.00
Arkansas Civil Liberties Foundation	$2,000.00
Arkansas Community Foundation	$150,000.00
Arkansas Delta Housing Development Corporation	$30,000.00
Arkansas Delta Housing Development Corporation	$35,250.00
Arkansas Department of Health	$2,000.00
Arkansas Department of Parks and Tourism	$1,200.00
Arkansas Development Finance Authority	$125,000.00
Arkansas Economic Corporation	$115,500.00
Arkansas Endowment for the Humanities/Humanities Council	$50,000.00
Arkansas Environmental Federation	$55,940.00
Arkansas Gay and Lesbian Task Force	$16,700.00
Arkansas Land and Farm Development Corporation	$44,500.00
Arkansas Low-Income Housing Coalition	$71,090.00
Arkansas Public Policy Panel	$63,015.00
Arkansas River Education Service Cooperative	$10,000.00
Arkansas River Valley Resource Conservation and Development	$15,350.00
Arkansas Rural Development Commission	$135,000.00
Arkansas School for the Deaf	$1,500.00
Arkansas Seniors Organized for Progress	$45,000.00
Arkansas Single Parent Scholarship Fund	$12,980.00
Arkansas Single Parent Scholarship Fund	$48,838.00
Arkansas State University	$30,000.00
Arkansas Tech University	$30,000.00
Arkansas Women on the Move	$1,500.00
Arkansas's Tax System	$50,570.00
Association for Children for Enforcement of Support	$20,000.00
Association for Supervision and Curriculum Development	$62,800.00
Atkins Public Schools	$1,500.00
Baxter County Library	$10,000.00
Beebe School District	$1,200.00

Beebe School District	$1,500.00
Benton Public Schools	$1,150.00
Bentonville Public Schools	$1,320.00
Bentonville Public Schools	$9,500.00
Bethel Crisis Community Development Center	$2,000.00
Block Grant Planning	$1,830.00
Boy Scouts of America	$96,000.00
Boys', Girls', Adults' Community Development Center	$40,000.00
Bradley, City of,	$2,000.00
Break the Mold Process Observers	$3,542.00
Brinkley School District	$1,500.00
Camden School District	$25,320.00
Camden School District	$9,500.00
Cassatot Technical College	$45,244.00
Cave City School District	$1,500.00
Center for Arkansas Legal Services	$1,500.00
Centers for Youth and Families	$64,553.00
Cleburne County Cares	$8,175.00
College Station Community Development Corporation	$1,500.00
Colt Community Development Corporation	$25,000.00
Community Coalition Corporation	$50,000.00
Community Economic Development Training	$12,000.00
Community Local Action Center	$76,904.00
Community Organization for Drug Education	$10,000.00
Community Resource Group	$2,000.00
Community Resource Group	$22,000.00
Community Services Network	$2,000.00
Conway Public Schools	$1,200.00
Conway Public Schools	$1,300.00
Conway Public Schools	$1,500.00
Conway Public Schools	$1,600.00
Conway Public Schools	$9,500.00
Cornerstone Project	$45,233.00
Corning Public Schools	$1,250.00
Crowley's Ridge Education Cooperative	$10,000.00
Danville Public Schools	$1,400.00
Dardanelle Public Schools	$9,500.00
Dawson Education Service Cooperative	$10,000.00
Deer Consolidated Schools	$1,700.00
Delta Community Development Corporation	$48,366.00
Delta Research, Education and Development Foundation	$2,000.00
Delta Special School District	$1,080.00
DeQueen-Mena Educational Cooperative	$10,000.00

Dermott Community Action	$1,500.00
Dewitt School District	$1,208.00
Dollarway School District	$500.00
Economic Opportunity Agency of Washington County	$25,300.00
El Dorado Public Schools	$1,500.00
El Dorado Public Schools	$9,500.00
Elizabeth McGill Drop-In Center	$55,000.00
Emma Elease Webb Community Center	$1,500.00
England Community Development Corporation	$2,000.00
Enterprise Corporation of the Delta	$50,000.00
EZ/EC Followup of Funded and Unfunded Sites	$9,714.00
Family Community Development Corporation	$33,323.00
Family Service Agency of Central Arkansas	$43,000.00
Farmington School District	$1,320.00
Fayetteville Public Schools	$600.00
Financial Management Workshops	$7,500.00
Florence Crittenton Home Services	$2,000.00
Fort Smith Public Schools	$1,500.00
Fort Smith Public Schools	$1,875.00
Fort Smith Public Schools	$19,000.00
Fort Smith Symphony Association	$19,300.00
Fouke School District	$1,250.00
Fountain Lake School District	$1,500.00
Future Builders	$45,231.00
Genoa Central School District	$1,400.00
Girl Scouts of America, Conifer Council	$13,675.00
Global Village Community Services	$10,000.00
Green Forest School District	$1,500.00
Greenbrier Public Schools	$9,500.00
Guardianship	$18,000.00
Hamburg School District	$1,300.00
Harrisburg School District	$1,500.00
Harrison School District	$1,000.00
Helena Community Renewal Corporation	$40,000.00
Henderson State University	$60,000.00
Historic Tourism	$5,000.00
Horatio School District	$1,000.00
Hot Springs Documentary Film Festival	$2,000.00
In Affordable Housing	$40,000.00
Jenkins Memorial Children's Center	$1,965.00
John Brown University	$30,000.00
Jonesboro Public Schools	$1,200.00
Junction City Industrial Development Corporation	$10,000.00
Junction City Industrial Development Corporation	$600.00
Kirby Public Schools	$1,325.00
Kirby Public Schools	$9,500.00
Lake Hamilton School District	$1,000.00
Lake Hamilton School District	$1,440.00
Lakeside School District	$1,200.00
Lakeside School District	$1,500.00
Lane House	$20,750.00
League of Women Voters Education Fund	$25,050.00
Leslie School District	$1,500.00
Little Rock Public Schools	$1,100.00
Little Rock Public Schools	$603.00
Little Rock Public Schools	$9,500.00
Little Rock–South Little Rock Community Development Corporation	$10,000.00
Lonoke Public Schools	$1,250.00
Lyon College	$30,000.00
Malvern Public Schools	$1,500.00
March of Dimes Birth Defects Foundation	$1,500.00
Martin Luther King Jr. Commission	$57,564.00
Micro-Loan Funds	$10,114.00
Monticello School District	$1,500.00
Monticello School District	$1,530.00
Murfreesboro Public Schools	$1,600.00
Museum of Science and History	$71,500.00
My House	$12,200.00
National Council of Contractors Association	$50,000.00
National Dunbar Alumni Association of Little Rock	$1,000.00
Natural Heritage Commission	$2,000.00
Nettleton Public Schools	$1,400.00
Nettleton Public Schools	$9,500.00
New Horizon Church and Its Ministries	$58,000.00
Newton County Housing Council	$30,000.00
Newton County Resource Council	$1,240.00
Newton County Resource Council	$50,000.00
Nonprofit Resources	$37,640.00
North Garland County Boys' and Girls' Club	$51,000.00
North Little Rock Public Schools	$1,400.00
North Little Rock Public Schools	$1,500.00
North-Central Arkansas Education Service Center	$10,000.00
Northeast Arkansas School District	$1,500.00
Northwest Arkansas Education Service Cooperative	$10,000.00
Oden School District	$612.00
Office of Human Concern	$2,000.00

Osceola School District	$1,500.00	Springdale School District	$1,500.00
Ouachita County Youth Aid	$100,000.00	Springdale School District	$1,500.00
Ozan-Inghram/Iron Mountain Neighborhood Development Corporation	$50,000.00	St. Vincent Development Foundation	$2,000.00
Parent-Teacher Association, Arkansas Congress	$17,941.00	Stamps Special School District	$1,000.00
		Star City Public Schools	$1,500.00
Pathways Community Development Commission	$1,400.00	Taylor School District	$1,300.00
		Temporarily Impaired Ministries	$2,000.00
Pathways Community Development Commission	$108,650.00	Training Community Organizations for Change	$115,250.00
Peaceable Kingdom	$250.00	U.S. Catholic Conference, General Counsel	$1,920.00
Pine Bluff Public Schools	$1,500.00	United Methodist Children's Home	$2,000.00
Pine Bluff Public Schools	$11,450.00	United Methodist Homeless Housing Mission	$10,000.00
Plainview-Rover School District	$1,200.00	United Way of Union County	$5,000.00
Plainview-Rover School District	$1,500.00	Universal Housing Development Corporation	$33,870.00
Public School Funding in Arkansas	$62,450.00	University of Arkansas for Medical Sciences	$69,326.00
Pulaski County Juvenile Services	$59,563.00	University of Arkansas Foundation	$99,860.00
Pulaski County Special School District	$1,375.00	University of Arkansas	$60,000.00
Pulaski County Special School District	$1,400.00	University of Arkansas, Little Rock	$1,000.00
		University of Arkansas, Little Rock	$30,000.00
Pulaski County Special School District	$1,500.00	University of Arkansas, Little Rock	$30,000.00
Pulaski County Special School District	$11,875.00	University of Arkansas, Pine Bluff	$1,300.00
		University of Arkansas, Pine Bluff	$60,000.00
Pulaski Metropolitan Initiative Neighborhood Development Corporation	$50,000.00	University of Central Arkansas	$60,000.00
		Victory Outreach	$2,000.00
Pulaski Metropolitan Initiative Neighborhood Development Corporation	$50,000.00	Viola School District	$1,500.00
		Watson Chapel School District	$1,350.00
Quapaw Quarter Association	$31,248.00	Weiner Public Schools	$9,500.00
RAIN Arkansas	$60,362.00	West Memphis School District	$1,400.00
Rogers Public Schools	$1,500.00	Western Arkansas Education Service Cooperative	$10,000.00
Russellville School District	$1,400.00	Westside Memphis School District	$900.00
Russellville School District	$1,500.00	White Hall School District	$755.00
Saving America's Future	$2,000.00	Wildwood Center for the Performing Arts	$152,000.00
SCAN Volunteer Services	$39,748.00		
Searcy Public Schools	$1,500.00	Winthrop Rockefeller Foundation, Networking Conference	$10,701.00
Second Genesis Ministries	$21,450.00	Witts Springs School District	$1,400.00
Second Look at Housing in Arkansas	$18,660.00	Woodruff County Economic Development Council	$15,000.00
Shepherd's Center of Little Rock	$21,300.00	Youth Home	$11,425.00
Shepherd's Ranch	$35,000.00	**TOTAL**	**$5,266,823.00**
Shirley Community Service and Development Corporation	$130,820.00	**1997**	
Shorter College	$1,500.00		
Sloan-Hendrix School District	$1,400.00	A Better Chance	$83,750.00
South Mississippi County School District	$1,500.00	Acorn School District	$1,750.00
		Advocates and Relatives for Kids	$1,150.00
Southside School District	$1,500.00	Arkansans for Drug-Free Youth, Union County	$17,500.00
Southwest Arkansas Community Development Corporation	$49,994.00	Arkansas ABLE	$21,385.00
Southwest Arkansas Community Development Corporation	$50,000.00	Arkansas Broadcasting Foundation	$49,660.00

Arkansas Community Foundation	$150,000.00
Arkansas Delta Housing Development Corporation	$34,250.00
Arkansas Development Finance Authority	$125,000.00
Arkansas Endowment for the Humanities/Humanities Council	$40,000.00
Arkansas Environmental Federation	$55,940.00
Arkansas Rural Development Commission	$135,000.00
Arkansas Seniors Organized for Progress	$40,000.00
Arkansas Single Parent Scholarship Fund	$12,980.00
Arkansas State University	$30,000.00
Arkansas Tech University	$30,000.00
Association for Children for Enforcement of Support	$20,000.00
Bentonville Public Schools	$9,500.00
Blytheville School District	$1,975.00
Boy Scouts of America	$25,000.00
Camden School District	$9,500.00
Cassatot Technical College	$24,337.00
Centers for Youth and Families	$57,367.00
Cleburne County Cares	$1,500.00
Community Coalition Corporation	$50,000.00
Conway Public Schools	$9,500.00
Cotter School District	$1,700.00
Dardanelle Public Schools	$9,500.00
Delta Community Development Corporation	$48,500.00
El Dorado Public Schools	$9,500.00
Elaine School District	$2,000.00
Emerson School District	$2,000.00
Enterprise Corporation of the Delta	$70,000.00
Family Community Development Corporation	$30,823.00
Family Service Agency of Central Arkansas	$28,181.00
Fort Smith Public Schools	$1,080.00
Fort Smith Public Schools	$9,500.00
Fort Smith Symphony Association	$19,800.00
Future Builders	$49,031.00
Girl Scouts of America, Conifer Council	$8,110.00
Greenbrier Public Schools	$9,500.00
Henderson State University	$60,000.00
In Affordable Housing	$35,000.00
John Brown University	$30,000.00
Kirby Public Schools	$9,500.00
League of Women Voters Education Fund	$21,550.00
Little Rock Public Schools	$2,000.00
Little Rock Public Schools	$9,500.00
Lyon College	$30,000.00
Magnet Cove School District	$2,000.00
Museum of Science and History	$42,000.00
My House	$7,340.00
National Council of Contractors Association	$50,000.00
Nettleton Public Schools	$9,500.00
New Horizon Church and Its Ministries	$50,000.00
Nonprofit Resources	$36,640.00
Nonprofit Resources	$65,000.00
North Garland County Boys' and Girls' Club	$44,000.00
Ozan-Inghram/Iron Mountain Neighborhood Development Corporation	$50,000.00
Pathways Community Development Commission	$80,750.00
Pulaski County Juvenile Services	$65,783.00
Pulaski County Special School District	$2,000.00
Pulaski Metropolitan Initiative Neighborhood Development Corporation	$25,000.00
Quapaw Quarter Association	$21,096.00
RAIN Arkansas	$53,038.00
Russellville School District	$2,000.00
Shepherd's Center of Little Rock	$15,400.00
Shepherd's Ranch	$25,000.00
Southwest Arkansas Community Development Corporation	$44,205.00
Southwest Arkansas Community Development Corporation	$50,000.00
Texarkana School District	$1,980.00
Training Community Organizations for Change	$115,250.00
United Way of Union County	$5,000.00
University of Arkansas for Medical Sciences	$61,601.00
University of Arkansas Foundation	$99,958.00
University of Arkansas	$60,000.00
University of Arkansas, Little Rock	$30,000.00
University of Arkansas, Little Rock	$30,000.00
University of Arkansas, Pine Bluff	$60,000.00
University of Central Arkansas	$60,000.00
Walnut Ridge School District	$1,937.00
Watson Chapel School District	$2,000.00
Weiner Public Schools	$9,500.00
Wickes School District	$1,000.00
Wildwood Center for the Performing Arts	$100,000.00
Yellville-Summit School District	$2,000.00
Youth Home	$13,925.00
TOTAL	**$2,928,722.00**

1998

A Better Chance	$196,350.00
Alread Community Resource and Development Council	$74,200.00
Alread School District	$25,800.00
Arkansas Arts Center Foundation	$20,000.00
Arkansas Community Foundation	$525,111.00
Arkansas Endowment for the Humanities/Humanities Council	$100,000.00
Aunt Jessie's House	$4,785.00
Bald Knob Public Education Foundation	$49,600.00
Bald Knob School District	$69,845.00
Brinkley School District	$20,000.00
Caddo Career Consortium	$39,000.00
Catticus Corporation	$75,000.00
Centerpoint School District	$85,600.00
Conway County Center for Exceptional Children	$5,725.00
Conway County Community Service	$6,000.00
Crawfordsville Community Development Corporation	$13,200.00
Crittenden and Mississippi County Economic Development	$13,200.00
Deer Volunteer Fire Association	$2,000.00
Delta Research, Education and Development Foundation	$32,500.00
Eastern Arkansas Community Outreach and Development Corporation	$13,200.00
Enterprise Corporation of the Delta	$1,500,000.00
Harmony House	$4,000.00
Humanity United Together	$13,200.00
Lawrence County Resources Council	$74,150.00
Leadership and Development for Children of the South	$13,200.00
Lee County Community Development Corporation	$19,919.00
Lurtron-Pelsor Volunteer Fire Association	$2,000.00
Morrilton Human Relations Council	$3,200.00
Mt. Judea Area Volunteer Fire Department	$1,000.00
New Horizon Church and Its Ministries	$20,000.00
Newton County Historical Society	$2,240.00
Newton County Housing Council	$4,000.00
Newton County Resource Council	$82,260.00
Newton County Resource Council	$12,000.00
Newton County Special Service Corporation	$8,000.00

Northwest Arkansas Economic Development District	$4,000.00
Ozark Conference Center	$8,798.00
Ozark Small Farm Viability Project	$1,500.00
Ozarka Technical College	$35,000.00
Ponca-Firetower Fire Department	$2,000.00
South Conway County Public School Foundation	$3,000.00
South Conway County School District	$90,500.00
Southern Christian Home	$3,548.00
Stone County Community Resource Council	$85,200.00
University of Arkansas Foundation	$6,800.00
Walnut Ridge School District	$50,850.00
Witts Springs School District	$25,000.00
TOTAL	**$3,446,481.00**

1999

A Better Chance	$84,700.00
Arkansas Arts Center Foundation	$10,000.00
Arkansas Arts Center Foundation	$100,000.00
Arkansas Arts Council	$100,000.00
Arkansas Commitment	$25,000.00
Arkansas Community Foundation	$5,000.00
Arkansas Community Foundation	$130,913.00
Arkansas Endowment for the Humanities/Humanities Council	$100,000.00
Arkansas Land and Farm Development Corporation	$17,000.00
Arkansas Land and Farm Development Corporation	$65,000.00
Arkansas Repertory Theater	$23,100.00
Arkansas River Valley Libraries for Literacy	$28,757.00
Arkansas River Valley Regional Library System	$8,420.00
Arkansas River Valley Regional Library System	$14,950.00
Arkansas River Valley Regional Library System	$20,000.00
Arkansas State University	$67,752.00
Boys' and Girls' Club of the Arkansas Valley	$55,574.00
Boys', Girls', Adults' Community Development Center	$17,428.00
Brinkley School District	$58,313.00
Catticus Corporation	$9,350.00
Central Arkansas Planning and Development	$22,340.00
Central Delta Historical Society	$12,495.00
Dardanelle Public Schools	$16,211.00
Enterprise Corporation of the Delta	$150,000.00

Enterprise Corporation of the Delta	$1,000,000.00
Fort Smith Symphony	$50,000.00
High Rocks Academy	$500.00
Ozan-Inghram/Iron Mountain Neighborhood Development Corporation	$25,000.00
Lee County Community Development Corporation	$38,000.00
Lee County Family Resource Center	$5,000.00
McNeal Funeral Home Workers Club	$13,245.00
Monroe County Child Development Center	$12,245.00
Neighborhood Reinvestment Corporation	$24,000.00
New Horizon Church and Its Ministries	$37,514.00
New Horizon Church and Its Ministries	$48,576.00
Southern Growth Policy Board	$20,000.00
T. I. Crudup Community Development Corporation	$31,119.00
Training Community Organizations for Change	$50,000.00
University of Arkansas	$12,340.00
University of Arkansas Foundation	$67,500.00
University of Arkansas Foundation	$99,999.00
University of Texas, Austin	$10,000.00
Wilburn School District	$22,750.00
Wildwood Center for the Performing Arts	$52,000.00
Wildwood Center for the Performing Arts	$100,000.00
Winrock International	$162,500.00
TOTAL	**$3,024,591.00**

Notes

Chapter 1: Introduction

1. Sam Harris, "Rockefeller Outlines His Plans," *Arkansas Gazette,* June 10, 1953, p. 2A.
2. David Rockefeller, *Memoirs* (New York: Random House, 2002), 37.
3. Sam Harris, "Rockefeller Outlines His Plans," *Arkansas Gazette,* June 10, 1953, p. 2A.
4. Winthrop Paul Rockefeller. Interview by author, February 1, 2001, pp. 2–3.
5. "Arkansas: Opportunity Regained," *Time Magazine,* December 2, 1966, pp. 24–25.
6. Winthrop Paul Rockefeller. Interview by author, February 1, 2001. p. 1.
7. *Family Weekly,* August 3, 1958, p. 14.
8. *A Letter to My Son.* Winthrop Rockefeller Collection, University of Arkansas at Little Rock Archives and Special Collections, pp. 32–33.
9. *A Letter to My Son.* Winthrop Rockefeller Collection, University of Arkansas at Little Rock Archives and Special Collections, p. 90.
10. *A Letter to My Son.* Winthrop Rockefeller Collection, University of Arkansas at Little Rock Archives and Special Collections, p. 90.
11. *A Letter to My Son.* Winthrop Rockefeller Collection, University of Arkansas at Little Rock Archives and Special Collections, pp. 91, 93.
12. *Family Weekly,* August 3, 1958, p. 14.
13. Melissa Smith, "The Rockefeller Legacy of Philanthropy." Presented at Winrock International Institute for Agricultural Development, May 9, 1991, p. 10.
14. Biographical sketch and press release on Winthrop Rockefeller's announcing his candidacy for governor, 1964. University of Arkansas at Little Rock Archives and Special Collections, Pamphlet No. 03904, p. 27.
15. Dictation transcribed Sep 27, 1951 for possible incorporation into *A Letter to My Son.* Winthrop Rockefeller Collection, University of Arkansas at Little Rock Archives and Special Collections—quote was never incorporated.
16. Editorial, "The Rockefeller Years," *Arkansas Democrat,* January 12, 1971.
17. Winthrop Paul Rockefeller. Interview by author, February 1, 2001, p. 4.
18. Winthrop Paul Rockefeller. Interview by author, February 1, 2001, p. 4.
19. Anne Bartley. Interview by author, February 15, 2000, p. 6.

20. Anne Bartley. Interview by author, February 15, 2000, p. 6.

21. Marion Burton. Interview by author, December 8, 1999, p. 2.

22. Marion Burton. Interview by author, December 8, 1999, p. 2.

23. *A Letter to My Son*. Winthrop Rockefeller Collection, University of Arkansas at Little Rock Archives and Special Collections, p. 26.

24. Carey Reich, *The Life of Nelson A. Rockefeller: Worlds to Conquer, 1908–1958* (New York: Doubleday, 1996), p. 26.

25. Marion Burton. Interview by author, December 8, 1999, p. 5.

26. G. Thomas Eisele. Interview by author, March 8, 2000, p. 3.

27. Biographical sketch and press release on Winthrop Rockefeller's announcing his candidacy for governor, 1964. University of Arkansas at Little Rock Archives and Special Collections, Pamphlet No. 03904, p. 27.

28. Marion Burton. Interview by author, December 8, 1999, p. 7.

29. Winthrop Paul Rockefeller. Interview by author, February 1, 2001, p. 12.

30. Rockwin Fund Review and Policy Statement, 1974, p. 2.

31. Rockwin Fund Review and Policy Statement, 1974, p. 2.

32. *A Letter to My Son*. Winthrop Rockefeller Collection, University of Arkansas at Little Rock Archives and Special Collections, p. 5.

33. *A Letter to My Son*. Winthrop Rockefeller Collection, University of Arkansas at Little Rock Archives and Special Collections, p. 6.

34. Winthrop Paul Rockefeller. Interview by author, February 1, 2001, p. 16.

35. Bruce Bartley. Interview by author, September 24, 2000, p. 2.

36. Editorial, "The Rockefeller Years," *Arkansas Democrat,* January 12, 1971.

37. Bruce Bartley. Interview by author, September 24, 2000, p. 2.

38. Bruce Bartley. Interview by author, September 24, 2000, p. 3.

39. Rockwin Fund Review and Policy Statement, 1974, p. 3.

Chapter 2: Racial Equality

1. Letter, Adolphine Fletcher Terry to Winthrop Rockefeller, June 11, 1958. Winthrop Rockefeller Collection, University of Arkansas at Little Rock Archives and Special Collections.

2. Anne Bartley. Interview by author, February 15, 2000, pp. 1, 4.

3. Henry Jones. Interview by author, November 29, 2000, p. 2.

4. Henry Jones. Interview by author, November 29, 2000, pp. 3–4.

5. Biographical sketch and press release on Winthrop Rockefeller's announcing his candidacy for governor, 1964. University of Arkansas at Little Rock Archives and Special Collections, Pamphlet No. 03904.

6. *A Letter to My Son*. Winthrop Rockefeller Collection, University of Arkansas at Little Rock Archives and Special Collections, pp. 14–15.

7. *A Letter to My Son*. Winthrop Rockefeller Collection, University of Arkansas at Little Rock Archives and Special Collections, p. 15.

8. "Arkansas Opportunity Regained," *Time Magazine,* December 2, 1966, p. 25.

9. Dictation transcribed September 27, 1951, for possible incorporation into *A Letter to My Son*. Winthrop Rockefeller Collection, University of Arkansas at Little Rock Archives and Special Collections—quote was never incorporated.

10. Robert Fisher. Interview by author, December 17, 1999, pp. 1–2.

11. Henry Jones. Interview by author, November 29, 2000, p. 7.

12. Henry Jones. Interview by author, November 29, 2000, p. 8.

13. William L. "Sonny" Walker. Interview by author, March 2, 2001, p. 6.

14. William L. "Sonny" Walker. Interview by author, March 2, 2001, p. 13.

15. Robert Fisher. Interview by author, December 17, 1999, p. 10.

16. William L. "Sonny" Walker. Interview by author, March 2, 2001, pp. 18–19.

17. William L. "Sonny" Walker. Interview by author, March 2, 2001, pp. 19–20.

18. Robert Fisher. Interview by author, December 17, 1999, p. 4.

19. Memo, Jane Bartlett to Frances Royston, August 2, 1971. Re: Plaque presented to Governor Rockefeller by the State Organization for Minority Involvement on April 24, 1971. Winthrop Rockefeller Collection UALR Archives and Special Collections.

Chapter 3: Education and Youth

1. Letter, John D. Rockefeller Jr. to Charles E. Sellers, July 8, 1929. Rockefeller Family Archives, Sleepy Hollow, New York.

2. *A Letter to My Son*. Winthrop Rockefeller Collection, University of Arkansas at Little Rock Archives and Special Collections, p. 28.

3. *A Letter to My Son*. Winthrop Rockefeller Collection, University of Arkansas at Little Rock Archives and Special Collections, p. 2 8.

4. Resolution by the Trustees of Ouachita Baptist University, December 21, 1965. Winthrop Rockefeller Collection, University of Arkansas at Little Rock Archives and Special Collections.

5. "Ouachita Dedicates Rockefeller Field House," *Arkansas Baptist Newsmagazine,* September 29, 1966, p. 11.

6. Biography of Winthrop Rockefeller, June 24, 1967. Winthrop Rockefeller Collection, University of Arkansas at Little Rock Archives and Special Collections, p. 30.

7. Letter, Winthrop Rockefeller to Henry Luce, April 25, 1940. Rockefeller Family Archives, Sleepy Hollow, New York.

8. Letter, Winthrop Rockefeller to Ansel E. Talbert, August 13, 1959. Winthrop Rockefeller Collection, University of Arkansas at Little Rock Archives and Special Collections.

9. "Statement by Governor Winthrop Rockefeller," March 25, 1968. Winthrop Rockefeller Collection, University of Arkansas at Little Rock Archives and Special Collections.

10. G. Thomas Eisle. Interview by author, March 8, 2000.

11. Letter, Jean Schmutz to Winthrop Rockefeller, July 15, 1964. Winthrop Rockefeller Collection, University of Arkansas at Little Rock Archives and Special Collections.

Chapter 4: Culture and the Arts

1. Anne Bartley. Interview by author, February 15, 2000.
2. Townsend Wolfe. Interview by author, January 12, 2000, p. 7.
3. "Jeane Mussman Hamilton," *Arkansas Democrat-Gazette,* February 20, 2000, p. 5D.
4. Letter, Winthrop Rockefeller to John Osman, April 11, 1960. Winthrop Rockefeller Collection, University of Arkansas at Little Rock Archives and Special Collections, p. 1.
5. Letter, Winthrop Rockefeller to John Osman, April 11, 1960. Winthrop Rockefeller Collection, University of Arkansas at Little Rock Archives and Special Collections, pp. 1–2.
6. Anne Bartley. Interview by author, February 15, 2000, p. 11.
7. Townsend Wolfe. Interview by author, January 12, 2000, p. 3.
8. "Jeane Mussman Hamilton," *Arkansas Democrat-Gazette,* February 20, 2000, p. 5D.
9. Townsend Wolfe. Interview by author, January 12, 2000, p. 6.
10. Townsend Wolfe. Interview by author, January 12, 2000, p. 8.
11. Townsend Wolfe. Interview by author, January 12, 2000, p. 12.
12. Townsend Wolfe. Interview by author, January 12, 2000, p. 12.
13. Steve Barnes, "The Star of Little Rock: An Arts Foundling Grows Up," *New York Times Magazine,* June 29, 2000.
14. Letter, Winthrop Rockefeller to Colonel T. H. Barton, May 9, 1960. Winthrop Rockefeller Collection, University of Arkansas at Little Rock Archives and Special Collections, p. 2.
15. Arkansas Arts Center, *Members Bulletin,* vol. 14, no. 4 (1973).

Chapter 5: Physical and Mental Health

1. Biographical sketch and press release on Winthrop Rockefeller's announcing his candidacy for governor, 1964. University of Arkansas at Little Rock Archives and Special Collections, Pamphlet No. 03904, p. 16.
2. "Area Cooperation in Medicine Urged," *New York Times,* April 16, 1950.
3. "New Building Ready in '53 as Hub of Bellevue," *New York Herald Tribune,* February 29, 1952.
4. "Rockefeller Honored at New York," *Arkansas Democrat,* February 4, 1966.
5. Memorandum, Winthrop Rockefeller to The Honorable Francis Cherry, February 16, 1954. Winthrop Rockefeller Collection, University of Arkansas at Little Rock Archives and Special Collections, p. 2.
6. Memorandum, Winthrop Rockefeller to The Honorable Francis Cherry, February 16, 1954. Winthrop Rockefeller Collection, University of Arkansas at Little Rock Archives and Special Collections, pp. 2–3.
7. ". . . Rockefeller's feeling: Cost of medicine has gotten to a point . . ." *Business Week,* August 20, 1955, p. 156.

8. "Perry County Doctor and Mr. Rockefeller," *Arkansas Democrat,* Sunday Magazine, January 30, 1955, p. 1.

9. "Perry County Doctor and Mr. Rockefeller," *Arkansas Democrat,* Sunday Magazine, January 30, 1955, p. 1.

10. "Perry County Doctor and Mr. Rockefeller," *Arkansas Democrat,* Sunday Magazine, January 30, 1955, p. 2.

11. KXLR Announcement—Dedication, Community Health Center, Perryville, July 11, 1955. Winthrop Rockefeller Collection, University of Arkansas at Little Rock Archives and Special Collections, p. 1.

12. KXLR Announcement—Dedication, Community Health Center, Perryville, July 11, 1955. Winthrop Rockefeller Collection, University of Arkansas at Little Rock Archives and Special Collections, p. 2.

13. Ben Hyatt. Interview by author, October 31, 2000, p. 3.

14. Ben Hyatt. Interview by author, October 31, 2000, p. 5.

15. Press Release on Winthrop Rockefeller's contribution, May 4, 1966. Winthrop Rockefeller Collection, University of Arkansas at Little Rock Archives and Special Collections.

16. Press Release on Winthrop Rockefeller's contribution, May 4, 1966. Winthrop Rockefeller Collection, University of Arkansas at Little Rock Archives and Special Collections.

17. "Rockefeller to Head National MH Campaign," *Morrilton Democrat,* March 21, 1963.

Chapter 6: Religion

1. Dictation transcribed September 27, 1951, for possible incorporation into *A Letter to My Son.* Winthrop Rockefeller Collection, University of Arkansas at Little Rock Archives and Special Collections—quote was never incorporated.

2. Dictation transcribed September 27, 1951, for possible incorporation into *A Letter to My Son.* Winthrop Rockefeller Collection, University of Arkansas at Little Rock Archives and Special Collections—quote was never incorporated.

Chapter 7: America's Place in the World

1. Rockefeller Brothers Fund, Annual Report, 1987.

2. Letter, Sidney Lovett to Winthrop Rockefeller, June 27, 1960. Winthrop Rockefeller Collection, University of Arkansas at Little Rock Archives and Special Collections.

3. "Rockefeller Hosts Meeting to Plan Infantry Museum," *Arkansas Democrat,* October 20, 1971.

Chapter 8: The Winthrop Rockefeller Foundation

1. Henry McHenry. Interview by author, January 31, 2001, p. 3.
2. Henry McHenry. Interview by author, January 31, 2001, pp. 4–5.
3. Henry McHenry. Interview by author, January 31, 2001, pp. 5–6.
4. Henry McHenry. Interview by author, January 31, 2001, p. 8.
5. Will of Winthrop Rockefeller. Filed February 23, 1973, Conway County, Arkansas.
6. Winthrop Rockefeller Foundation, Annual Report, 1975.
7. Tom McRae. Interview by author, November 1, 2000.
8. Winthrop Rockefeller Foundation, Annual Report, 1976.
9. Tom McRae. Interview by author, November 1, 2000.
10. Winthrop Rockefeller Foundation, Annual Report, 1977.
11. Winthrop Rockefeller Foundation, Annual Report, 1978.
12. Winthrop Rockefeller Foundation, Annual Report, 1981.
13. Winthrop Rockefeller Foundation, Annual Report, 1982.
14. Winthrop Rockefeller Foundation, Annual Report, 1982.
15. Winthrop Rockefeller Foundation, Annual Report, 1982.
16. Winthrop Rockefeller Foundation, Annual Report, 1983.
17. Winthrop Rockefeller Foundation, Annual Report, 1983.
18. Winthrop Rockefeller Foundation, Annual Report, 1984.
19. Winthrop Rockefeller Foundation, Annual Report, 1986/1987.
20. Winthrop Rockefeller Foundation, Annual Report, 1992.
21. Winthrop Rockefeller Foundation, Annual Report, 1993.
22. Sybil Hampton. Interview by author, January 31, 2001.
23. Sybil Hampton. Interview by author, January 31, 2001.
24. Sybil Hampton. Interview by author, January 31, 2001.
25. Sybil Hampton. Interview by author, January 31, 2001.
26. Winthrop Rockefeller Foundation Annual Report, 1994.

Chapter 9: The Winthrop Rockefeller Charitable Trust

1. Will of Winthrop Rockefeller. Filed February 23, 1973, Conway County, Arknasas, p. 1.
2. Will of Winthrop Rockefeller. Filed February 23, 1973, Conway County, Arkansas, p. 8.
3. Will of Winthrop Rockefeller. Filed February 23, 1973, Conway County, Arkansas, pp. 8–9.
4. Will of Winthrop Rockefeller. Filed February 23, 1973, Conway County, Arkansas, p. 9.
5. Marion Burton. Interview by author, December 8, 1999, p. 7.
6. Letter, David Rockefeller to Carlisle Humelsine, July 19, 1977.

7. Marion Burton. Interview by author, December 8, 1999, p. 12.

8. Letter, Dr. Trudie Kibbe Reed to Marion Burton, November 8, 1999. WR Trust, Little Rock.

9. Letter, Dr. Trudie Kibbe Reed to Marion Burton, November 8, 1999. WR Trust, Little Rock.

10. "$2 Million Buoys College Fund," *Arkansas Democrat-Gazette,* Aug 29 2000.

11. Activities Report of the National Rural Center, Report Number 4, January 1978, pp. 5–9.

Chapter 10: *Building Arkansas*

1. "WR Promises State Water Study," *Hot Springs Sentinel Record,* January 8, 1967.

2. "WR Promises State Water Study," *Hot Springs Sentinel Record,* January 8, 1967.

3. "Arkansas: Opportunity Regained," *Time Magazine,* December 2, 1966, p. 24.

4. "Arkansas Catalyst," *Time Magazine,* March 11, 1957, p. 94.

5. "Magazine Hails Rockefeller as Arkansas' No. 1 Salesman," *Arkansas Democrat,* March 7, 1963.

6. "Magazine Hails Rockefeller as Arkansas' No. 1 Salesman," *Arkansas Democrat,* March 7, 1963.

7. "Rockefeller Begins Second Decade in State with New Project," *Arkansas Democrat,* n.d., 1963, p. 2.

8. Obituary/Press Release, February 22, 1973. Winthrop Rockefeller Collection, University of Arkansas at Little Rock Archives and Special Collections, p. 1.

Bibliography

Oral Interviews

Bartley, Anne. Interview by author, February 15, 2000.
Bartley, Bruce. Interview by author, September 24, 2000.
Burton, Marion. Interview by author, December 8, 1999.
Eisele, G. Thomas. Interview by author, March 8, 2000.
Fisher, Robert. Interview by author, December 17, 1999.
Hampton, Sybil. Interview by author, January 31, 2001.
Hyatt, Ben. Interview by author, October 31, 2000.
Jones, Henry. Interview by author, November 29, 2000.
McHenry, Henry. Interview by author, January 31, 2001.
McRae, Tom. Interview by author, November 1, 2000; February 14, 2001.
Rockefeller, Winthrop Paul. Interview by author, February 1, 2001.
Walker, William L. "Sonny." Interview by author, March 2, 2001.
Wolfe, Townsend. Interview by author, January 12, 2000.

Manuscript Collections

Biographical sketch and press release on Winthrop Rockefeller's announcing his candidacy for governor, 1964. University of Arkansas at Little Rock Archives and Special Collections, Pamphlet No. 03904.
KXLR Announcement—Dedication, Community Health Center, Perryville, July 11, 1955. Winthrop Rockefeller Collection, University of Arkansas at Little Rock Archives and Special Collections.
A Letter to My Son. Winthrop Rockefeller Collection, University of Arkansas at Little Rock Archives and Special Collections.
Letter, Adolphine Fletcher Terry to Winthrop Rockefeller, June 11, 1958. Winthrop Rockefeller Collection, University of Arkansas at Little Rock Archives and Special Collections.

Letter, David Rockefeller to Carlisle Humelsine, July 19, 1977. Unknown source.

Letter, Dr. Trudie Kibbe Reed to Winthrop Rockefeller Trust, November 8, 1999. WR Trust.

Letter, Jean Schmutz to Winthrop Rockefeller, July 15, 1964. Winthrop Rockefeller Collection, University of Arkansas at Little Rock Archives and Special Collections.

Letter, John D. Rockefeller Jr. to Charles E. Sellers, July 8, 1929. Rockefeller Family Archives, Sleepy Hollow, New York.

Letter, Sidney Lovett to Winthrop Rockefeller, June 27, 1960. Winthrop Rockefeller Collection, University of Arkansas at Little Rock Archives and Special Collections.

Letter, Winthrop Rockefeller to Ansel E. Talbert, August 13, 1959. Winthrop Rockefeller Collection, University of Arkansas at Little Rock Archives and Special Collections.

Letter, Winthrop Rockefeller to Colonel T. H. Barton, May 9, 1960. Winthrop Rockefeller Collection, University of Arkansas at Little Rock Archives and Special Collections.

Letter, Winthrop Rockefeller to Henry Luce, April 25, 1940. Rockefeller Family Archives, Sleepy Hollow, New York.

Letter, Winthrop Rockefeller to John Osman, April 11, 1960. Winthrop Rockefeller Collection, University of Arkansas at Little Rock Archives and Special Collections.

Memo, Jane Bartlett to Frances Royston, August 2, 1971. Re: Plaque presented to Governor Rockefeller by the State Organization for Minority Involvement on April 24, 1971. Winthrop Rockefeller Collection, University of Arkansas at Little Rock Archives and Special Collections.

Memorandum, Winthrop Rockefeller to The Honorable Francis Cherry, February 16, 1954. Winthrop Rockefeller Collection, University of Arkansas at Little Rock Archives and Special Collections.

Obituary/Press Release, February 22, 1973. Winthrop Rockefeller Collection, University of Arkansas at Little Rock Archives and Special Collections.

Press Release, December 5, 1960. Unknown source.

Press Release on Winthrop Rockefeller's contribution, May 4, 1966. Winthrop Rockefeller Collection, University of Arkansas at Little Rock Archives and Special Collections.

Resolution by the Trustees of Ouachita Baptist University, December 21, 1965. Winthrop Rockefeller Collection, University of Arkansas at Little Rock Archives and Special Collections.

"Statement by Governor Winthrop Rockefeller," March 25, 1968. Winthrop Rockefeller Collection, University of Arkansas at Little Rock Archives and Special Collections.

Articles and News Clippings

"Area Cooperation in Medicine Urged," *New York Times,* April 16, 1950.

Arkansas Arts Center, *Members Bulletin,* vol. 14, no. 4, 1973.

"Arkansas Catalyst," *Time Magazine,* March 11, 1957.

"Arkansas: Opportunity Regained," *Time Magazine,* December 2, 1966, pp. 24–28.

Barnes, Steve. "The Star of Little Rock: An Arts Foundling Grows Up," *New York Times Magazine,* June 29, 2000.

"Blacks Look at Gains under WR; Many Optimistic about Bumpers," *Arkansas Gazette,* n.d.

Family Weekly, August 3, 1958, p. 14.

"Governor's 'Furniture Factory' Operating with Volunteers," *WR70 Campaigner,* October 16, 1970.

"Hospital Gets $500,000 Gift," *Arkansas Gazette,* January 31, 1970.

"Jeane Mussman Hamilton," *Arkansas Democrat-Gazette,* February 20, 2000.

"Magazine Hails Rockefeller as Arkansas' No. 1 Salesman," *Arkansas Democrat,* March 7, 1963.

"New Building Ready in '53 as Hub of Bellevue," *New York Herald Tribune,* February 29, 1952

"Ouachita Dedicates Rockefeller Field House," *Arkansas Baptist Newsmagazine,* September 29, 1966.

"Perry County Doctor and Mr. Rockefeller," *Arkansas Democrat,* Sunday Magazine, January 30, 1955

"Rockefeller Begins Second Decade in State with New Project," *Arkansas Democrat,* n.d., 1963.

". . . Rockefeller's feeling: Cost of medicine has gotten to a point . . ." *Business Week,* August 20, 1955.

"Rockefeller Honored at New York," *Arkansas Democrat,* February 4, 1966.

"Rockefeller Hosts Meeting to Plan Infantry Museum," *Arkansas Democrat,* October 20, 1971.

"Rockefeller to Head National MH campaign," *Morrilton Democrat,* March 21, 1963.

"The Rockefeller Years," Editorial, *Arkansas Democrat,* January 12, 1971.

"$2 Million Buoys College Fund," *Arkansas Democrat-Gazette,* August 29, 2000.

"WR Promises State Water Study," *Hot Springs Sentinel Record,* January 8, 1967.

Annual Reports

Rockefeller Brothers Fund, Annual Report, 1987

Winthrop Rockefeller Foundation, Annual Report, 1975

Winthrop Rockefeller Foundation, Annual Report, 1976

Winthrop Rockefeller Foundation, Annual Report, 1978

Winthrop Rockefeller Foundation, Annual Report, 1982

Winthrop Rockefeller Foundation, Annual Report, 1983

Winthrop Rockefeller Foundation, Annual Report, 1984

Winthrop Rockefeller Foundation, Annual Report, 1987

Winthrop Rockefeller Foundation, Annual Report, 1992

Winthrop Rockefeller Foundation, Annual Report, 1993
Winthrop Rockefeller Foundation, Annual Report, 2000

Miscellaneous

Activities Report of the National Rural Center, Report Number 4, January 1978.
Reich, Carey. *The Life of Nelson A. Rockefeller: Worlds to Conquer, 1908–1958*. New York: Doubleday, 1996.
Rockefeller, David. *Memoirs*. New York: Random House, 2002.
Rockwin Fund Review and Policy Statement, 1974.
Smith, Melissa. "The Rockefeller Legacy of Philanthropy." Presented at Winrock International Institute for Agricultural Development, May 9, 1991.
Will of Winthrop Rockefeller. Filed February 23, 1973, Conway County, Arkansas.

Index

12–13; approach to changing world's view of America, 67–76; approach to philanthropy, 9–10, 19–22, 32, 38–39, 42–43; as board member of Urban League, 29–30; on board of New York University Medical Center, 55–56; café society life and, 4, 114; changes initiated for racial equality, 28, 30–34; character judgment of, 20–21, 23; charitable contributions of, 123–47; contributions for better health care, 20, 57–61, 62; contributions to arts, 19, 45–49, 51–53, 113, 119; contributions to Colonial Williamsburg, 49–51; contributions to cultural endeavors, 51–53; contributions to education, 17, 20, 30–31, 36–37, 39, 42–44, 44; contributions to Williamsburg area, 49–51; death of, 122; donation of blood during World War II, 71, 72; education of, 35–36, 114; family automobile collection, 121; family relationships, 3–4, 14, 114; fight against Arkansas's inferiority complex, 11–12, 17–18; at Fort Benning fund-raising event, 74, 75; fund-raising style, 10, 19, 47–48; as governor, 114–17; honorary degrees of, 40, 56; impact on Arkansas, 17, 113–22; interest in aviation, 37–39; interest in Duke Ellington, 52; interest in Eyrie Garden sculpture, 52–53; involvement in Middle East, 71–72; last days of, 113; at Loomis preparatory school, 13; marriages of, 15; military service, 4, 72–73, 75, 114; move to Arkansas, 1–4, 14–15, 16; organizations contributed to, 118; payment of supplements to state workers, 11–12, 33; philanthropic background, 7–9; politics and, 9, 10–12, 17–18; relationship with Winthrop Paul, 64–65; religion and, 63–66; as seen by others, 4,

118–19; sense of values, 26; view of racial equality, 23–30; will of, 78–79, 105–7; Winrock Farms projects and, 68–70; work for Greater New York Fund, 5–7, 8, 113; work for mental health care, 61–62; work for veterans' affairs, 73, 75–76, 76; work in Texas oil fields, 4–5, 6, 114; work on IBEC, 72, 73, 75; work on industrial development, 18–19, 117, 119–20, 120

Rockefeller, Winthrop Paul: book written to, 64–65; purchase of Winrock Farm, 106; on Winthrop Rockefeller's approach to change in Arkansas, 17–18; on Winthrop Rockefeller's form of philanthropy, 9–10, 19–20; on social difficulties of Hudson, 24; studies at TCU, 111; as trustee of Winthrop Rockefeller Charitable Trust, 105; on views of Winthrop Rockefeller, 4; work of, 5

Rockefeller Brothers Fund: concern about America's place in world, 67–68; contributions to Arkansas Arts Center, 48; contributions to Arkansas Baptist Medical Center, 61; establishment of Worldwatch Institute, 111; investment in Arkansas, 36; Winthrop Rockefeller Charitable Trust and, 107

Rockefeller family: philanthropy of, 7–9, 14; relationships within, 3–4; training of, 12–14; views on racial equality, 28. *See also specific Rockefeller or Rockefeller organization*

Rockefeller Family Fund, 107
Rockefeller Foundation, 69
Rockefeller Institute for Medical Research, 7
Rockefeller Sanitary Commission, 7
Rockwin Fund: contributions to education, 42–44; contribution to mental health care, 62; financial support of, 79; function of, 39; study of education

water resources study, 115–17
Welfare Rights Organization, 32
White Citizens Council, 24
Winrock Enterprises, 12, 121
Winrock Farms: cattle breeding at, 68;
  documentary about, 14, 114; housing
  projects of, 12; Hudson as manager of,
  24; information sharing, 71; as part of
  Rockefeller estate, 106; as training
  center, 110; water supply for, 115
Winrock International Agricultural
  Development Institute, 12, 69–70, 107
Winrock International Livestock Research
  and Training Center, 12, 69
Winthrop Rockefeller Archaeology
  Museum, *50, 51*
Winthrop Rockefeller Charitable Trust:
  agricultural development projects of,
  69–70; contributions of, 107–11,
  149–87; donation to Colonial
  Williamsburg, 51; function of, 39;
  Rockefeller's wishes for, 12, 105–7;
  Winthrop Rockefeller Foundation and,
  78–79
Winthrop Rockefeller Foundation: 1975
  grants, 79–81; 1976 grants, 81–82;
  1977 grants, 82; 1978 grants, 82–83;
  1979 grants, 83–85; 1980 grants, 85;
  1981 grants, 85–86; 1982 grants,
  86–87; 1983 grants, 87–89; 1984
  grants, 89–90; 1984 policy shifts, 89;
  1985 grants, 90–92; 1986 grants,
  92–93; 1987 grants, 93–94; 1988
  grants, 94–95; 1990 grants, 97; 1991
  grants, 97–98; 1992 grants, 98–99;
  1993 grants, 99; 1994 grants, 99–100;

1995 grants, 100; 1996 grants,
  100–101; 1997 grants, 101–2; 1998
  grants, 102–3; 1999 grants, 103; agricultural programs, 81; approach of,
  78–80, 82–84, 86–87, 98; attempts to
  improve community awareness, 82;
  contributions to black colleges, 31;
  educational programs, 79–80, 81;
  goals for 1990s, 99; grants from
  Winthrop Rockefeller Charitable Trust,
  107; health care programs of, 81–82;
  mission of, 103; ownership of Eyrie
  Garden sculpture, 53; policies of, 12;
  racial equality and, 80–81; transition
  from Rockwin Fund, 77–78; year of
  reevaluation, 101–2
Winthrop Rockefeller Gallery, 47
Wolfe, Townsend, 45, 47, 48
Wolstenholme Towne, 50
Women's Project, 94
Worldwatch Institute, 111
Worth, William and wife, 25

Yale-in-China program, 70
Yale University, 44, 107
Young, Whitney, 29–30
youth: contributions to programs for, 37;
  general programs for, 42; programs in
  agriculture, 40, 101; programs in aviation, 37–39; programs in China, 70;
  response to Jonesboro tragedy, 102;
  Winthrop Rockefeller Charitable Trust
  grants for, 110; Winthrop Rockefeller
  Foundation programs for, 81, 86, 95
Youth Enterprise in Agriculture Project,
  101